AEB 1966–2016

I dedicate this book to all who have trusted us
to realise their vision.
To our children, and their children.
To our future generations.

Ibrahim Mohamed Jaidah

Luca Molinari

AEB
1966–2016

Fifty years
of architectural design
in Qatar

SKIRA

Project Initiative
Ibrahim Mohamed Jaidah

AEB Editor
Lejla Nikšić

Architectural Drawings and Technical Adaptation
Fatma Abdullah Khalfani
Artemio D. Quijano
Edwin L. Gregorios

Sketches
Ahmed Gad
Macario Cammanong
Mohamed Fangary

Photography
AEB
Filippo Romano

Cover
Barzan Tower

Back Cover
Al Dhayaan Municipality

Design
Marcello Francone

Editorial Coordination
Alessandro Benetti
Emma Cavazzini

Editing
Andrew Ellis

Layout
Antonio Carminati
Serena Parini

First published in Italy in 2016 by
Skira editore S.p.A.
Palazzo Casati Stampa
via Torino 61
20123 Milano
Italy
www.skira.net

Printed and bound in Italy.
First edition

ISBN: 978-88-572-2880-8

Distributed in USA, Canada, Central & South America by Rizzoli International Publications, Inc., 300 Park Avenue South, New York, NY 10010, USA.
Distributed elsewhere in the world by Thames and Hudson Ltd., 181A High Holborn, London WC1V 7QX, United Kingdom.

Acknowledgement

As a firm, we owe our success to individuals who entrusted us with their projects, and have constantly believed in our ability to turn their visions into realities.

While remembering late Gamal Abdul Halim, who founded AEB back in 1966, I would like to take this opportunity and thank all of my colleagues for their constant challenges and support in being dedicated to setting the architectural trends in Qatar. Without you, none of this would be possible.

I would like to express my sincerest gratitude to that special group of individuals from the AEB team who made it possible to complete this book.

And, while marking the 50th anniversary of architectural practice in Qatar, we pledge to continue with our mission to translate the unique identity of our vernacular architecture into the contemporary Gulf style.

Ibrahim Mohamed Jaidah

Contents

Evolutionary Interventions. In Search of National Architectural Identity

Ashraf M. Salama
Chair Professor and Head of the School of Architecture
University of Strathclyde Glasgow
United Kingdom

During the second half of the twentieth century Qatar witnessed its first period of modern urbanisation, which was spurred by the rapid increase of oil production. Today's new development strategies are instead geared to diversifying the country's economy in new directions, and mark a second major phase of urban transformation. In the middle of the twentieth century, Doha, the capital city of Qatar, rapidly evolved from a small fishing hamlet to a vibrant emerging regional urban centre that now boasts over 2.1 million inhabitants. Here I will present selected works from AEB and discuss them within the urban development processes as a whole.

During the bustling 1960s settlement patterns were determined by the development of modern infrastructure such as roads and the supply of fresh water and electricity. At the time, modern public administration, housed in various buildings scattered across the city, was in its infancy. Despite the introduction of the first public housing law in 1964, planning and regulations still had limited impact on the city's general development. With Qatar's release as a British protectorate and its declaration of independence in 1971 – and in response to rising internal demand – the city's streets were widened in central areas to provide access by car, while the old courtyard buildings were replaced by modern structures made of concrete and brick. In order to accommodate expatriate labourers as well as Qatari nationals moving from other parts of the country to Doha, new housing areas were developed around the former city boundaries. In this first period of Doha's urban development, incentives such as land reclamation of an area around Doha's port and the construction of the Al-Corniche Road on the waterfront around the attractive bay, would later become defining elements of urban development. Rectangular grid settlement patterns and modern cement buildings included the addition of a development belt around the old centre and its harbour; these in turn were gradually replaced by modern urbanisation. Thus, Doha's traditional urban environment faced a rapid decline as a direct result of these first investments in modern infrastructure, and the increasing purchasing power of the city's population. In addition, cars and air-conditioning units furthered the emergence of a new type of urban structure comprised of low building densities, extensive road grids, and cement-block architecture.

The year 1969 saw the completion of Government House on reclaimed land to the east of the traditional market area; this was followed by the construction of the Headquarters of Qatar National Bank and the Ministry of Foreign Affairs nearby. The most significant landmark at that time was the Emiri Diwan palace, completed in 1972, which replaced Government House as the official seat of the Emir and his government. The Emiri Diwan occupies a prominent location at the point where the reclaimed Corniche begins and the old centre in the west ends. To its west, the Grand Mosque and the Clock Tower were built to complete a modern architectural ensemble intended to indicate a clear break with Doha's traditional style of building. In 1983 a hotel and conference centre – today known as the Sheraton Hotel Complex – was developed at the northern end of the Corniche as a landmark and pioneering project of the NDOD development. With its innovative pyramidal shape, the fifteen-storey hotel introduced a new standard of modern architecture in Doha. Together with the Al Jaidah office tower in the city centre core, until the early 1990s these two projects remained the tallest structures in Doha.

During the late 1960s the early works of AEB displayed overt admiration for modernism while attempting to balance the regional heritage with the tastes of the time. AEB's brand of modernism expressed itself in simple lines, cubic volumes, and a purity of form and surface treatment. This is evident in the design of a wide spectrum of projects ranging from private houses to public buildings. The villa of HE SH Khalifa Bin Hamad Al Thani and the National Oil Distribution Company are two examples of AEB's designs that manifest an inclination towards Modernism. However, during the same period an early quest for national identity is manifested in some of AEB's key projects, such as in the private residence of Mr Ali Al Attiya, in which an early blend of tradition and modernity was effected through the use of shading techniques and symbolic elements.

Villa of HE Sheikh Khalifa Bin Hamad Al Thani, 1970
Front Elevation

National Oil Distribution Company, 1969
Right Elevation

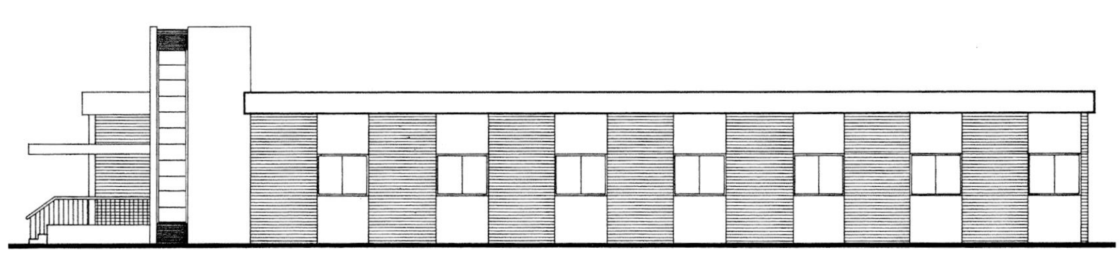

Mr Ali Al Attiya House, 1969
Front Elevation and Ground Floor Plan

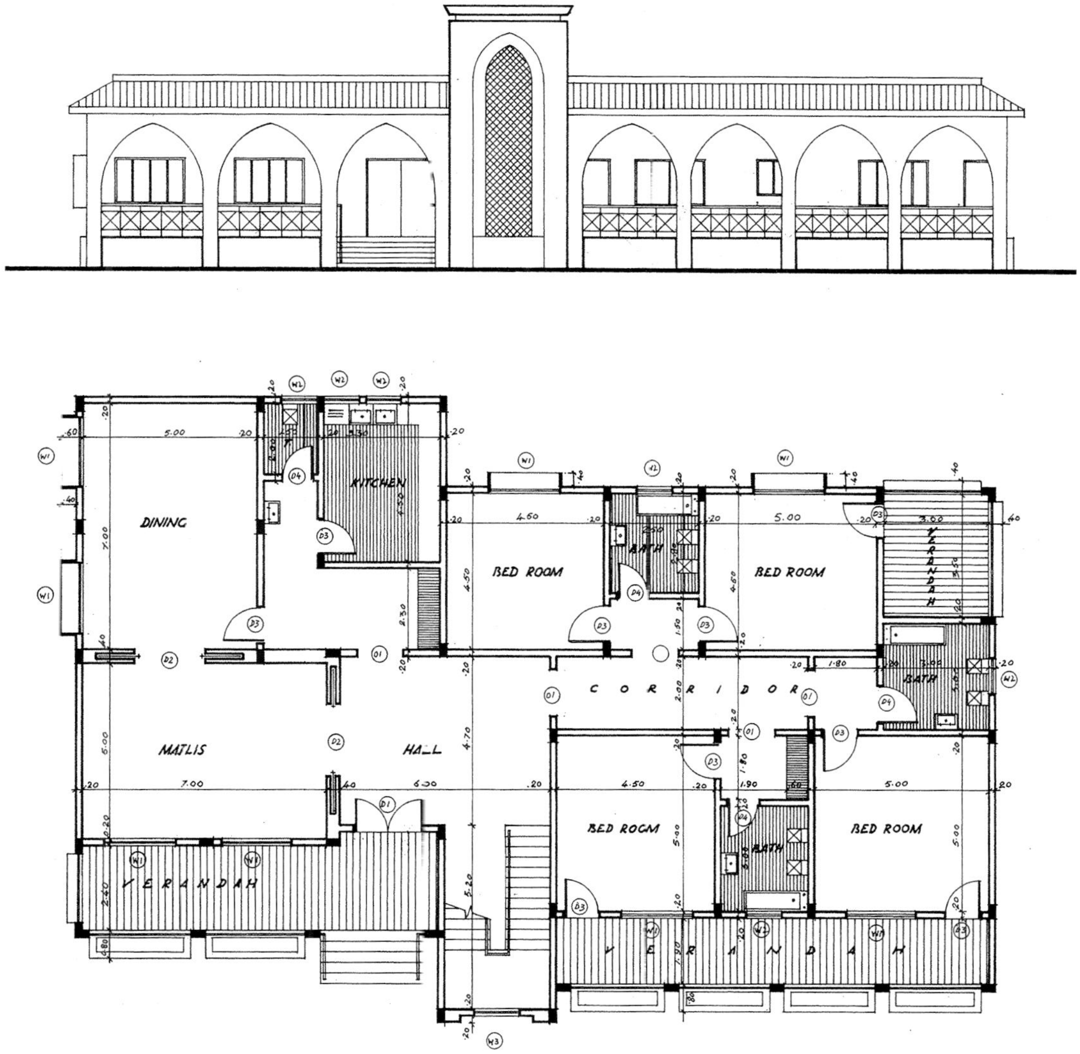

During the early 1970s many international consultants involved in the first phase of Qatar's urban planning began arriving in the city. In 1972 an interdisciplinary team comprised of planners, economists, sociologists, traffic engineers as well as urban designers was appointed by the Ministry of Municipal Affairs and Agriculture (MMAA) to develop a comprehensive study of Qatar and its inhabitants in order to identify the main challenges facing the city's development. This study was based on the first census of 1971; one of its main focuses was a socio-anthropological study of Qatari society of the time; this served as the basis for an initial structure plan for Qatar and its capital, Doha. Additionally, this study included the first comprehensive transportation master plan, drafted by Peat Marwick Mitchell and Company, plus a series of local action plans for selected areas, in combination with a proposal of phased developments.

In 1974 the British consultant Llewelyn Davis was appointed by the new town-planning authority within the Ministry of Municipal Affairs and Agriculture to design the first master plan of Doha, projected for 1990. His plan was based on a ring-road concept with a clear definition and a functional distribution of land uses regarding each ring, and the division of the total urban area into sixty-nine administrative zones. By the end of the 1970s most of the old Qatari neighbourhoods had been demolished or replaced, and the indigenous population had moved to new suburban developments such as Al Rayyan, Madinat Khalifa or Al Gharrafa in the north-west of the city. Three main initiatives of public housing programmes – known as Popular Housing, Senior Staff Housing, and Intermediate Staff Housing – were introduced: while the Popular Housing programme provided land and interest-free loans for Qataris who until then had no property of their own, the Senior Staff Housing programme was designated for more educated Qataris with university degrees, or for indigenous senior staff in the public sector. In addition to these two programmes, which were carried out through the cooperation of several ministries, the Intermediate Staff Housing programme launched by the Emiri Diwan was designed to supply expatriates working in the public sector with suitable housing units.

As Llewelyn Davis continued his planning efforts toward the development of the city centre until 1977, the American planning consultancy William L. Pereira Associates was commissioned in 1975 to develop in parallel a new master plan for an extension area in the north, known as North District of Doha (NDOD), or West Bay. The plan included the development of Qatar University and housing for its staff, along with new residential districts further inland. Coastal development at the northern end of the Corniche included a proposed large hotel development for conferences, a diplomatic and ministries area, and a new business district surrounded by a large park. While the hotel development and several embassies were completed during the early 1980s, to a large extent the commercial centres remained unbuilt due to the focus of commercial activities in and around the city centre. At the same time as the NDOD was being developed in the early 1980s, foreign consultants were engaged to review and adjust the zoning plan for existing urban areas in order to accommodate future population growth and improve the urban environment in the city centre. In 1985 the Lebanese company Dar Al Handasah Consultants was assigned to conduct detailed surveys of Doha's city centre, and to create a list of possible interventions to improve urban quality. However, in reality, the majority of these plans had very little impact on the actual urban development.

The projects AEB undertook during the continuous urban development process of the 1970s attempted to implement symbolism as a means to foster a sense of national identity. It is argued by historians that the acts of symbolisation and cultural and personal attachment to what we call "symbols" are recognised modes of thinking, feeling, behaving, associating, and understanding ourselves and our identity. Two sources of symbolism arise in the context of this discussion: the social and spontaneous creation of new places or buildings by the public itself, and the planning or intentional actions of those who have the power and authority to introduce change in the urban environment. If an organism or a component of a social structure is able to intentionally introduce change in the environment, one can argue that it is wielding power. This purposive action aims at endowing space with shape, structure, elements, and name, with an attempt to highlight certain values, aesthetics, or facts to lodge in the minds of the public. It is intended to create a symbolic space or building with preconceived meaning that may or may not be comprehended and assimilated by the public as a point of reference, and which might possibly become a shared symbolic element. Examples of AEB projects of this type in Qatar include the Ministry of Foreign Affairs and the Rulers Palace, both of which place emphasis on the use of symbols that conflate the various different influences the city enjoys, from Persian to Indian to Arab-Mediterranean.

Ministry of Foreign Affairs, 1974
Main Elevation

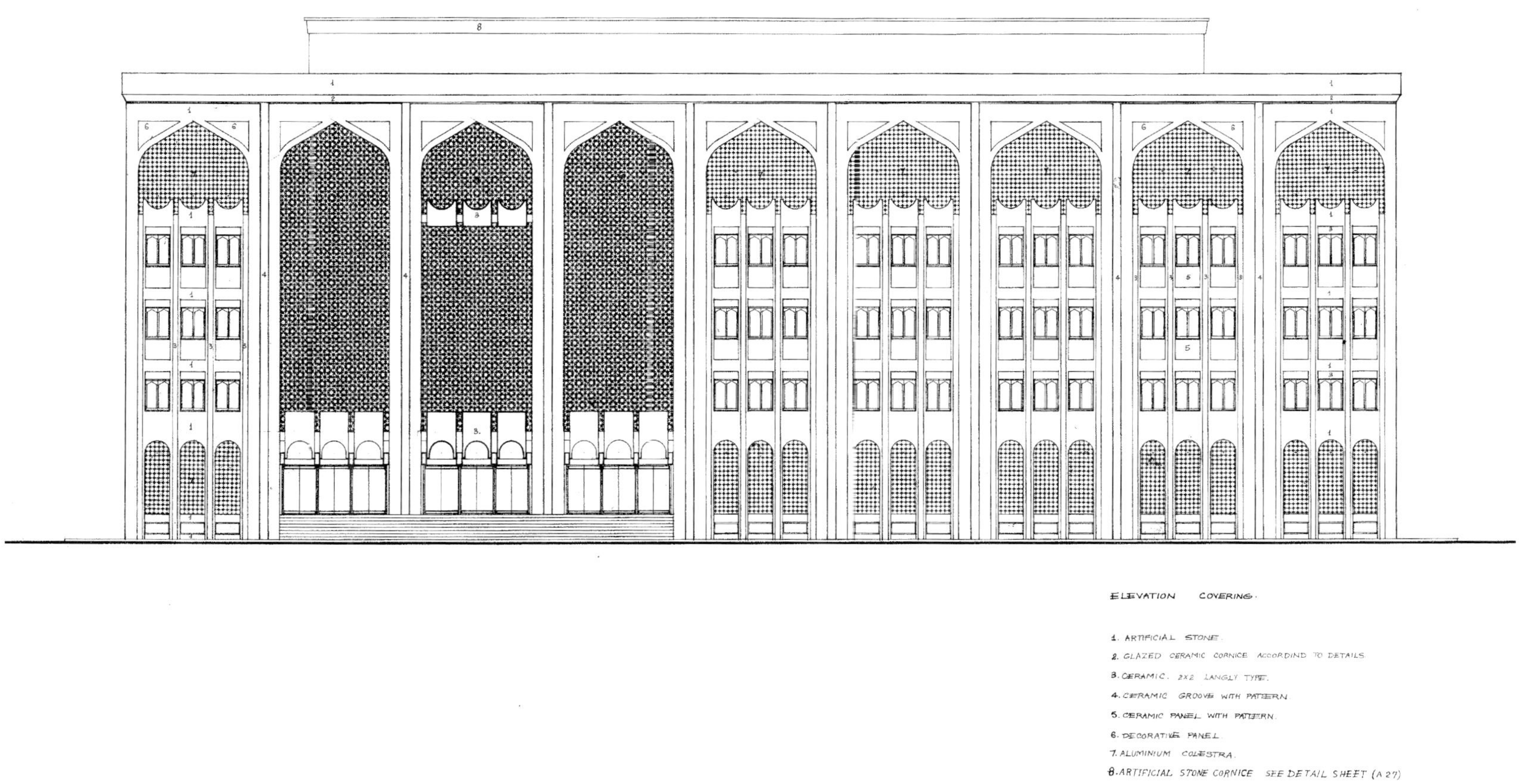

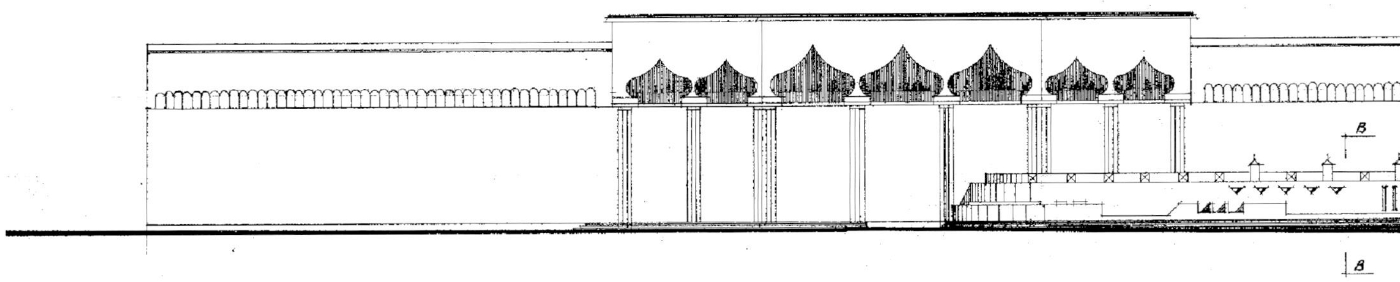

The Rulers Palace, 1972
Front Elevation and Interior Entrance Elevation

Through the judicious use of arches, patterned screens, and different types of shading, the ultimate goal is to establish an architectural and spatial language that speaks to the public and the context. No doubt, the search for historical and discernible symbols can foster a sense of identity while promoting a desired type of intimacy between a community and its physical surroundings. It is argued that the use of symbols derived from architectural heritage nurtures public awareness, along with the preservation of traditions and the tangible elements of cultural heritage. In fact, this desire to instill a sense of belonging by replicating the visual attributes, signs, and symbols of historical or traditional architecture through the built environment has encouraged professionals – and AEB is no exception – to increase the inclusion of historic symbols in their work.

During the 1980s and the early 1990s, AEB's works comprised office buildings, bank headquarters, mosques, and private homes. Notably, with its adoption of stylistic elements

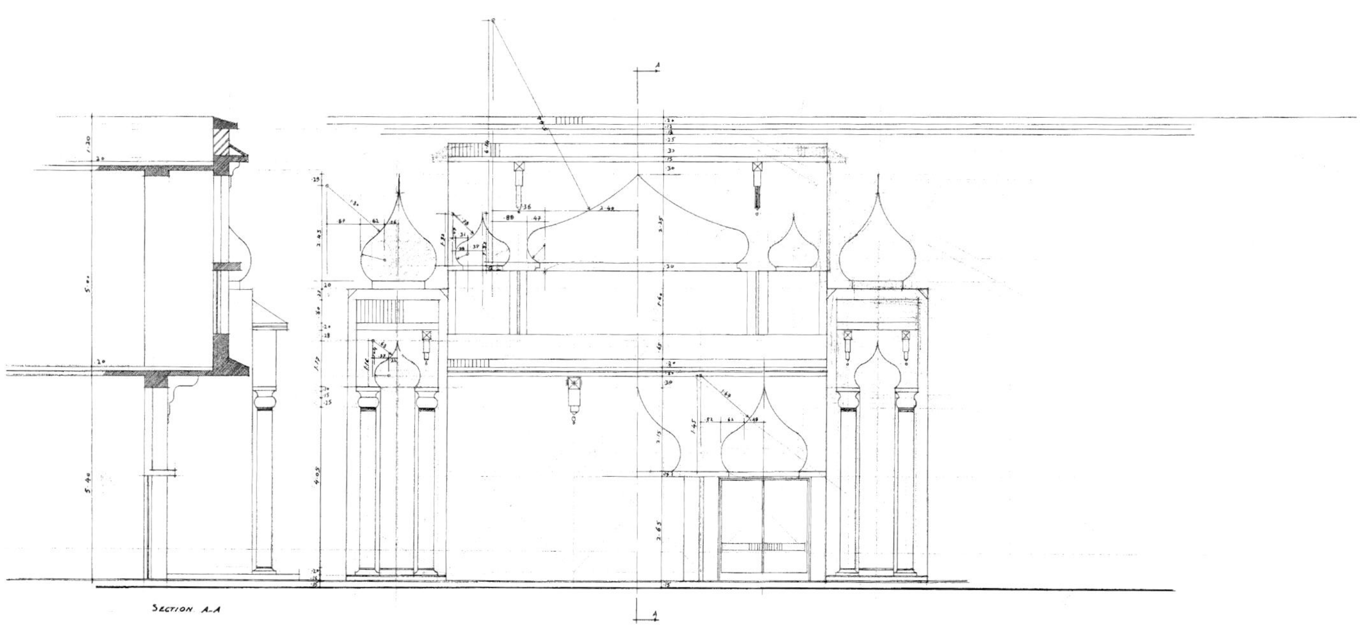

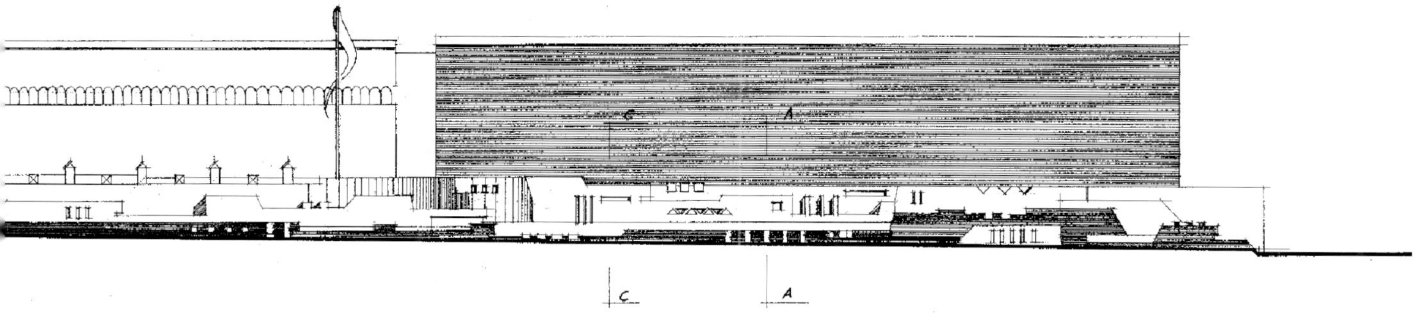

from the Mamluk culture, the Ahmed Bin Ali Mosque is one of the most significant projects designed by AEB during the period in question. The transformation of Doha from a vernacular settlement to an expanding oil-producing city was as sudden and precipitous as the oil boom that instigated it. The modernisation of the city was rapidly and effectively executed by importing the necessary expertise and labour from outside the country. This accelerated transition to modernity was reflected in the architecture and urban design of the period, which abruptly broke away from the vernacular traditions to adopt new and different design principles imposed by the state authorities, keen to establish a new and thoroughly modern identity for the growing nation. This can best be seen in the wholesale elimination of the traditional neighbourhoods with their courtyard houses and winding streets and indigenous population, and their replacement with modern suburban dwellings rising on uniform rectangular plots accessed via an orthogonal grid of roads. Unsurprisingly, the Western consultants engaged for Doha's transformation applied their own stand-

Ahmed Bin Ali Mosque, 1992. Main Elevation

ards of modern architecture and urbanism to the modernisation of the city. Little wonder, then, that the private vehicle became the main means of transport, and turned Doha into a car-dependent and car-oriented society, a shift of approach that impacted on all subsequent urban design and development plans. Hence, the incorporation of geometrical grids with various road hierarchies and space for roads and parking sites meant the end of the classic Qatari high-density type of building, altering also human interrelations and urban behaviour patterns.

In the current context of rising international competition between the world's major cities, diverse new challenges are emerging as each metropolis tries to find ways to sustain its growing populace, expand its economy, and extend its influence. With these aims in mind, there is no doubt that architecture and the urban environment as a whole are among the vital tools at the disposal of governments and decision-makers to help cities survive and keep abreast of the intense global competition, ensuring they establish themselves as key geographical and economic locations and destinations. Like its fellow high-growth capitals in the Gulf region, Doha has made clear its ambitions and aspirations in this competitive global economy, showing the city's determination to distinguish itself on the world map: to this end, Doha's new architecture has proved to be a dynamic tool and manifestation of these aspirations.

Since the end of the 1990s, the goal of attracting visitors and promoting culture and tourism has been acknowledged as crucial in establishing of Doha as an emerging hub in the Gulf, while diversifying the economy and fostering the city's brand appeal as an investment magnet. Actually, even before the 1990s there were schemes to develop Doha as a cultural centre and venue for international sports events. Qatar fortune with sporting events began with the first "Qatar Open" held in January 1993 as part of the World Series of the Association of Tennis Professionals (ATP). This success was later followed by the selection of Qatar to host the hugely successful 2006 Asian Games, which then led to the development of the 250-hectare Aspire Zone, also known as Doha Sports City. This space includes the Khalifa International Stadium as well as the 300-metre-high Aspire Tower. The increasing participation of Qatar's high-profile families in the Fédération Internationale de Football Association (FIFA) led to an official bid for the 2022 World Cup, which was awarded in 2010 and is thus far the biggest success of all of Qatar's sporting ambitions. As part of

Bank Al Mashrek, 1972.
Perspective

these developments, the AEB has expanded and diversified its output to include a wide spectrum of undertakings. Of particular note are several municipal projects – including the Barzan Tower – which simulate heritage values as part of the studio's drive to affirm national identity.

During the same period many new hotel developments were completed, particularly along the waterfront. This phase of expansion was followed by various initiatives to revitalise the core of Doha's downtown in order to highlight the city's perceived and actual traditions. Despite the fact that Doha's original historic settlement was entirely replaced during the modernisation period, the country's rulers decided to promote the capital as a cultural centre so as to extend tourism beyond sporting events. Subsequently, over the period 2004–2008 the old city core – including the traditional market Souq Waqif – was reconstructed in its original location using traditional building materials and techniques. In addition to the roofed market area with its small shops, the old walkway along the Wadi Al Sail was rebuilt as a paved pedestrian boulevard with restaurants and souvenir shops. More recently a number of exclusive boutique-hotels have been added to attract tourists. Other cultural projects are the nearby Museum of Islamic Art, which was completed in 2008 on redeveloped reclaimed land at the old port, along with Katara Cultural Village on the northern coast of the city in the prestigious West Bay area. In addition to making Doha more appealing, these developments were intended to attract stopover tourists on intercontinental flights, as well as visitors from neighbouring countries. Further support for the nation's tourism strategies includes the new airport project, known as the Hamad International Airport (Phase 2 is under way), which constitutes a driving force for the current strategy to establish Doha as an international transit hub. By the year 2020 the airport is scheduled to deal with a turnover of 50 million passengers per year.

The tourism industry was the first new oil-independent economy to be established in Qatar; in addition, there have been parallel attempts to develop Doha into an important centre of knowledge-economies in the region. This strategy is seen as a long-term plan, and its most prominent driving force is the Qatar Foundation, which was established in 1995 as a non-profit organisation to develop a centre for new economies by focusing on three fundamental concepts, namely, education, science, and community development. Its first project, Education City, was established in the late 1990s on a plot of 2,500 acres in the northwest of the city. The master plan comprises diverse educational facilities and assorted

Ministry of Foreign Affairs, 1974. Perspective

residential projects, and it is expected that approximately 100,000 people will eventually reside, study, and work there. Today it boasts numerous educational and administrative buildings that currently house a number of renowned American universities. Science and research are promoted by its subsidiaries, the Qatar National Research Fund and the Qatar Science and Technology Park, whose tax-free environment has attracted global cooperation and sponsors such as Shell, General Electric, and Microsoft. The community development aspect is being implemented in the form of various social initiatives to safeguard and reposition Qatar's culture, as well as establish a new architectural language for Qatar that stems from its cultural traditions and tangible heritage. The most prominent example of these is the Msheireb project, a 35-hectare mixed-use development, south of Souq Waqif, which is intended to showcase examples of modern Islamic architecture.

Addressing the sensitive relationship between tradition and modernity is AEB's constant attention to endorsing and conserving the nation's unique architectural identity. In this respect, tradition manifests itself both as a natural, internal force, and as resistance to external agencies. In essence, the result of this interaction between internal and external forces generates an evolving identity. Ever attentive to these subtle shifts in perception and style, the work of AEB manifests this quest for identity in its wide range of interventions, from the Doha Diplomatic Club to the Kempinski Residences and Suites and the Sharq Hotel and Spa, the expression of cultural identity through architecture and urban form is one of the hallmark leitmotifs of AEB's architectural and consulting practices.

Architectural Identity in a State of Impermanence. AEB & Qatar 1991–2016

Luca Molinari

There are certain books and research works that provide valuable opportunities when weighing up complex situations that are ripe and ready to be tackled.

At times, reading about the history of an architectural firm such as AEB allows us to look at the history of a country through a single lens, and identify some of the key issues and urgent matters that are taking place in this intense and troubled historical phase of transition.

I believe that using a transversal and open approach to read what has happened over these last decades in some Gulf countries is not only a necessity but also an important opportunity.

Over the last thirty years, this part of the world has been viewed by designers as a dazzling Shangri-La where everything was possible: monumental works for which budget was not a problem have pandered to the most extravagant whims and forbidden dreams of both architects and their clients.

Then the spell started to break. The global financial crisis of 2008 heralded a widespread slowdown to large construction sites, and not just in the Gulf states. Investments came to be seen in a different light, and environmental issues gained more emphasis. The question of identity and traditions was deeply reconsidered, and these new metropolitan cities came to be viewed not only as whimsical objects of design, but above all as fragments of likely cities.

The wider context is changing deeply. It is no longer possible to speak of this sector in general terms, since each Gulf state is now pursuing many different approaches and strategies, revealing extremely interesting energy and cultural independence. New generations of local designers, planners, artists, intellectuals and clients are emerging and contributing to enhance a framework that is undergoing drastic change, and establishing its central geographical and cultural role.

Strangely, the sudden reduction in resources has increased the critical ability to select and choose, prompting a more attentive focus on general strategies and defining a picture with a different growth prospect.

COMMERCIAL BANK

We are also witnessing a scenario that is usual in many countries that are just emerging from an initial phase of overwhelming growth. This moment urges a critical reading of recent events, and the need to slow down and understand which direction to take. The role of production, created by local generations of designers and architects, must also be questioned, as it offers a glimpse of a scenario that is less globalised and assumes an independent nature still in the making.

At the 2014 Venice Biennale, the United Arab Emirates and Bahrain pavilions raised the delicate issue of modern roots in Arab architecture, with two very interesting projects. These projects clearly focused on the issue of the difficult historiographical reading of at least fifty years of growth and changes in this region.[1]

Taking a step back historically, a first period commenced during the 1960s with the start of oil extraction activities and the rise of modern and independent states in the Gulf. This vitally important phase produced the first modern works of great interest, even though they have almost completely disappeared.

These complex events gave rise to a first generation of modern Arab and Middle Eastern architects who worked alongside British (above all), French, Italian and German designers, and developed the first large-scale public works in the modern style in this part of the world.

In the majority of cases, such works were influenced by Anglo-Saxon Brutalism or by a problematic form of International Style. Yet attempts at neo-vernacular also appeared, in which, for the first time in the history of this area, the question of the linguistic and cultural matrices of local architecture was addressed with a different and open approach.[2]

The Arab Engineering Bureau was founded at this point in history, a few years before the State of Qatar gained independence and underwent its first, consistent phase of modernisation. The modernity of institutions together with the rise of professional and creative environments that made modernity possible were the processes that emerged, alongside the willingness to give independent shape to a growth that at times was difficult to control.

This first decisive phase for establishing a taste and new construction techniques in such a difficult geographical and climatic area was followed by a second phase in the 1990s. It featured powerful acceleration, corresponding to the political and financial desire to turn this part of the world into an influential magnet for capital investments and human and creative resources that could transform a portion of desert into a place of extraordinary opportunities on a global scale.[3]

The result is there for all to see: the majority of urban centres have multiplied their population at least fourfold, with a ratio of three-to-one between the expatriate labour force and the local population. Abu Dhabi, Doha, Dubai, Kuwait City, Manama and Jeddah are recognised as metropolitan hubs and global economic catalysts. Some of the richest Sovereign Wealth Funds in the world are concentrated in these states. Dubai has been awarded Expo 2020 and Qatar the 2022 FIFA World Cup. A significant part of the most important investments in the field of museum and educational culture is being developed in this area. Tourism grows every year at a very fast pace, and is strictly linked to the enormous infrastructural and airport efforts in the Gulf.

What is happening to architecture in this new phase?

After a series of works that passively portrayed the euphoria of the early 2000s, combining energy and language that led to easy forms of consumption, new lines of research and experiences have taken shape, linked to diverse players and alternative cultural conditions. These projects and research works have moved hand-in-hand with the continuous production of contemporary works, especially in the services and retail sector, which have continued to expand in the Gulf and have revealed the potential topics on which many architects and designers belonging to the new local generations have been showing great enthusiasm: the restoration of existing heritage, original discussions on the role of tradition, the growing weight of community life and the application of a sustainable, widespread and pervasive thinking in the new projects.

Under the guidance of the Ministry of Culture and of Noura Al-Sayeh, the young architect in charge of the architecture programmes, Bahrain has started an urban-scale experiment to reclaim the ancient pearl fishing district, involving some of the best young contemporary designers such as OFFICE Kersten Geers David van Severen and Atelier Bow-Wow.[4] The

projects focus on context, reflect upon the role of contemporary public space and evince an environmental sensitivity that shows that it is possible to take action in a different way than similar, parodistic projects developed in other city centres.

Abu Dhabi is hastening the construction of an impressive international museum complex, supported by great stars of global architecture. Of even greater significance is the decision to develop Masdar City, the first fully sustainable city, designed by Norman Foster and symbolising the desire to rethink the issue of environmental impact in this region.

The situation in Qatar is more interesting and complex, due to the presence of leading public clients who are capable of influencing and supervising the work of important designers, and the rise of a new generation of local architects and artists. Over the past fifteen years, the Qatar Foundation has significantly invested in the construction of Education City, a new urban hub that covers 1,500 hectares and includes university campuses and schools of excellence, with the aim of placing education at the centre of the Qatar's political agenda.[5] Another large construction project – Msheireb Downtown in Doha, adjacent to the old Souq and designed by a joint British and local team – reveals an interesting reversal of trend, with a stricter architecture that is attentive to the quality of urban space.[6]

At the same time, major local firms are gaining ground. This is the case with AEB. Taken over at the start of the 1990s by Ibrahim Mohamed Jaidah, AEB is regarded today as one of the most advanced and best-organised firms in the region. Its economic and cultural importance in the Gulf is of great relevance since a new generation of local architects and designers has emerged which has been capable, on the one hand of putting into practice the lessons learned from the leading international firms working in the area, and on the other of developing an approach that is more attentive and sensitive to the context in which they work.

The recent construction of the State Grand Mosque in Doha, alongside other examples of government architecture in which the goal is to knowingly forge a dialogue between modern architecture and the tradition of vernacular architecture, are some of the most original and significant projects of a new season of Qatari architecture.

In all of these cases, dialogue is linked to a concept of history and tradition that needs to be fully re-established in an overall framework that promotes questioning and a sincere quest for the cultural and formal identity of a nation and its people.

From this viewpoint, the research and publications that Ibrahim Mohamed Jaidah has developed over the past years on local architectural languages and materials are of particular interest, as they express the growing need of a leading artist and of institutions to go beyond stereotypes and start building an archive of references together. The recent project involving the Doha Fire Station, designed in the 1970s by a British firm, opens another stimulating scenario: the need to restore what remains of the country's modern architectural heritage, and regard it as a cultural and material resource. All of these works unfold in a dynamic political and cultural context that is attentive to the significant transition that Muslim countries are undergoing (especially in the Gulf), and which carefully considers the growth prospects for the following years and its relevant identity.

Today, the Gulf is turning into an interesting laboratory that must be viewed attentively and without prejudice. It is one of those places in the world where new local identities and globalisation can shape important and original initiatives for our future.

[1] *Lest We Forget. Structures of Memory in the UAE*, National Pavilion UAE, edited by Michele Bambling (Venice, 2014); *Fundamentalists and Other Arab Modernism*, Kingdom of Bahrain National Participation, edited by George Arbid and Bernard Khoury (Venice, 2014).

[2] See the catalogues created for the two Venetian exhibitions: Michele Bambling (ed.), *Structures of Memory in the UAE* (Venice/UAE, 2014); George Arbid (ed.), *Architecture from the Arab World* (Italy, 2014).

[3] Archis+AMO+C-Lab+Pink Tank+NAi (eds.), *Al Manakh* 2, vol. 23, 2010; Kelly Hutzell, Rami el Samahy, Adam Himes, "Inexhaustible ambition. Two eras of planning in Doha/Qatar", in George Katodrytis, Kevin Mitchell (eds.), *UAE and the Gulf, Architectural Design* 233 (January/February 2015): 80–91.

[4] See Noura Al Sayeh, "A field of possibilities. The Post-Oil Future of Bahrain", in op. cit., pp. 136–41.

[5] Kevin Mitchell, "Design for the Future. Educational Institutions in the Gulf", and "Ameena Ahmadi, City for Education", in op. cit., pp. 38–53.

[6] Varkki Pallathucheri, "New Hearts for two Gulf Cities", in op. cit., pp. 92–99.

Rediscovering Qatari Vernacular

Local Tradition as an Inspiration for Contemporary Design

Luca Molinari
in conversation with
Ibrahim Jaidah

Luca Molinari: When we first met in July 2014, I was impressed by the efforts of your research and systematic investigation to reconstruct the history of traditional Qatari architecture, which is only a few centuries old, but suffers a lack of information because of its perishable component materials, especially in its more ancient expressions. Despite this typical feature, your book, *The History of Qatari Architecture*, is an amazing analysis of different building types according to their end-use.
So I would like to start with the book, because I think it's a theoretical milestone which offers a yardstick for approaching and understanding Qatar's architecture and urban development. The last time we met you told me you felt like an archaeologist, that you needed to rediscover your local culture, to come back to it. I am curious to know what your reasons and objectives were, and why a brilliant professional with a big company decided to devote so much time and energy in this direction. What were the cultural goals of that book, and what were you aiming at?
Ibrahim Mohamed Jaidah: Okay, I will go back to the past a little bit, and try to explain where this passion came from. I grew up in the old part of town, in the area called Al Jasra, where the old souq is. I lived in a courtyard house and absorbed all these traditional architectural elements from an early age. Later I attended the University of Oklahoma School of Architecture in the United States, where we were taught about all the different schools of architecture (regional, periodical, etc.), but the Qatari form of architecture was never documented, listed, or even mentioned in any of the history books. What we studied was from the Renaissance to the Bauhaus, the history of mankind from the Greeks to the Modern Movement.
So I came back with an open mind and much knowledge obtained through this formal education of the world's architectural history, and as a result I gained a new appreciation of what has remained of our vernacular architecture here in Qatar. I especially enjoyed visiting the ancient sites. And although I was fascinated by the traditional architecture and have photo-documented many of these projects, I myself never really attempted to recreate any traditional architecture or use that particular language – at least not until later on. Three or four years later, when I was working for the government, I had the opportunity to design the old Al Dana Club – which still exists, by the way – and this is where my eyes were truly reopened. I looked back to our vernacular architecture for inspiration.
Turning to Greek architecture evolution, or reasoning as an academic by simply analysing ancient styles of architecture, you realize that everything is the result of transition. But there was a point when the development of the Qatari traditional architecture stopped. It developed

Umm Slal Mohammad Fort, Umm Slal, late 19th century

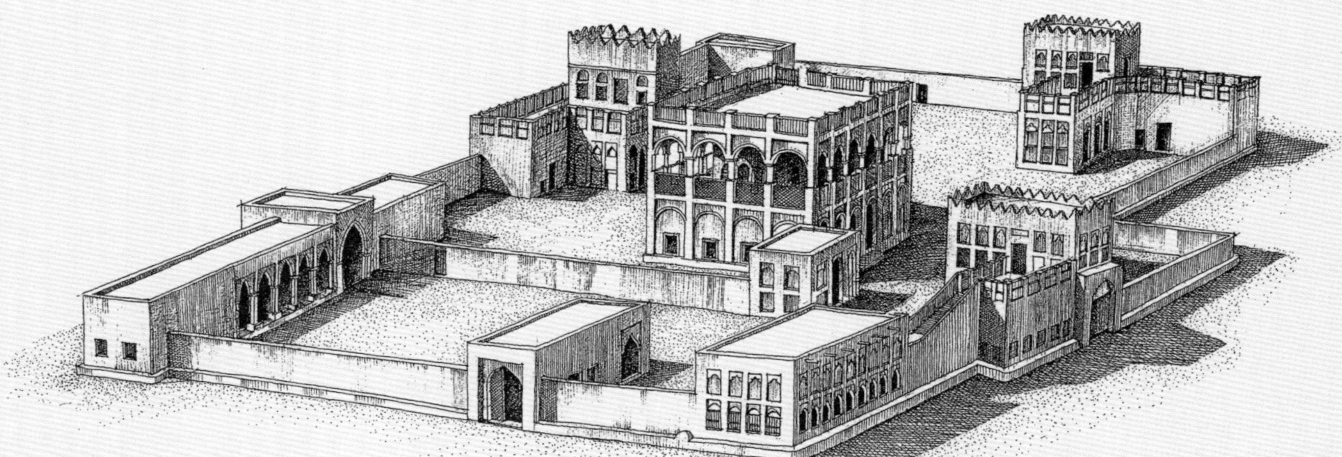

The Old Amiri Palace, Doha

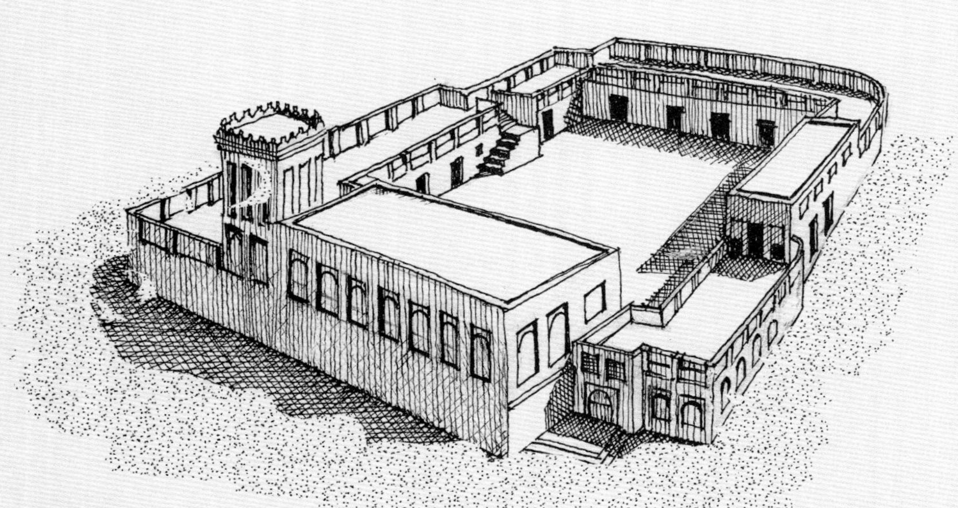

Mohammed Said Naserallah House, Doha, 1920

over the centuries, but it came to a halt with the discovery of oil. There was therefore no smooth transition, so I traced things back to where the development had been interrupted and focused my attention on that specific moment. From the moment I had this flash of realisation I started building up not only my personal library, but also my passion and research into Qatari architecture. I collected a lot of data, photographs and documents.

Incidentally, in the early 1990s policymakers and designers began a big debate on how we could revive our local vernacular. There weren't many people actually interested in attempting this, however, so I happened to be in the right place at the right time when I conceived the Al Dana Club. In that case I referred to vernacular architecture in a more direct way, rather than contemporary. Some intellectuals accused me of copying, of taking aesthetic features of the past and developing them into remakes, but my response always was that we were missing the transition phase. Maybe I felt that my generation needed to make sacrifices and delve back into our past, so that the next generations would be able to appreciate their traditions. In this sense I had taken on the responsibility of bridging the gap, of being a sort of a missing link that would help them better relate to their past in order to be better equipped for their future.

In fact, given the speed and sheer amount of building we were experiencing in Qatar in the ten years at the turn of the century, we were basically cramming all the experience of three generations into one.

Instead of waiting for the next generation, after more than twenty years of practice I decided to take a more contemporary approach to vernacular architecture myself. So I performed a sort of "fast-rewind" back to Qatari traditional architecture. I know for a fact that at the time in Qatar there was only a handful of practising local architects, and the country's architecture was actually being developed by some big international names. Although our government did advocate that the Qatari identity should be reflected in the new buildings in one way or another, those foreign designers actually had little or nothing to refer to. Some critics said that the only available sources were picture postcards – actually the very few existing postcards were of the old souq! – and referred to this derisively as "postcard research". Apart from those old pictures, there were no tools or materials available for understanding the past. So I realised that an in-depth study on Qatari architecture was essential – not just for what was about to be built, but mainly to offer new generations a knowledge base that would provide the real means to analyse and understand the traditional elements of typical Qatari architecture, and enlighten them toward more contemporary approaches while also making

our heritage their own. I realised it was something of great importance, and I wished I'd had such a book in my hands when I graduated. Maybe it would have dramatically changed the directions of my thinking, or sped up my understanding.
These are the reasons why I think the book turned out to be an extremely important reference work for what was going to happen in the following years. I received compliments from Santiago Calatrava and other acknowledged colleagues, who recognised that my study is worth a PhD. Of course, it is a great honour and pleasure to hear that eleven years of passionate research, study, and hard work are so appreciated.

LM: The shift between what you call vernacular architecture and the contemporary reinterpretation of it is very interesting. There's a big difference between the two, isn't there?
IMJ: There is indeed, and this relationship is still evolving today. In fact, in the last twenty years the evolution of Qatari architecture has been on fast-forward, even more rapidly than when I made my first attempts to get back to vernacular architecture and integrate it with contemporary technologies (like air-conditioning, new materials, etc.).
Now imagine if what I did in 1990 had happened in 1960. It would have significantly affected the architectural evolution over the next thirty years, taking it in a totally different direction that would now be more conscious and respectful of the specificities of Qatari local building design.
The big challenge therefore is going back to the past, but at the same integrating state-of-the-art technologies into these vernacular buildings.
As you proceed, you realise that you are gradually starting to design with a more minimalist attitude, recalling the original Qatari minimalism, which is an intrinsic prerogative of our architecture.
This is noticeable, for instance, when it comes to respecting a building's orientation – which was ignored in the early period of Qatari contemporary architecture – but also to finding more effective solutions in relation to environmental issues (such as materials, sustainability strategies, etc.).
So now, as a mature architect, I'm trying to use these elements as qualities of the local vernacular, rather than typical, straightforward architectural features.

LM: This brings me to my next question: we're both interested in the matter of vernacular and the interpretation of traditional features, not merely as linguistic elements, but as enduring

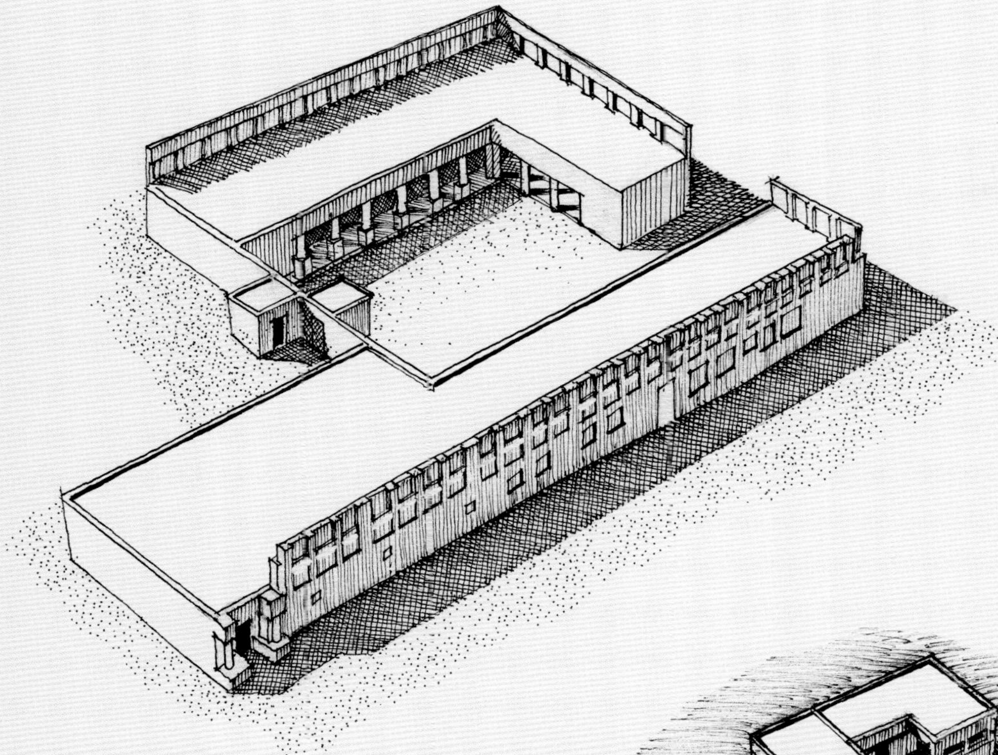

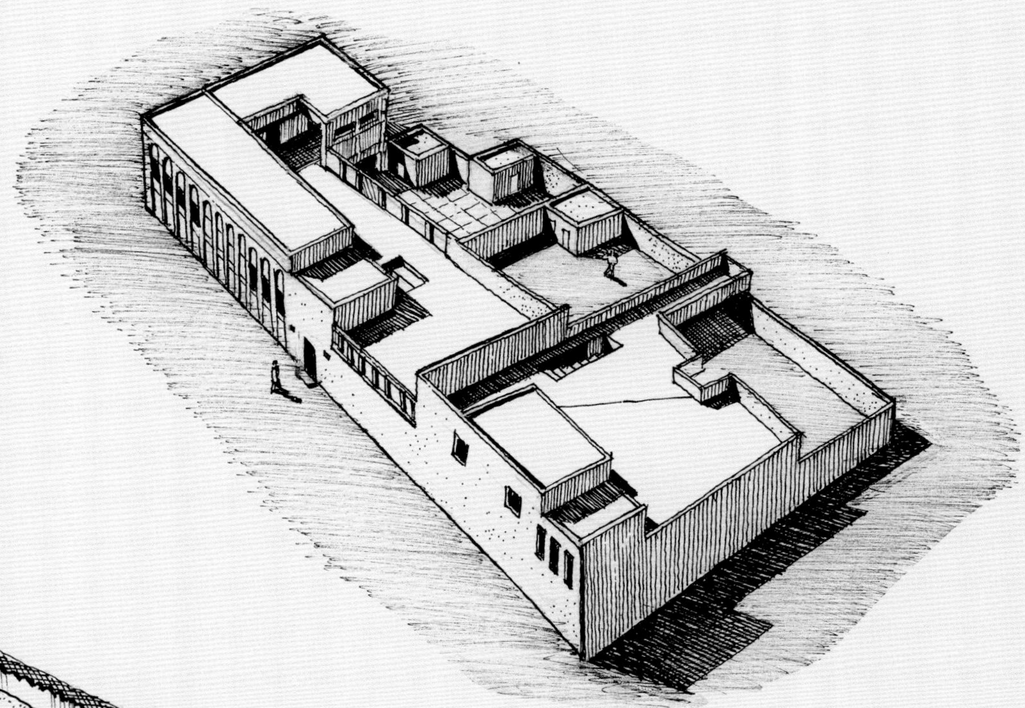

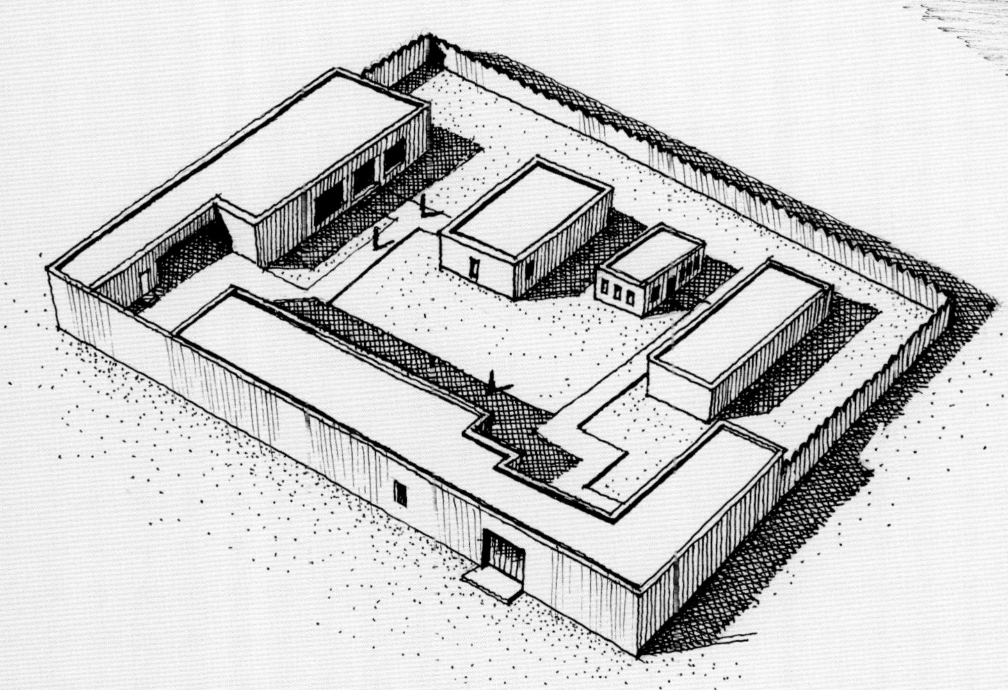

Nasser Bin Ahmed Obeidan House, Al Jasra, Doha, 1940

Al Asmakh House, Al Asmakh, Doha, 1930

Al Khulaifi House, Doha, 1940

Al Subaiei Mosque,
Al Wakrah, 1940

Zekreet Mosque, Madinat
Zekreet, 1940

Old Al Khor Police Station,
Al Khor, 1945

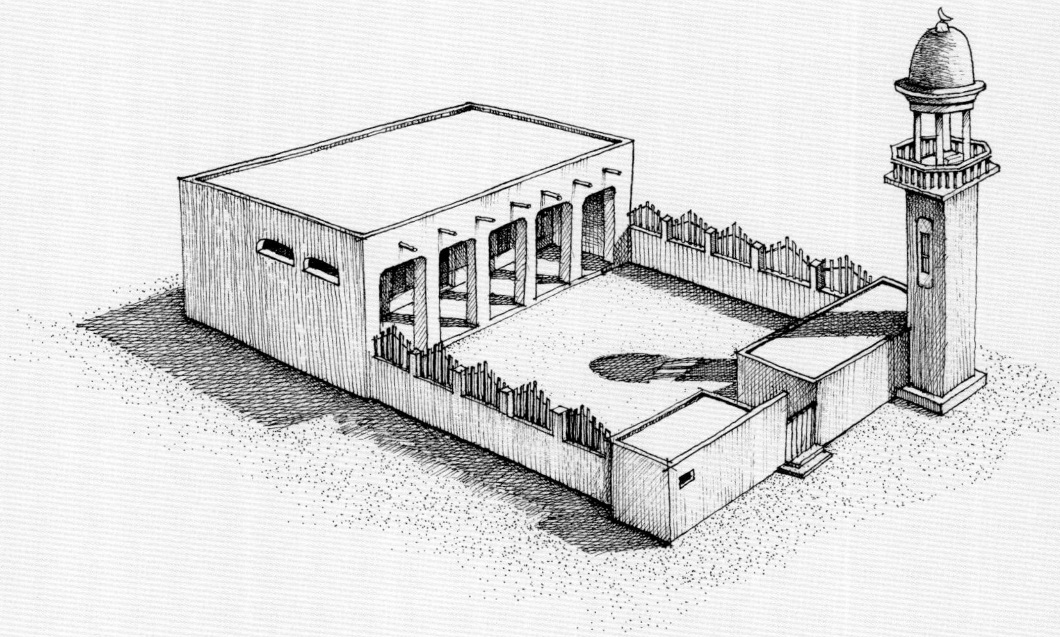

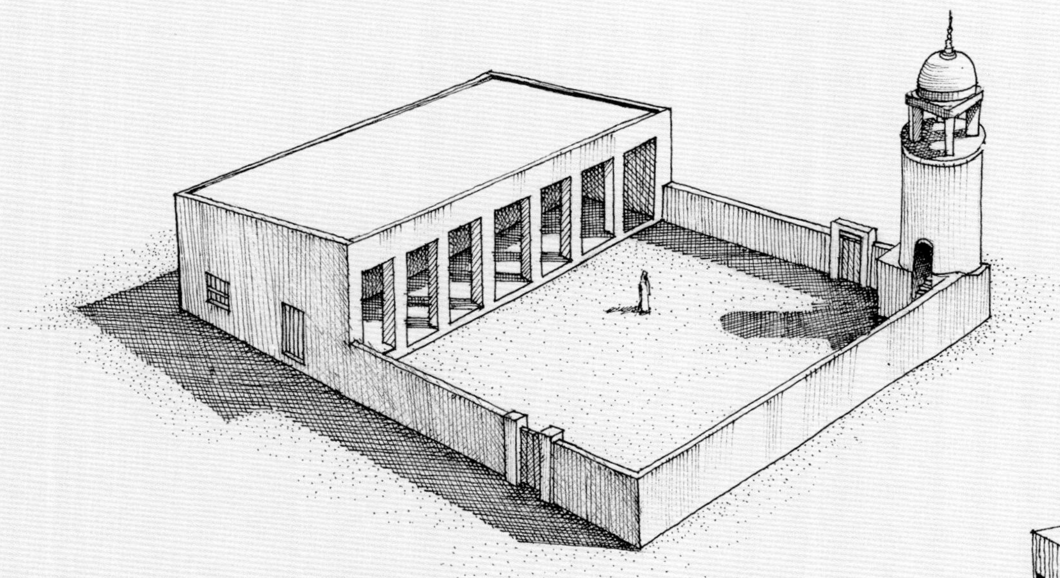

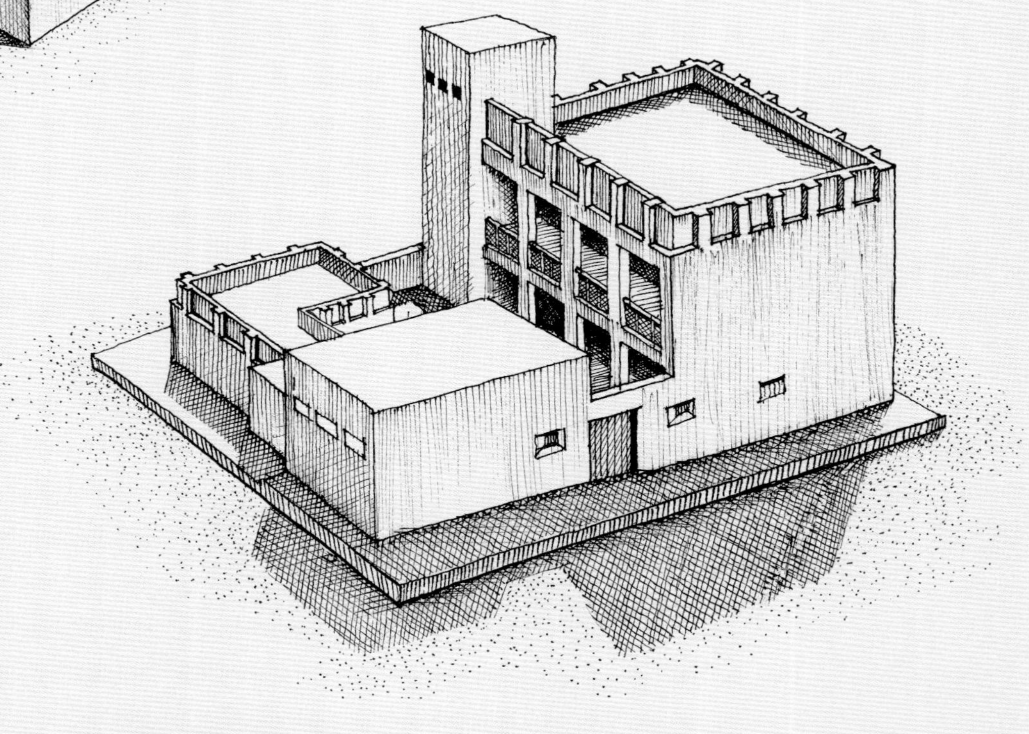

features of founding architecture. I believe that certain elements of traditional architecture can still be used in a very challenging way. So my question is, which features of traditional Qatari architecture do you believe can still be applied today?

IMJ: If we set aside our emotions and the aesthetics of traditional elevations, then you have such elements as the layout, density and orientation in respect to the sun and the winds. These are what have always been and still remain successful features of our local architecture. In terms of floorplan, the theme of the courtyard fits with the need for privacy while respecting the sun's movement and taking advantage of every little breeze.

Now, interestingly, in public buildings these are used for the purpose of controlling the shade. In my lectures, I refer to their use as "going back to basics". Let's take these basic elements of our old mansions, which were originally built without any real planning regulations. If we put together these "ingredients", we're respecting our culture – in terms not so much of aesthetics, as of employing the most intelligent elements that successfully adapt to such a rigid environment. This is the great heritage we should borrow from our tradition.

LM: Do you think that these elements can be successfully applied to contemporary architecture?

IMJ: Indeed I do.

LM: Which of your projects best express this kind of idea?

IMJ: Well, I'd say some buildings that we are concluding very soon, but also many completed projects – such as the municipalities of Al Dhayaan and Al Rayyan, Al Sharq village and spa, and the headquarters of Contraco and Qatari Diar.

LM: Your work is often pioneering. How do local and cultural institutions receive and deal with your ideas? Do you think that in the future they will continue to apply the new awareness of traditional architecture that you have introduced?

IMJ: Actually this is happening already. We have conducted some wonderful research in conjunction with Harvard University on the old Gulf cities, on both sides of the Gulf. The study involved an analysis of the old neighbourhoods, and the results are incredible. It shows that there were many excellent liveable places, thanks to their taking account of orientation and wind factors. Respect of privacy was another argument central to the analysis carried out by Harvard University.

I hope this new focus will continue, and that Qatar University will explore these topics further. I touched upon these issues in my book as well, but there are many more buildings still to be preserved, and a great deal of studies to be done yet.

Further analysis will provide proper guidelines for people on how to build their houses, and provide them with a reference of useful rules that explain how to orientate a building, how many openings it should have, how to build a sustainable house and an energy-efficient living space, and so on. Many of us tend to build houses that do not respect orientation, or have large double windows facing west that require curtains because of the heat and to provide much-needed privacy. So there are so many lessons to be learnt, and I'm hoping that eventually I will find the time to study this in greater detail.

LM: Looking back through your book and reading about materials used in the Gulf area architecture, the region offers an incredible and very stimulating laboratory. I believe we are moving from the production of buildings as *objects* (strange ones sometimes) to the idea that the area offers an environment in which you can build something quite different. This is very interesting. In relation to the so-called "rehabilitation of traditional architecture", we are moving away from the outside world's perception of "Arabian identity" – or of what looks Arabic (I'm Italian, so I know very well the "postcard effect") – to the concrete realisation of how Qatar is envisioning and building its future. I think this shift is hugely relevant today, and it's one of the main challenges for the next decades. Don't you agree?

IMJ: I agree. The present situation in Qatar is very interesting. On one hand, the government has very little control over the private sector. Of course, there are some guidelines that need to be respected, but they are far more flexible than those affecting state buildings. This is why, when it comes to the West Bay, the downtown, there's more freedom for clients to do whatever they want – even though a lot of private sector clients are naturally influenced by the public.

On the other hand, if you look at state buildings, where the government has full control, the direction is very clear. State buildings are recommended to have evident vernacular elements, but at the same time they require working on a larger scale appropriate for modern facilities, and to include the most advanced technologies available.

A perfect example of this is what we have done with the Ministry of Interior, the Traffic Department HQ and several other government buildings for which we were commissioned to explicitly follow these instructions. In these cases, the straightforward interpretation

Suq Al Baker, Doha, 1950

Al Shagab Water Well,
Al Rayyan, 1935

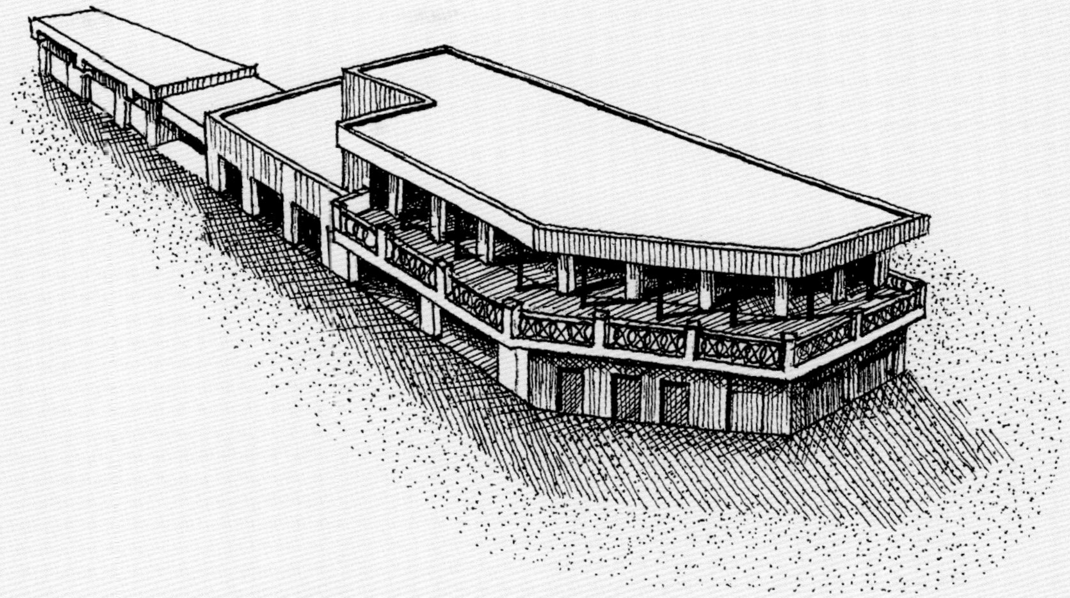

that screams "Qatar" is preferred, so we have designed monumental buildings reflecting the authorities in question. For instance, when I drove by the MoI with my eight-year-old daughter, she was astounded by the sheer scale of the complex.
So this is the direction being taken for certain government buildings.
Parallel to this, we have seen that some of the world's most famous architects are being challenged to respect the host culture – and the results are incredible, with a switch from an abstract approach to the contextual redefinition of what is local. By that I mean that "local" can be the colour of the sea, the desert rose, etc.

LM: Right, such as the National Museum of Qatar, by Jean Nouvel...
IMJ: Yes! Isn't it brilliant? That's as local as it gets. Its inspiration reaches deep into the roots of our nation.
Another approach is the Museum of Islamic Art designed by I. M. Pei, where the general Islamic architecture approach fits into a context it really belongs to.
The international architects usually have a very personal style, but when you challenge them to deal with native features the results are often unbelievable.
I think that between the school that I set up and these projects, a wonderful architectural vocabulary is being created for a new generation to develop an original identity, which is composed of and influenced by Qatari imagery.
Many ingredients are part of this imagery, starting with typological features like floorplan and building orientation, and the retrieval of ancient settlements such as the typical *dhow*, and including a wide range of possible sources of inspiration, like the colour of the sea or a microscopic blow-up of grains of sand.

LM: These aspects are indeed fascinating, and show that the economic upturn brought together the right moment with the right people, making it possible to explore something different. I'm curious about the next stage, and whether it will bring a truly new and original Qatari identity. It's all very exciting.
IMJ: Sure. Take the Msheireb project, for example, that's designed by international firms. It belongs to the type of architecture we're talking about here, even though it is common knowledge that it's the work of international firms.
The British architect John R. Harris was the first international architect who practised extensively in the Gulf in the 1950s. This is exactly what he did. His early works have

been copied at a much larger scale. Harris realised that vertical elements with recessed openings reduce the glare and provide a more visual cue than the strictly traditional openings. Moreover, they are also suited for new uses, such as corporate buildings. The Msheireb architects have used these elements, which are becoming very popular. For example, we use these elements even in high-rise buildings, and sometimes we alter the density of openings to regulate air circulation, heat gain, and glare.

LM: Would you start considering early modern architecture as part of your cultural heritage? I think that the first period of modernism is quite exciting.

IMJ: The first period of modernity showed far greater awareness of the environment than this latest one does. Our studio made three important renovations. One was the Fire Station, where we preserved this very early 1980s building, and designed a contemporary annex alongside it, extending the roof to create extra shading. The new building is actually quite neutral, so it does not compete with the original building that we restored. We also did a complete makeover of the Ministry of Finance building and the central Post Office. I'm extremely proud and happy to have preserved these monuments of our early modern history, because they can now be enjoyed and visited by everyone. At the same time I'm pleased that the government realized that this too is history, even these modern buildings. For a long time it was believed that whatever was not built in mud could not be considered historical. Consequently, a lot of gorgeous neighbourhoods that were built in the late 1960s have been completely demolished. Fortunately, I documented some of them before their destruction.

Qatar Foundation HQ (Al Shaqab)

Qatar Foundation HQ (Al Shaqab)

Education City, Doha, Qatar

Completed, 1997

Client: HH The Emir's office

Awards
- Aga Khan Award for Architecture (2001, nominated)
- Arab Towns Organisation Award (2002, 2nd place)
- Honoured on Qatari's 100 riyal banknote

AEB's Al Shaqab Institute for Girls in Doha, directly commissioned by HH The Emir's office, was completed in 1997. Along with the neighbouring Qatar Academy and Shaqab College for Design Arts, the new college building offered a response to the development of the surrounding areas, which were lacking a proper educational infrastructure, one that could enable students to continue up to university level.

A few years after its construction, as Doha expanded and the authorities deemed it not only necessary but fundamental to the growth and development of both Qatar and the Gulf region to establish a centre of educational excellence, the Institute's building was chosen as the central hub of what would become an extensive Education City. As a consequence, nowadays the building serves as the headquarters for the Qatar Foundation, which is responsible for the continued expansion of the country's entire educational sector.

Despite the building's important new role, the Institute's spaces easily adapted to the evolution and change of function, thanks to a lucid design strategy, which takes inspiration from traditional Islamic architecture.

Its elementary layout is centred on the main courtyard, which originally functioned as a vast full-height gathering room for students, teachers, and visitors.

Accesses to all facilities, both on the ground level and on the first floor, connect directly to the main courtyard itself, making it a key element in the management of people's movements inside the building.

Few architectural elements define its quiet and contemplative atmosphere: plain, gently decorated white walls reflect the light entering from the arched openings located just below ceiling level; selected wooden details make the ambiance more welcoming; lastly, the octagonal star of the central fountain, together with the four colonnades, suggest a possible spatial structure and hierarchy.

The significance of AEB's project has been recognized with many awards, such as the Aga Khan Award for Architecture (nominated in 2001) and the Arab Towns Organisation Award (2nd place in 2002). As a further acknowledgement of its cultural relevance for the development of the country, the Qatar Foundation HQ is currently honoured on the QR100 banknote.

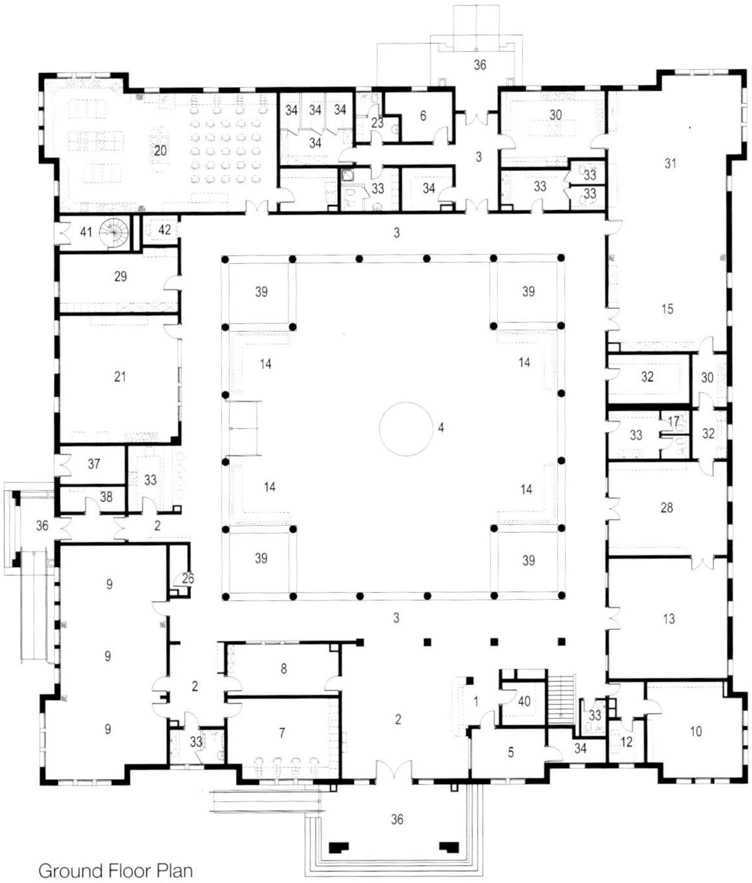

Ground Floor Plan

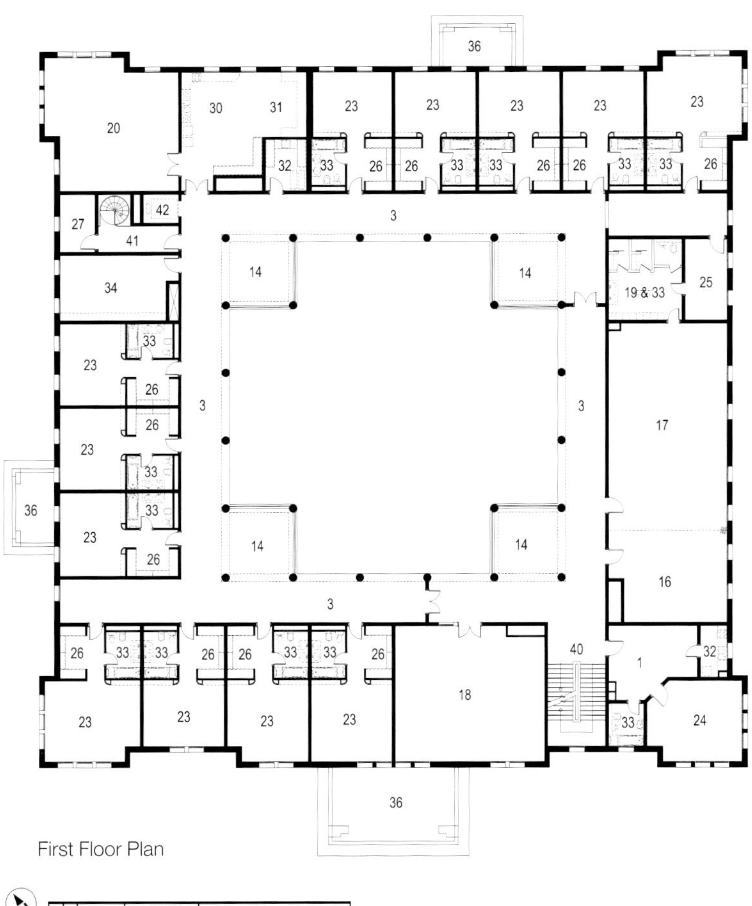

First Floor Plan

Legend

1. Reception
2. Lobby
3. Corridor
4. Covered Student Hall
5. Registration Office
6. Staff Room
7. Teachers Office
8. Principle Office
9. Classroom
10. Library
11. Archive and Filing Room
12. Photocopy Room
13. Visitors' Sitting Room
14. Sitting Area
15. Multi-Purpose Hall
16. Music Room
17. Fitness Room
18. Prayer Room
19. Locker Room
20. Demonstration Kitchen
21. Ironing Class
22. Boarders' Sitting Room
23. Typical Double Bedroom
24. Housemother Bedroom
25. Assist. Housemother Bedroom
26. Dressing Room
27. Luggage Room
28. Elegant Dining Room
29. Laundry
30. Kitchen
31. Dining Room
32. Pantry
33. Toilet
34. Store
35. Food Store
36. Entrance Porch
37. Technical Room
38. Tele and Comp. Room
39. Interior Landscape
40. Staircase
41. Fire Escape Staircase
42. Lift

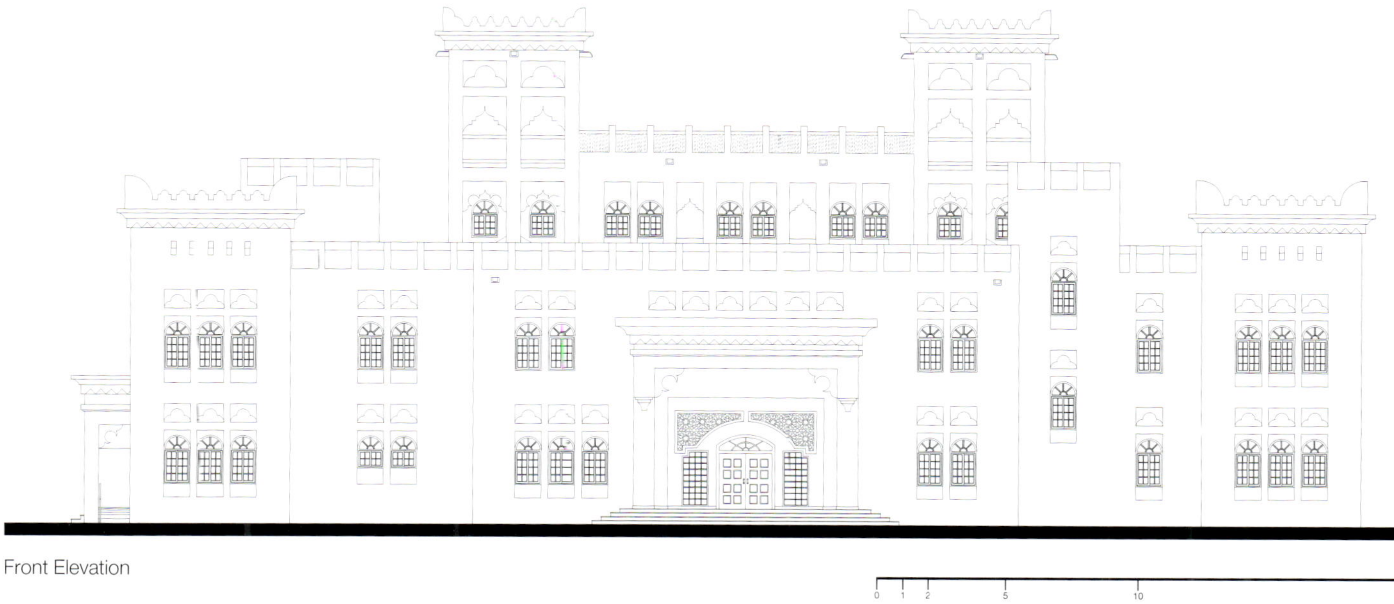

Front Elevation

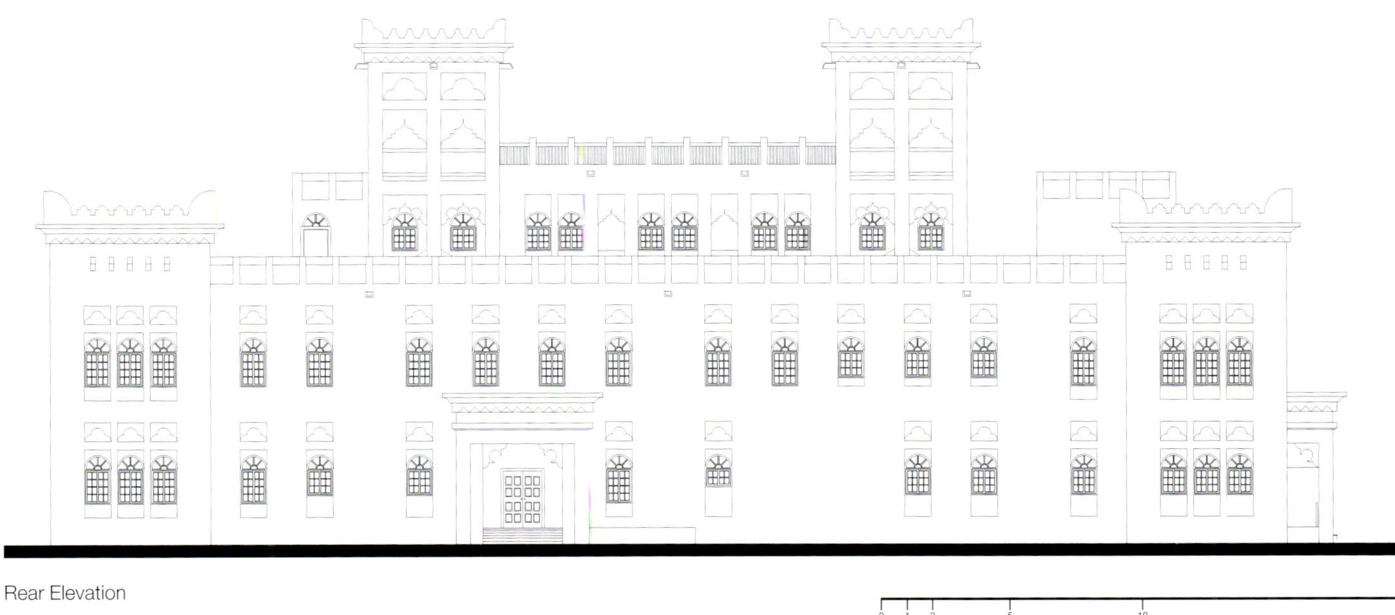

Rear Elevation

Barzan Tower

Barzan Tower

West Bay, Doha, Qatar

Completed, 2000

Client: H.E. Abdullah bin Khalifa Al Attiyah

Award
- Aga Khan Award for Architecture (2004, nominated)

The original Barzan Towers were built at the turn of the twentieth century by Sheikh Mohammed bin Jassim Al Thani, as part of the defensive system that was being developed along the Qatari coast. They were named after the Arabian word *barzan*, which literally means "high place", and they served both to conserve rainwater collected in the area, and to oversee the activities of pearl divers. Their typical square core consists of the tower volume emerging at the centre of a wider base enclosed in an external staircase and tapering upwards. As they were exclusively intended for military purposes, the towers have very few openings and decoration is simple, the parapets around the crown being their only relevant feature.

Most of the above-mentioned characteristics can be also found in AEB's contemporary Barzan Tower – located in West Bay, Doha – which addresses the client's request for a building that would integrate well with a modern business district, but would at the same time retain some traditional features.

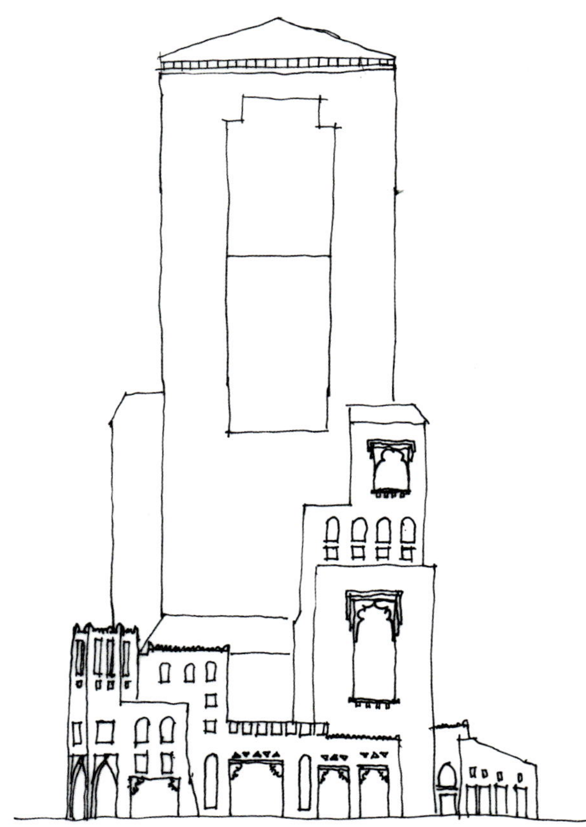

For this, a progressive approach to historical architecture was essential, as an outspoken vernacular style would clash with its bold contemporary surroundings. This is why AEB's design exhibits a clear double identity, unexpected and somehow radical, which aims to be the literal metaphor of modern Qatar growing alongside tradition.

On one side, at the ground level, a small village is reproduced, where different heights and typologies coexist and rise up to the eighth floor. Here, the Barzan Tower associates with precious decorative patterns, thus summarising in a single building the different themes of Qatari architectural history. In contrast, the pure geometry of the glass curtain wall envelop the simple shapes of the high-rise, peaking 22 levels above ground, as a symbol of the cosmopolitan Qatar of the twenty-first century.

Not only has the design of the Barzan Tower earned it a nomination to the prestigious Aga Khan Award for Architecture in 2004, but its distinctive language has also turned it into the personification of the debate on the relationship between tradition and modernity in the Middle East, directly inspiring a long-lasting architectural movement in the Gulf region.

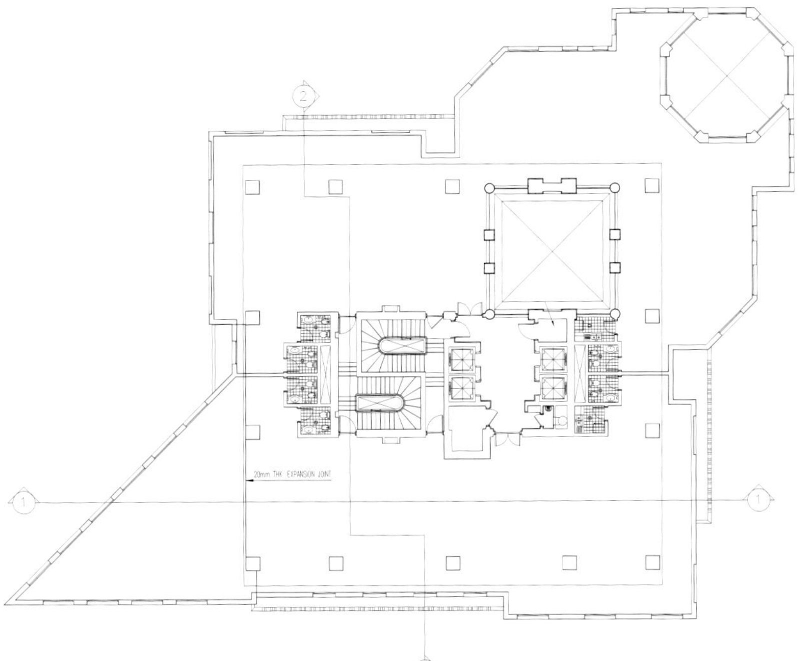

First Floor Plan

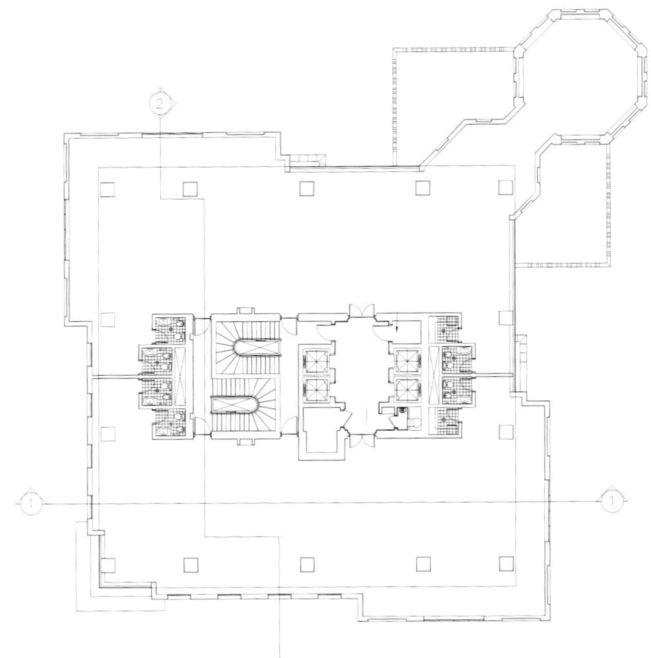

Fourth Floor Plan

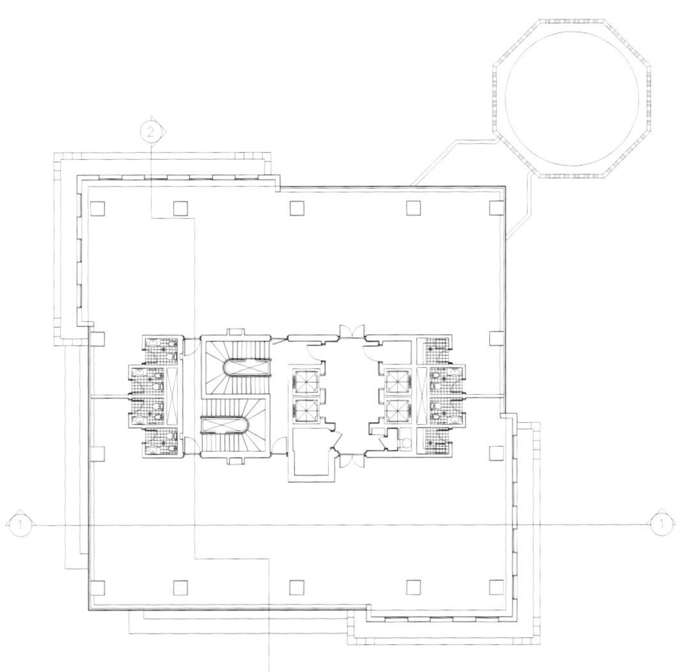

Fifth Floor Plan

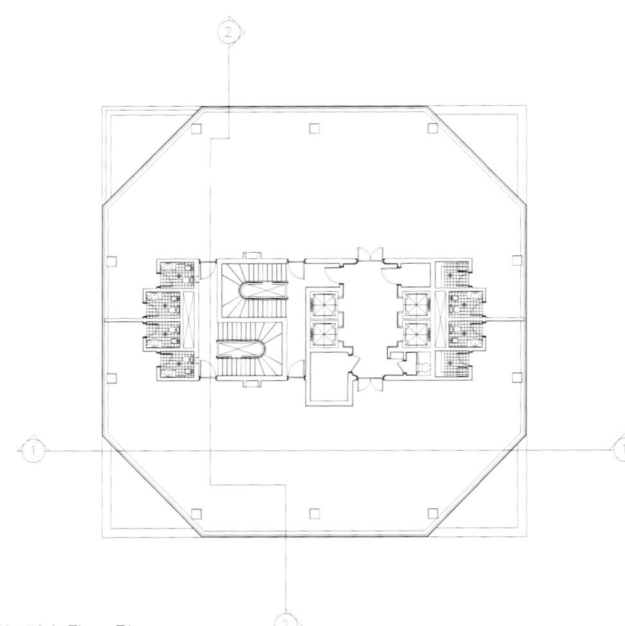

Typical 16th-19th Floor Plan

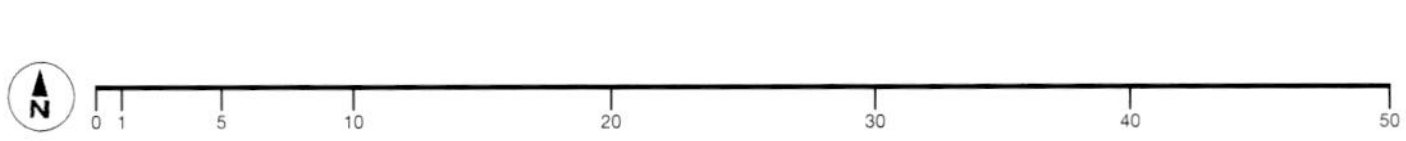

Cross Section

Longitudinal Section

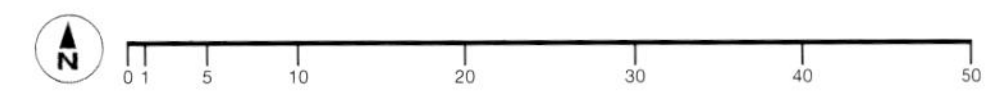

BARZAN TOWER

East Elevation

North Elevation

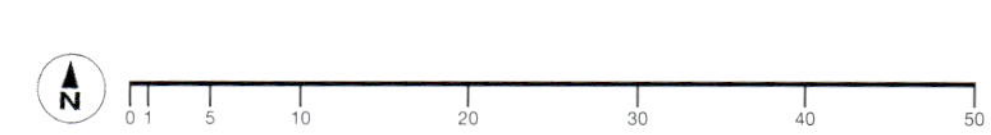

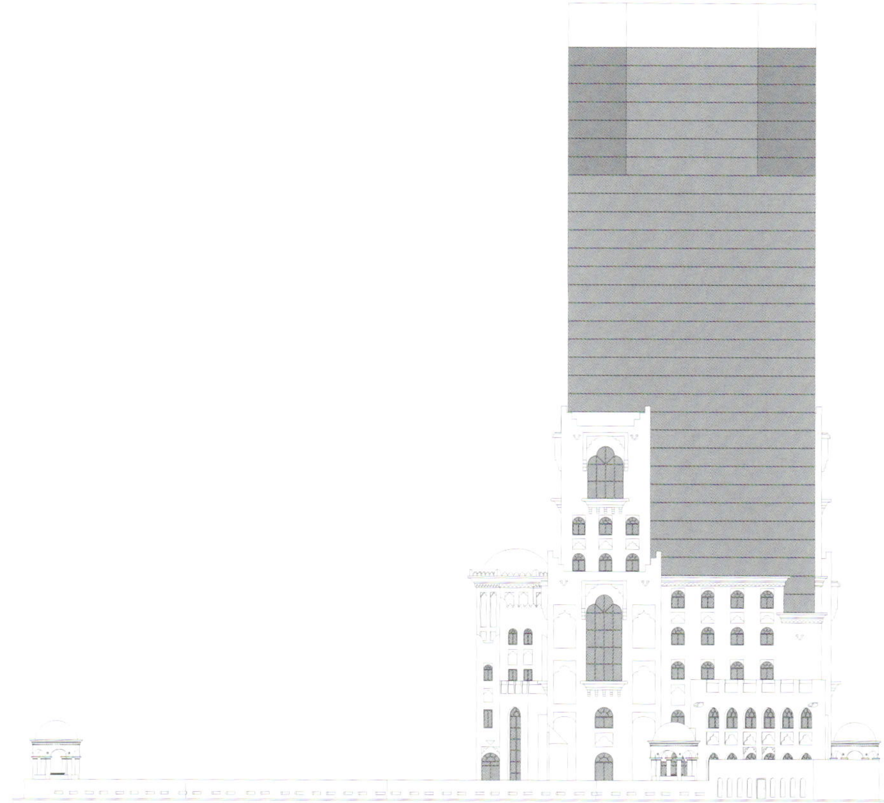

West Elevation

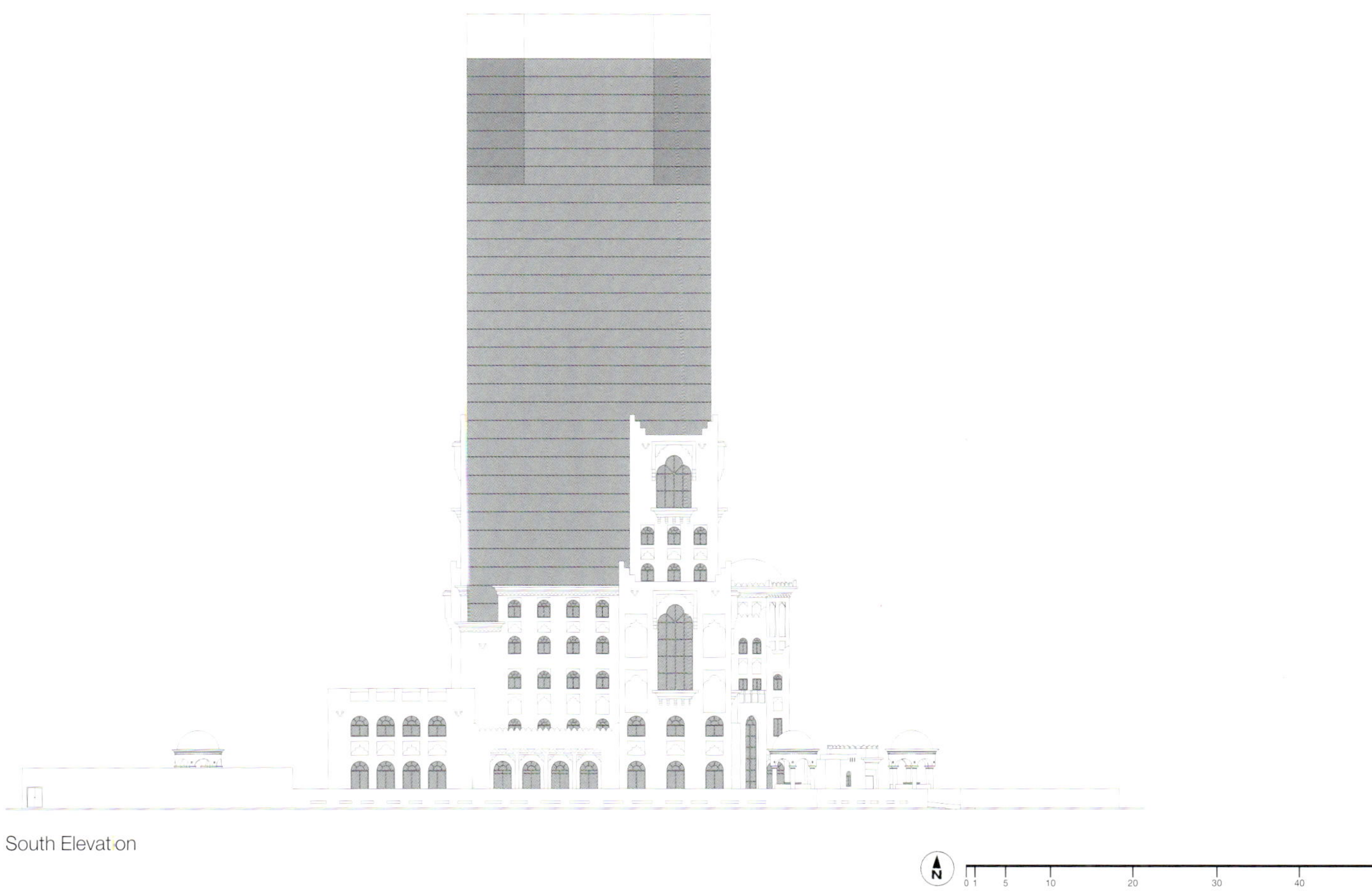

South Elevation

Barzan برزان
TOWER

Diplomatic Club

Diplomatic Club

West Bay, Doha, Qatar

Completed, 2001

Client: Ministry of Foreign Affairs

Award
- Organisation of Islamic Capitals and Cities in the Architectural Projects Category (2004, 2nd place)

The Diplomatic Club marks an important step in the development of AEB's architectural language and the rediscovery of Qatari building tradition. When it was completed in 2001, the club was the largest pure vernacular building of its type, surpassing the size of anything built previously, and on a scale that was not achievable in the past. Here the typologies and motifs of local tradition merge seamlessly with modern materials and techniques, which allow reproduction on a bigger scale that is more suited to the needs of a contemporary building.

At the turn of the millennium this crucial stylistic evolution coincided with a wholesale revision of Qatari hospitality standards, whereby the Club became the country's very first clubhouse for diplomats and VIPs from the Gulf and other parts of the world. Strategically located along the waterfront in the West Bay district, even today the clubhouse offers the best combination of the country's landscape and architectural aesthetics. The building's amenities include a restaurant, a café room, a ballroom for celebrations, a beauty salon and spa, a garden and a swimming pool.

The Club's layout reproduces the typical plan of the early palaces of the region with their typical sequence of courtyards, and the design utilises a vast range of "fundamentals" of Qatari traditional architecture, such as arcades, dome-shaped roofs, *mashrabiyah*-like openings, and parapets.

In spite of the many large-scale construction projects completed in West Bay in recent decades, the Club's front façade, overlooking the parking lots, continues to stand out thanks to its elegant and balanced composition of a main entrance at the centre with two towers framing the sides. The Club's interiors feature rich decorations, inspired by the patterns of the local tradition, which include high-quality carvings of the finest Qatari craftsmanship.

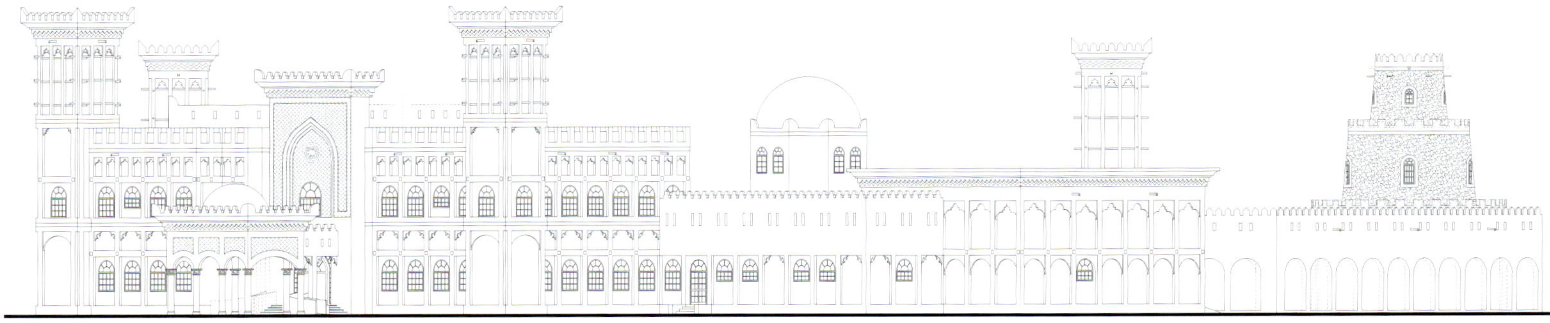

Right Elevation

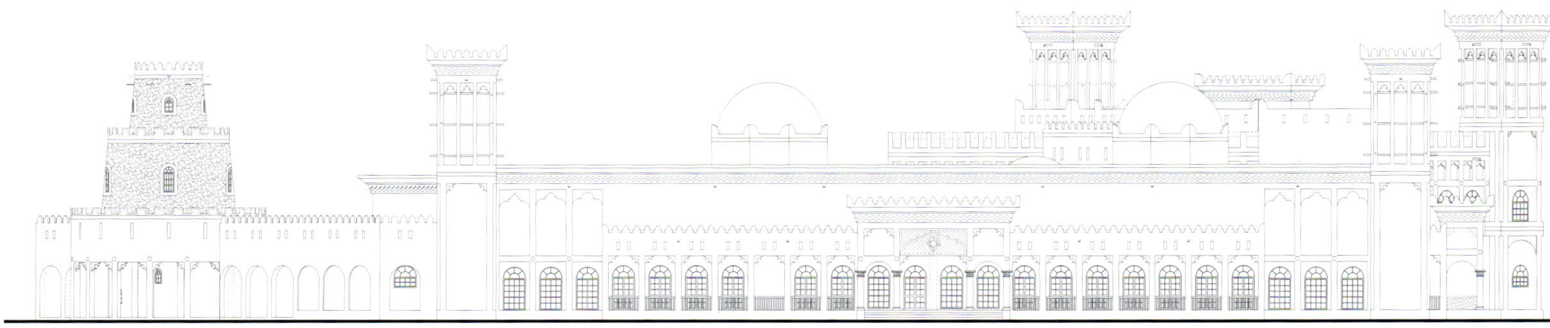

Left Elevation

Front Elevation

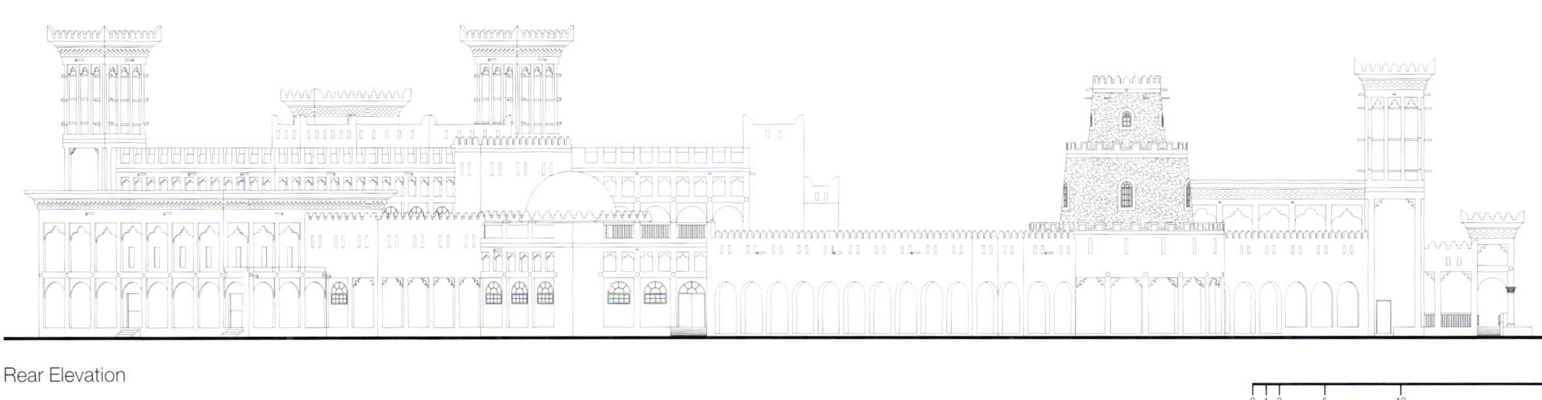

Rear Elevation

Jaidah Mosque

Jaidah Mosque

New Salata, Doha, Qatar

Completed, 2004

Client: Private

The Jaidah Mosque is one of the many religious building projects with which AEB was able to explore the possibilities of sacred architecture. Here, the main focus is the role of the mosque at the local scale, and how the building acts as both a landmark and a gathering point for the community.

To enhance the mosque's presence, the design aims to make it stand out clearly as a material body. The building is clad entirely in pale natural stone, its polished walls enriched by a lower band of ashlar masonry surmounted by a strip of abstract geometrical decorations, and a widespread use of niches and recesses.

Despite its relatively small size, the building's overall effect is one of great solidity and strength, allowing it to emerge as a long-lasting monument in Doha's rapidly evolving neighbourhood of New Salata.

The mosque's clear layout evokes some of the classic features of Islamic places of worship: the entrance gate, the open courtyard and the main prayer hall are all aligned on the same axis, with ablution areas set to one side, and the Imam's house and Muazzin's chamber clustered together.

Lastly, the minaret rises separate from the principal building, signalling the mosque's presence from a distance and marking out the daily prayers. Its walls comprise the *Sabeel*, a profound symbol of sharing, providing free drinking water for worshippers and passers-by.

For this project AEB critically reflected on the effective uses of the mosque's spaces, and reconsidered some of the activities performed in the building, deciding to retrieve a long-lost feature from old Ottoman and Egyptian religious buildings, whereby the ablution areas were commonly located outdoors. This idea was applied to the Jaidah Mosque, where the ablutions occupy an open-air pavilion that is accessed through a sequence of two arcades, and shaded by a wooden pergola, which enhances the calm and reflective atmosphere of this highly symbolic space.

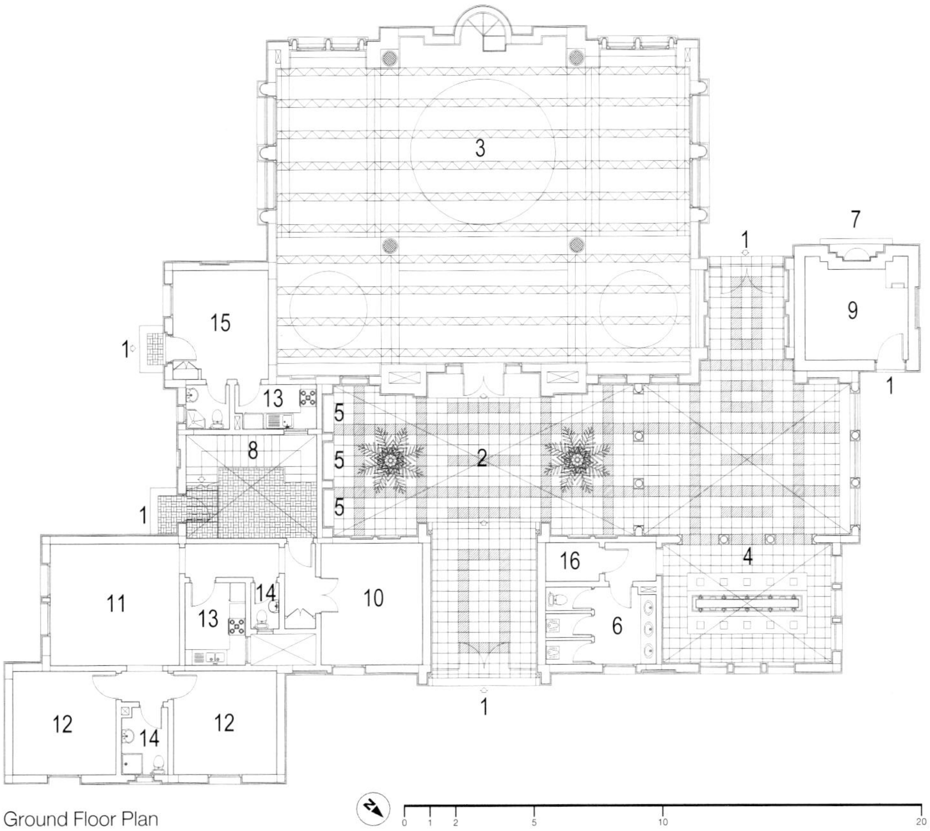

Ground Floor Plan

Legend

1. Main Entrance Gate
2. Open Courtyard
3. Praying Hall
4. Ablution Area
5. Shoe Rack
6. Wash Room
7. Sabeel (Drinking Fountain)
8. Staircase
9. Minaret
10. Imam's House Majlis
11. Living Room
12. Bedroom
13. Kitchen
14. Wash & Bath
15. Muazzin's Bedroom
16. Services

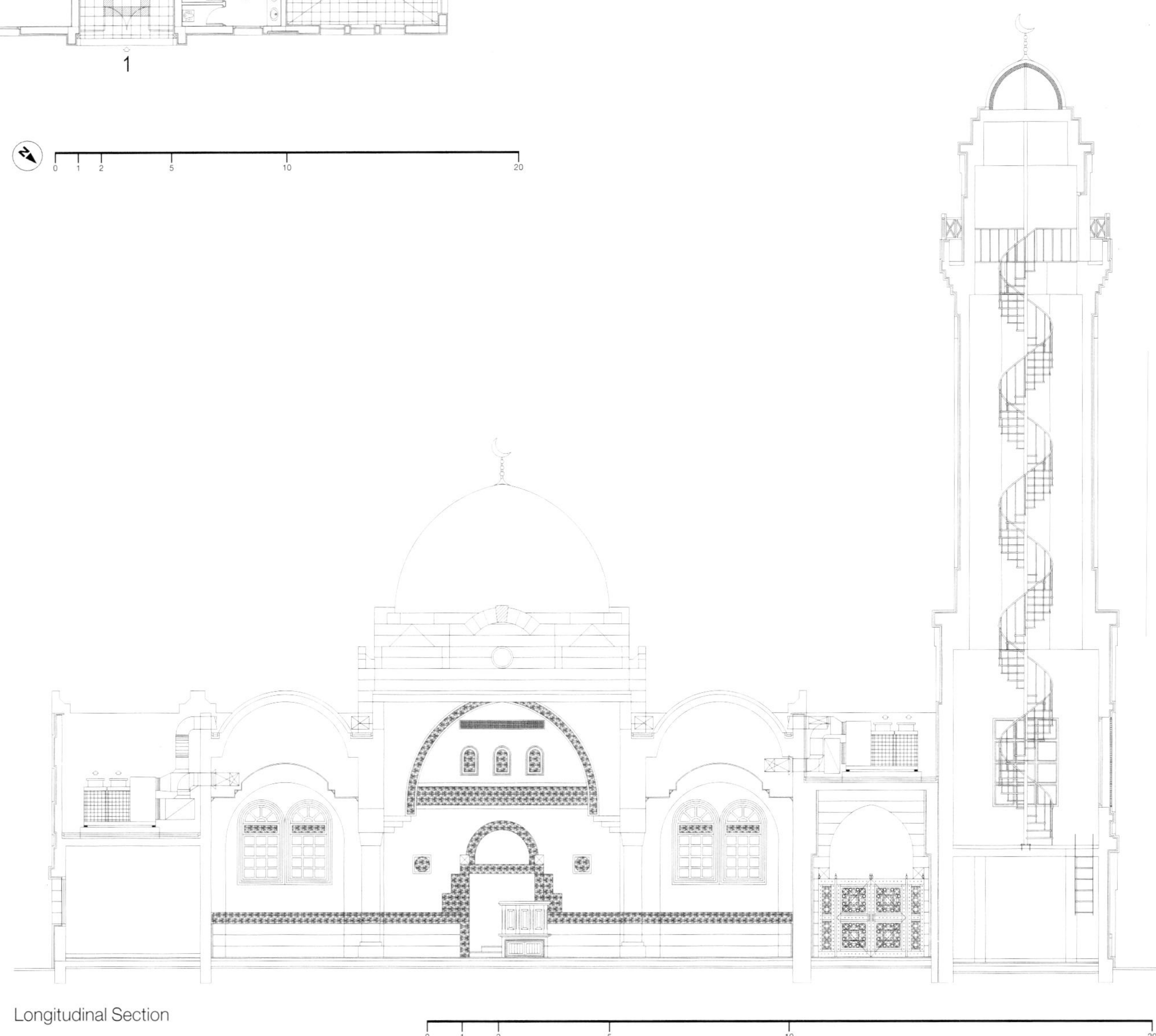

Longitudinal Section

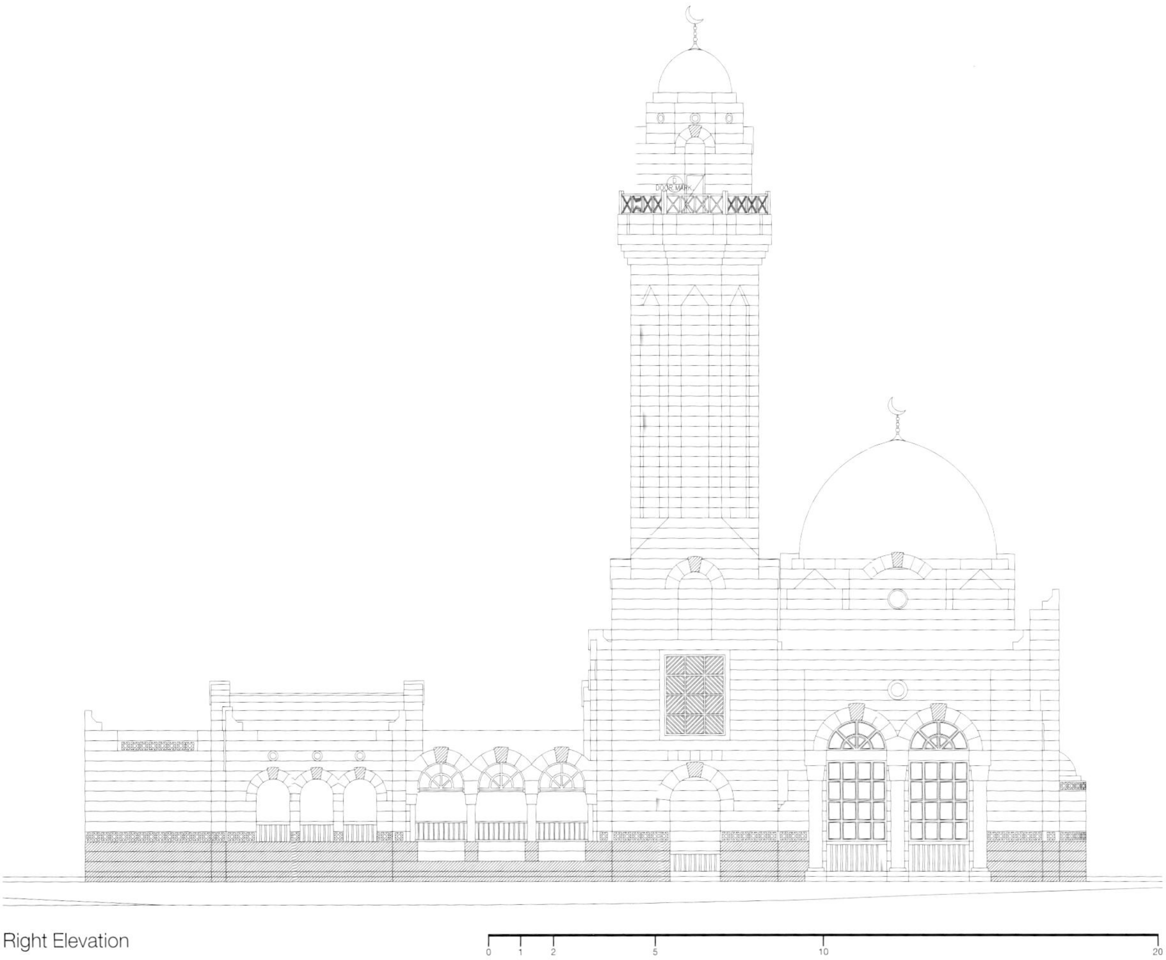

Right Elevation

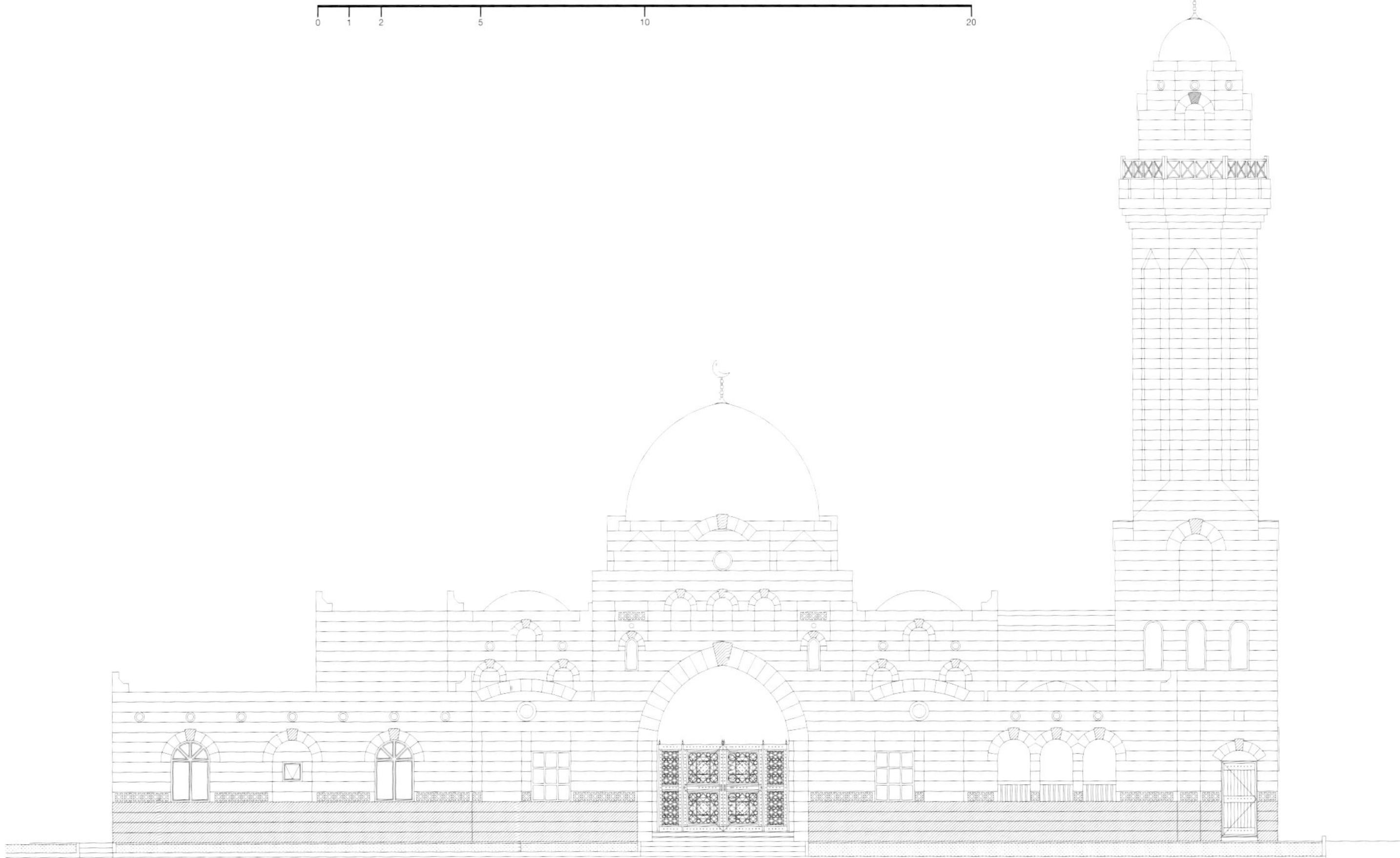

Front Elevation

Najadah Mosque

Najadah Mosque

Al Najadah, Doha, Qatar

Completed, 2005

Client: Ministry of Awqaf

AEB designed the Najadah Mosque following a competition promoted by the Ministry of Awqaf. The building is situated in a fairly complex context: on one side it is very close to the bustling intersection between the busy Banks Street and Ali Bin Abdullah Street; while on the other it overlooks the Souq Wafiq, with its varied traditional buildings and bustling street life.

The mosque's site posed a challenge during its construction, as the allotment had an irregular shape and a considerably limited space. This made the area – often congested with traffic – difficult to access.

This strategic position now provides the Najadah Mosque with the utmost visibility, providing the bearings for cars and pedestrians.

The mosque itself is composed of a cluster of several architectural volumes of different heights, with the minaret dominating all of them. As a result, the image of the complex changes according to one's vantage point.

The plain walls with sand nuances are punctuated by arched windows and dark wooden *mashrabiya*, and are crowned with gentle castellated parapets.

In plan, the mosque offers a sequence of indoor/outdoor spaces, including an intimate garden of palms, which provides worshippers with a much-needed oasis of calm and peace.

The design of the Najadah Mosque does not reference the local vernacular, drawing instead from the larger Islamic world. In doing so, it not only enhances the cultural exchange between Qatar and its neighbours, but also creates a contemporary building that serves as an example for a larger area united by the same creed.

NAJADAH MOSQUE

NAJADAH MOSQUE

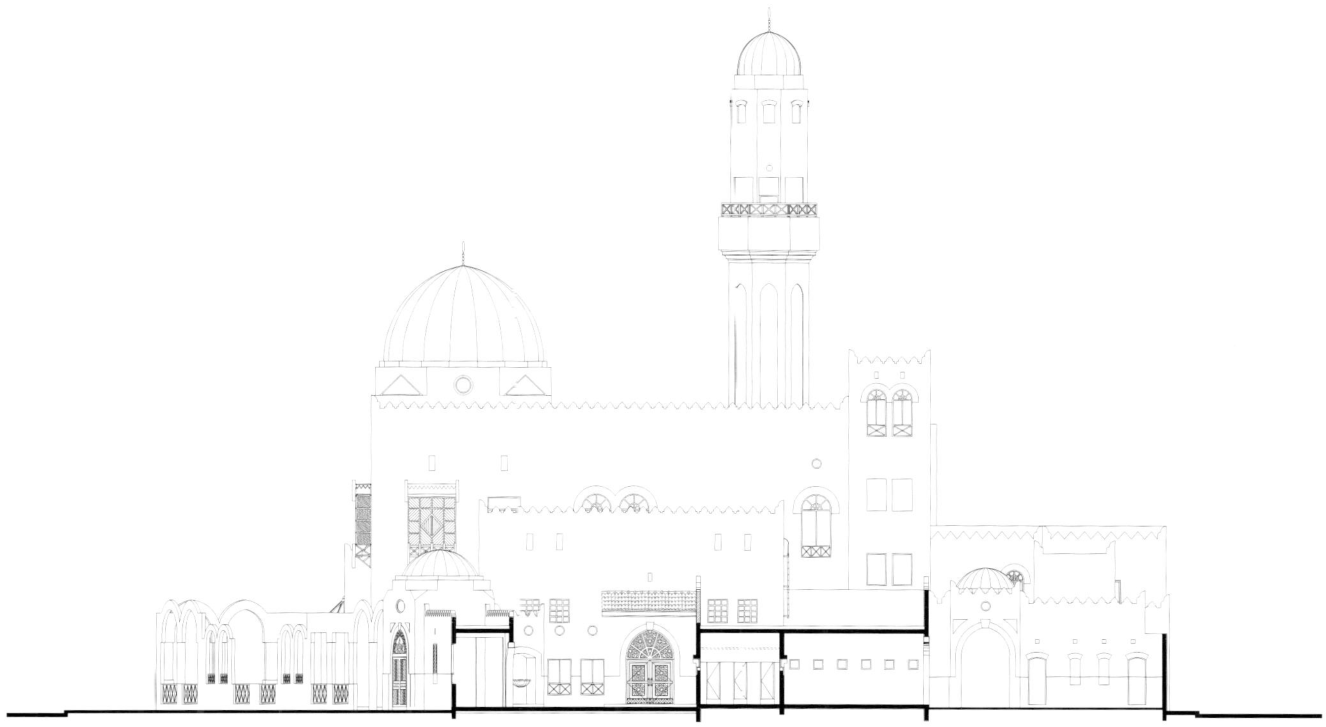

Cross Section

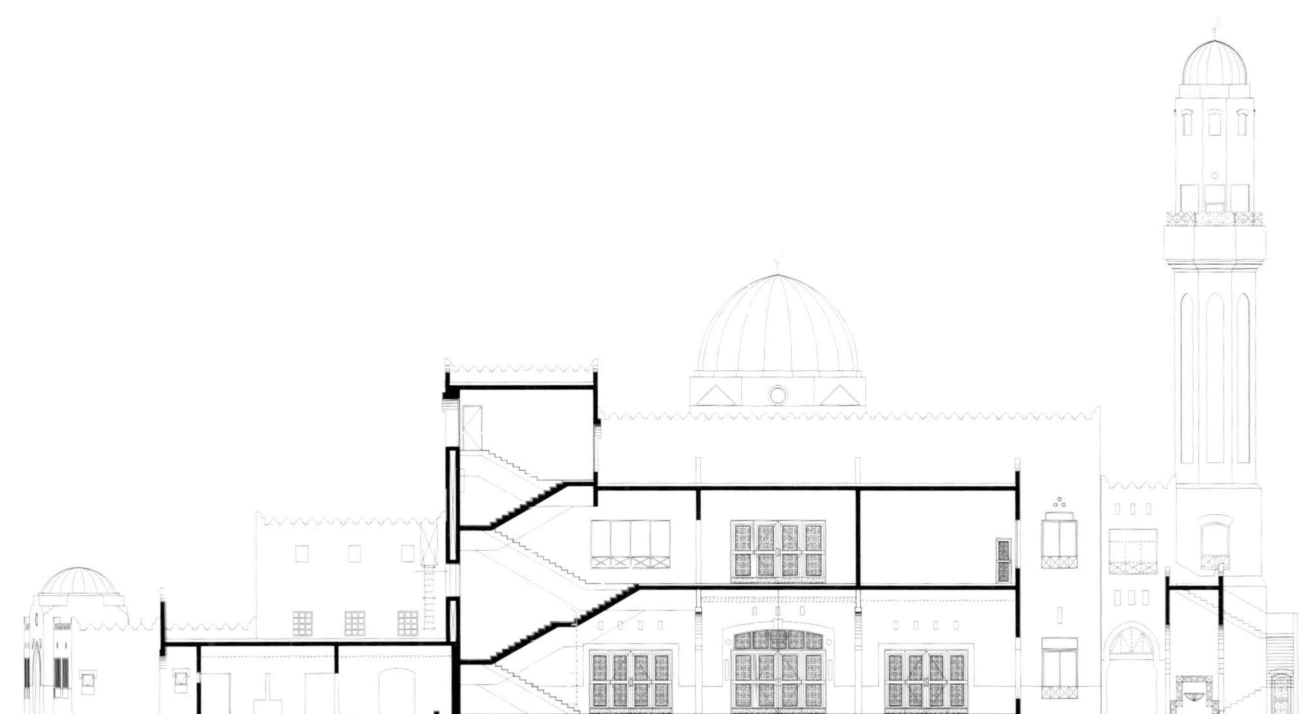

Longitudinal Section

0 1 5 10 15 20

WORK ACCESS

Najada
AL ANNABI

North Elevation

South Elevation

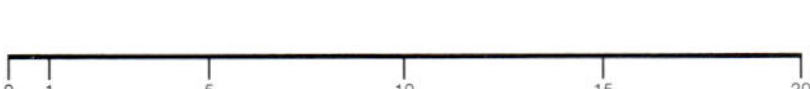

East Elevation

West Elevation

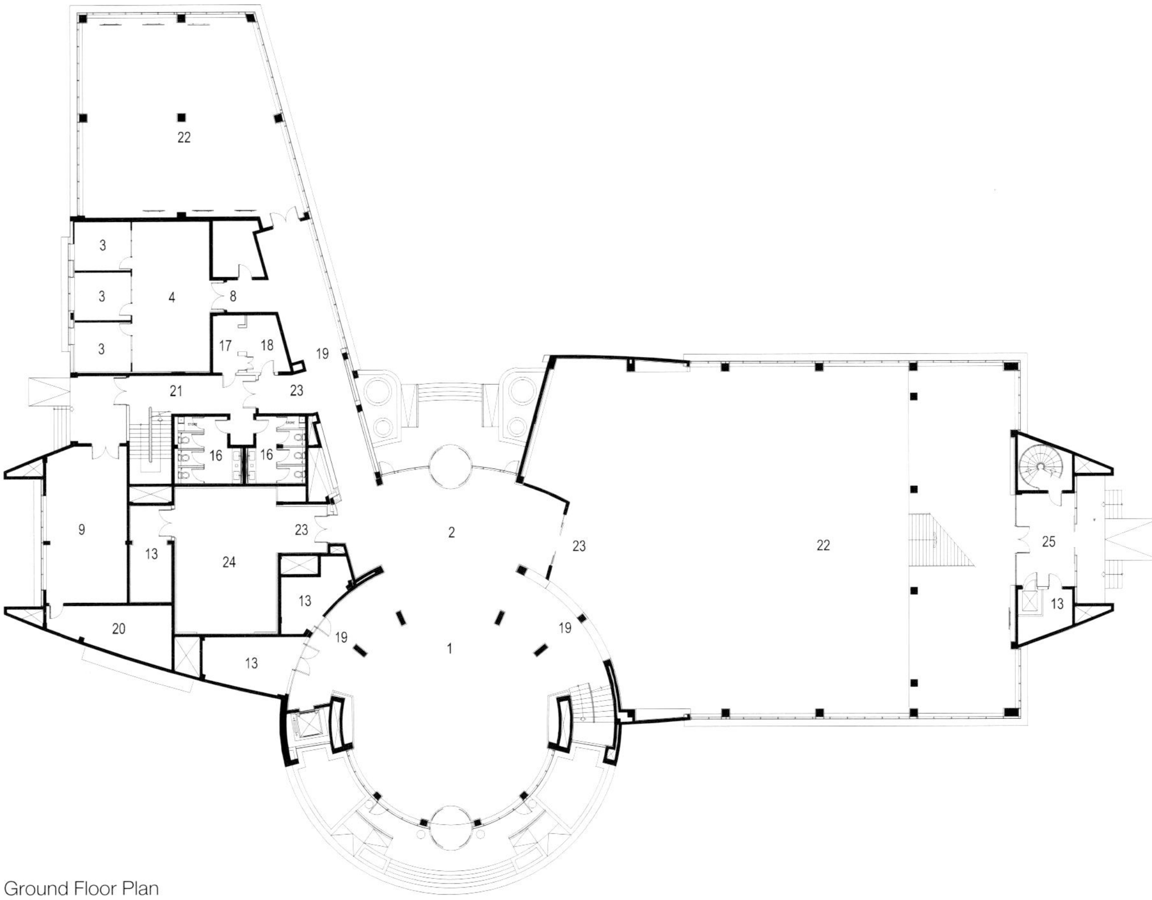

Ground Floor Plan

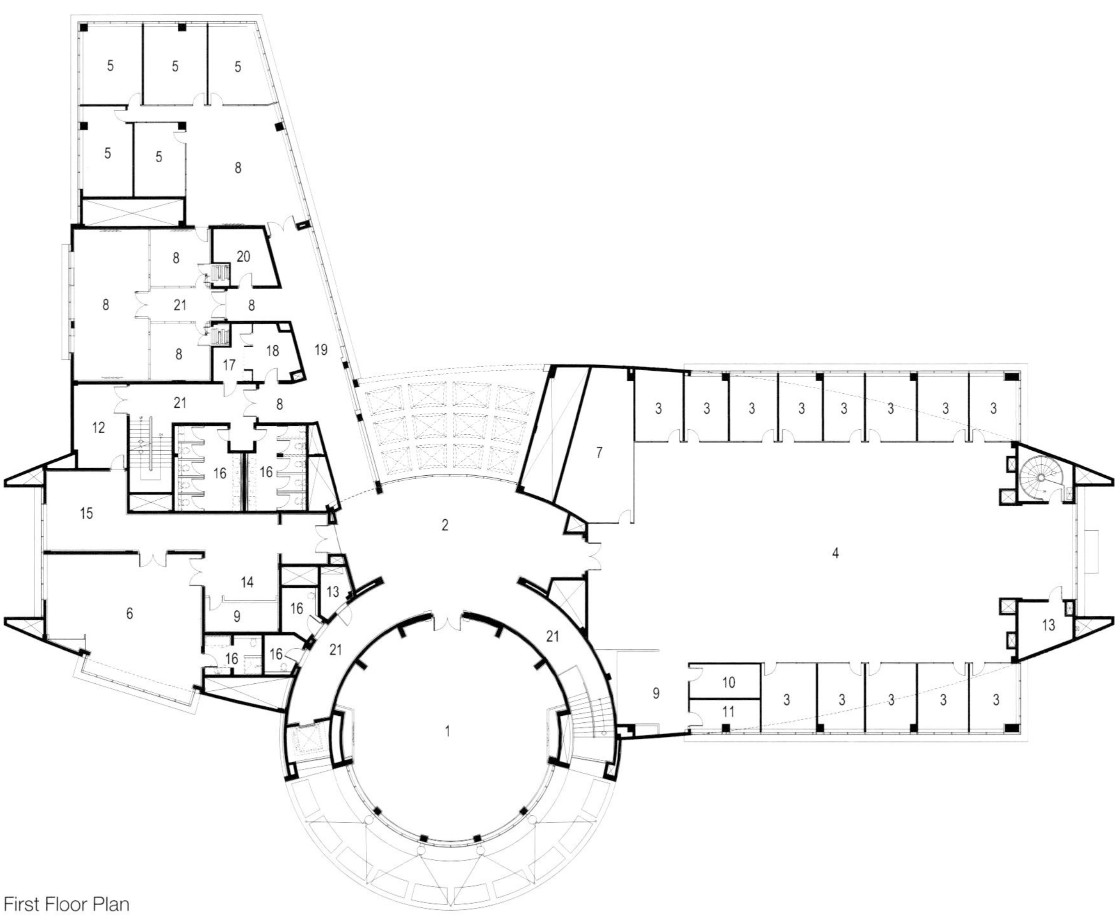

First Floor Plan

Legend

1. Entrance Porch
2. Entrance Lobby
3. Office
4. Open Offices
5. Executive Office
6. General Manager Office
7. Meeting Room
8. MED Conference Room
9. Filing Room
10. Copy Room
11. Janitor Kitchen
12. Store & Janitorial Service
13. Technical Room
14. Reception
15. Waiting Room
16. Toilets
17. Pantry
18. Coffee Bar
19. Corridor
20. Storage
21. Hallway
22. Exhibition Hall
23. Foyer
24. AV Theatre
25. Vestibule
26. Kitchen
27. Servery

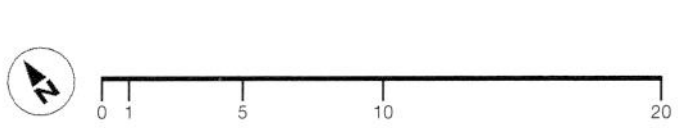

Qatar Financial Centre

Qatar Financial Centre

West Bay, Doha, Qatar

Completed, 2006

Client: Qatar Insurance Company

The Qatar Insurance Company commissioned AEB to design the Qatar Financial Centre in the heart of West Bay, one of the many high-rises that define the complex landscape of the area.

It rises 22 floors above-ground (plus two underground levels), and its total construction cost amounted to QR 120 million. In response to the request to build a headquarters that would express the many activities carried out by the company, AEB provided the building with a highly iconic Q-shaped floor-plan, indicating the trademark first letter of the client's logo.

While only perceivable from the ground level, the gigantic extruded Q stands out from overhead, and is visible from planes flying over the Bay. Its tail actually includes the volume of the fire escapes: therefore, while being based on a formal concert, the layout of the Qatar Financial Centre also effectively responds to the client's request for a fully flexible open space.

The main building's typical floor plan approximately corresponds to an ellipse, showing a clear hierarchy between service and served spaces: elevators, stairs, restrooms, and technical rooms are all concentrated at the extremes of the ellipse's longer axis, leaving its core almost entirely free.

This solution also ensures unimpeded views of the panorama outside, which is another important theme of AEB's project. In fact, when it was being designed, the Qatar Financial Centre was already scheduled to be part of a row of skyscrapers, most of which were yet to be built. In order to prevent the new constructions from interfering with the tower, the project turns its blind walls to the neighbouring lots and orients the curtain walls of its main façades towards the open, unobstructed landscape.

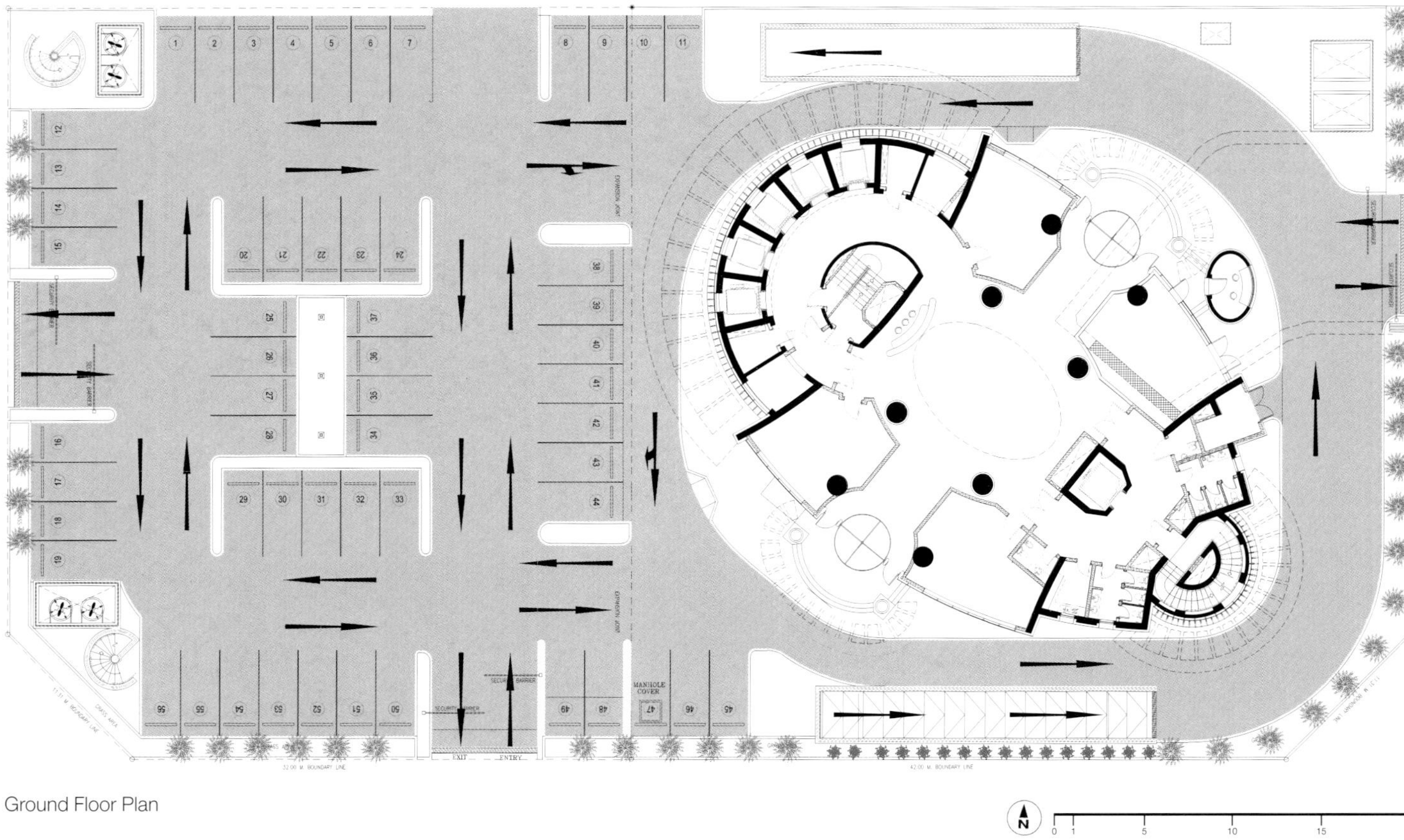

Ground Floor Plan

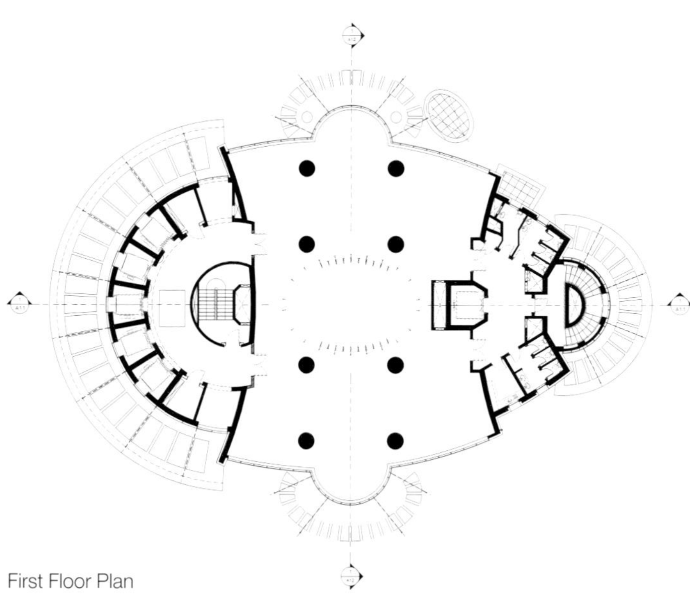

First Floor Plan

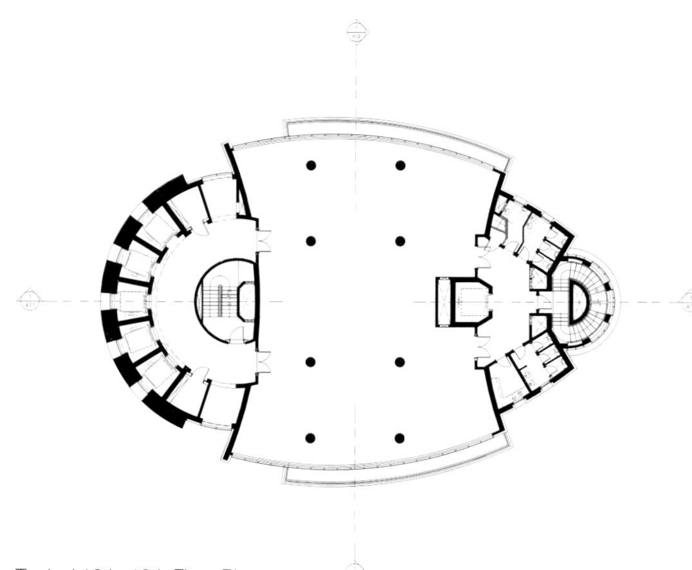

Typical 16th–18th Floor Plan

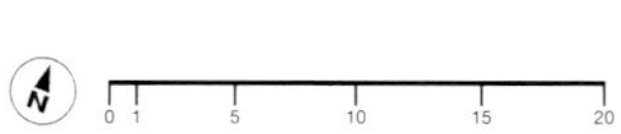

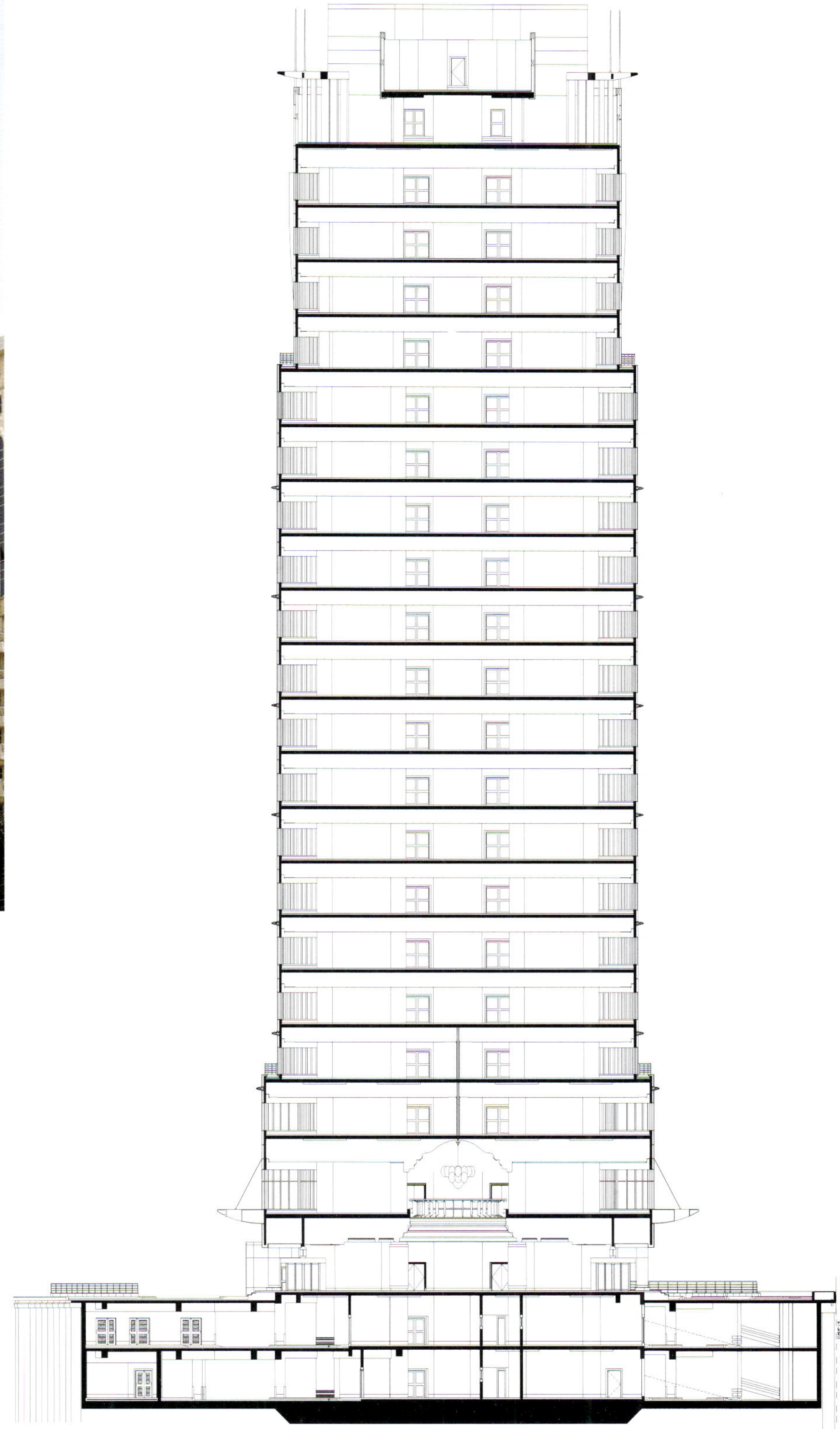

Cross Section

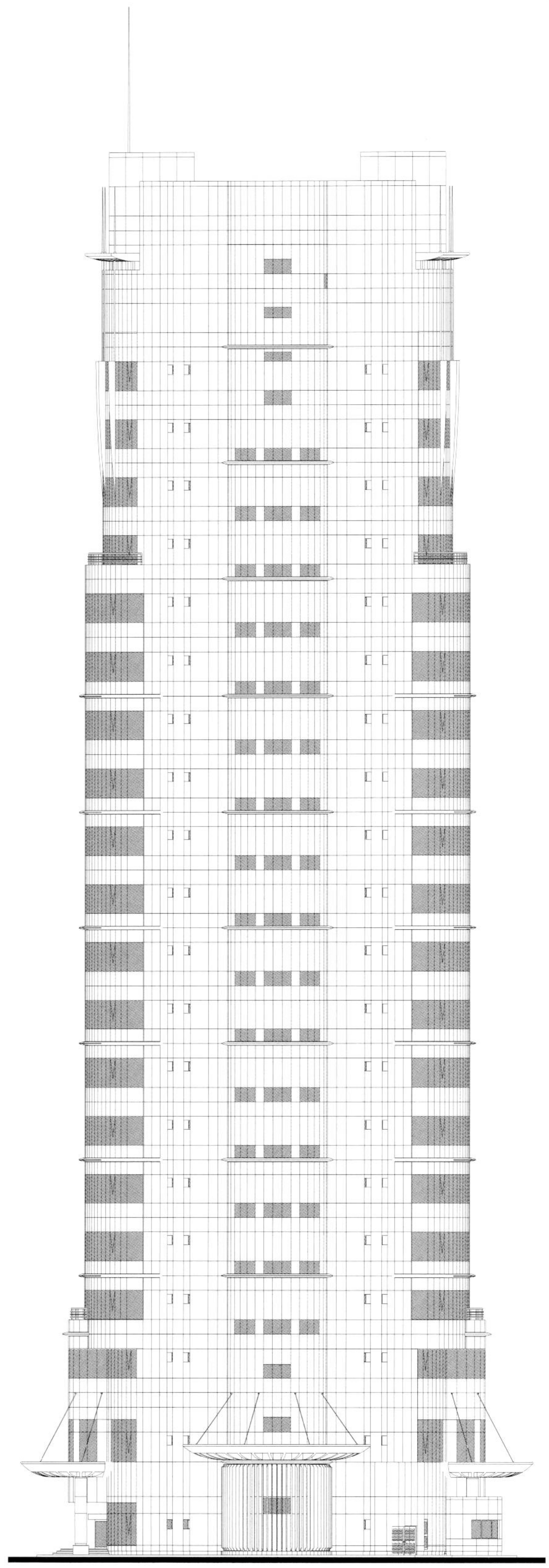

Front Elevation

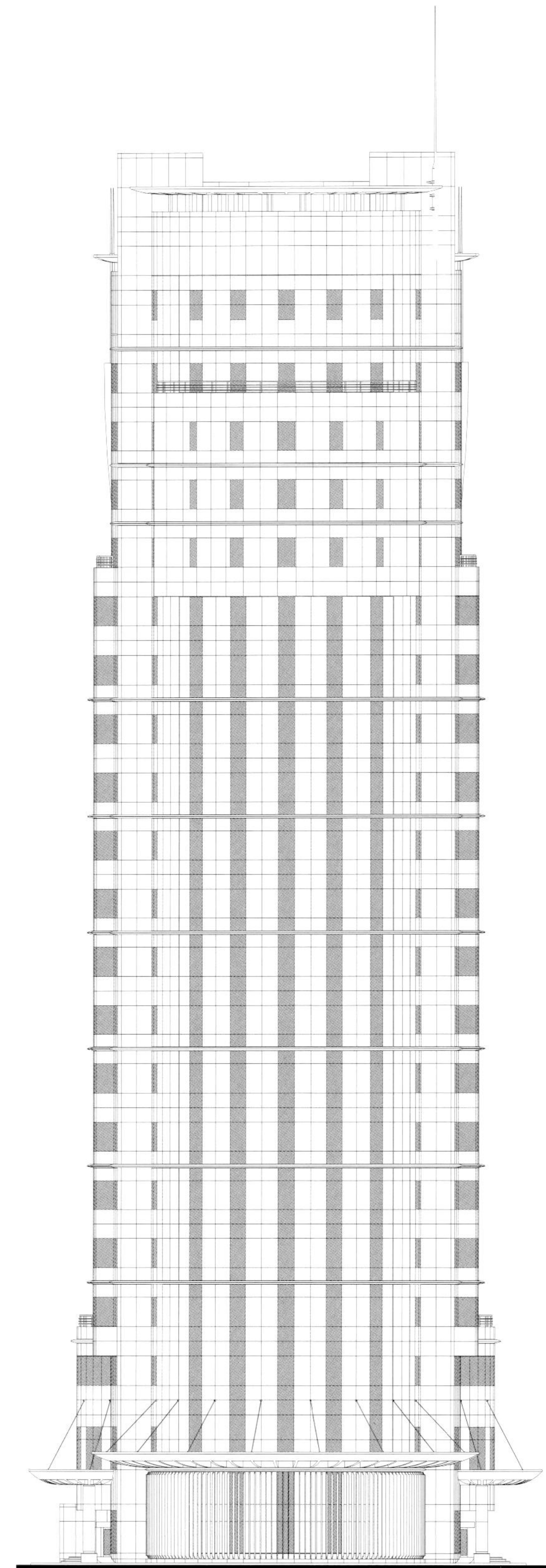

Rear Elevation

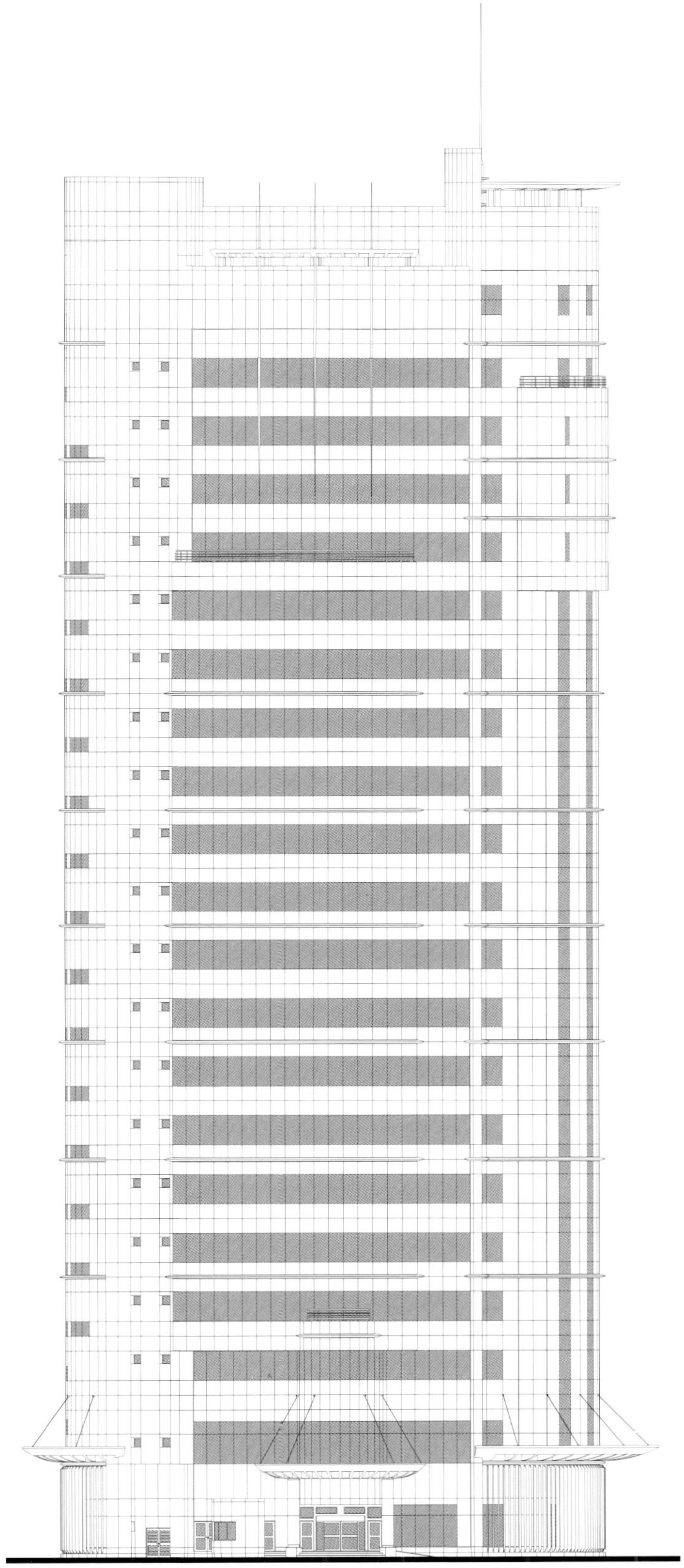

Right Elevation

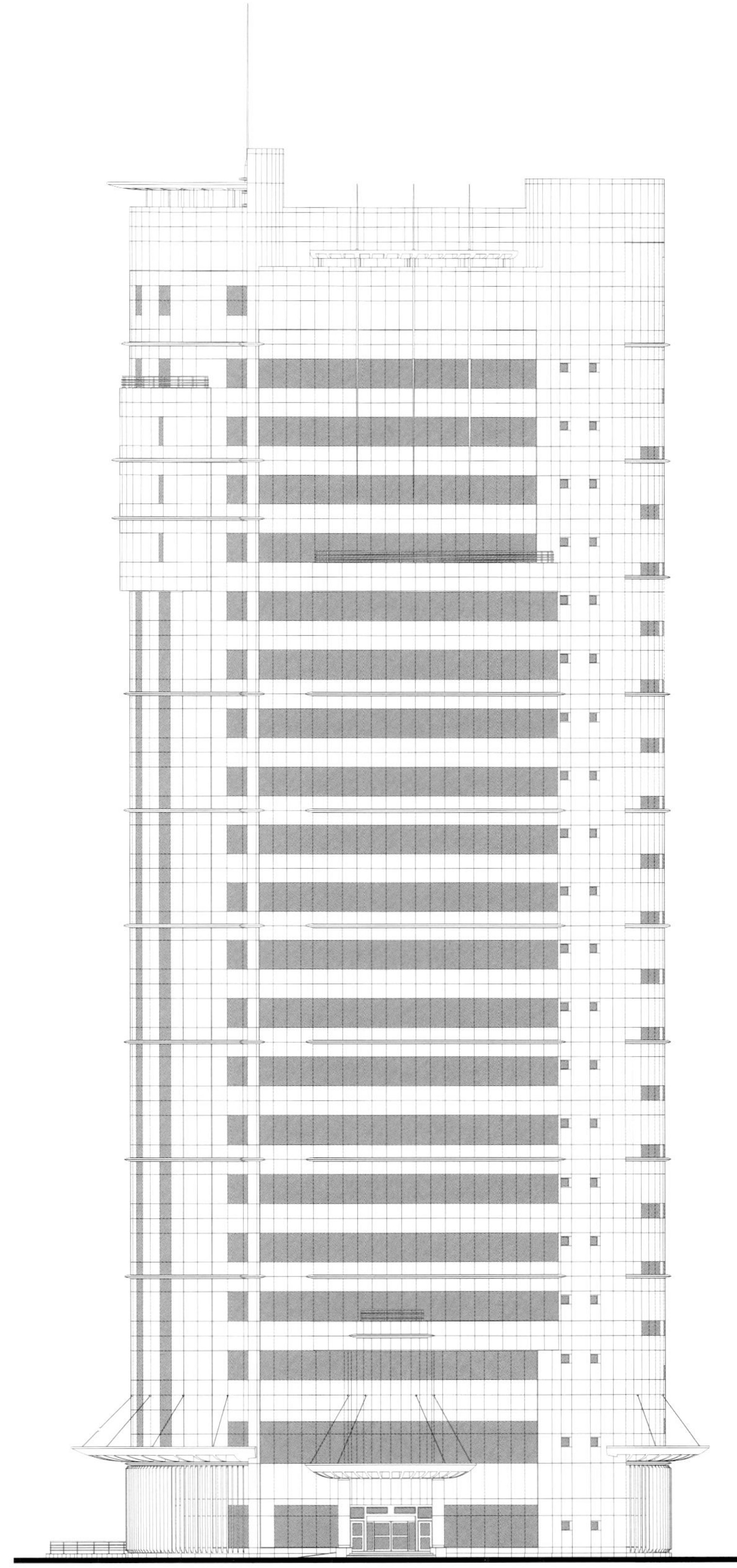

Left Elevation

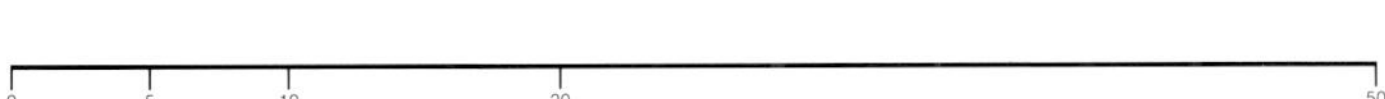

qatar

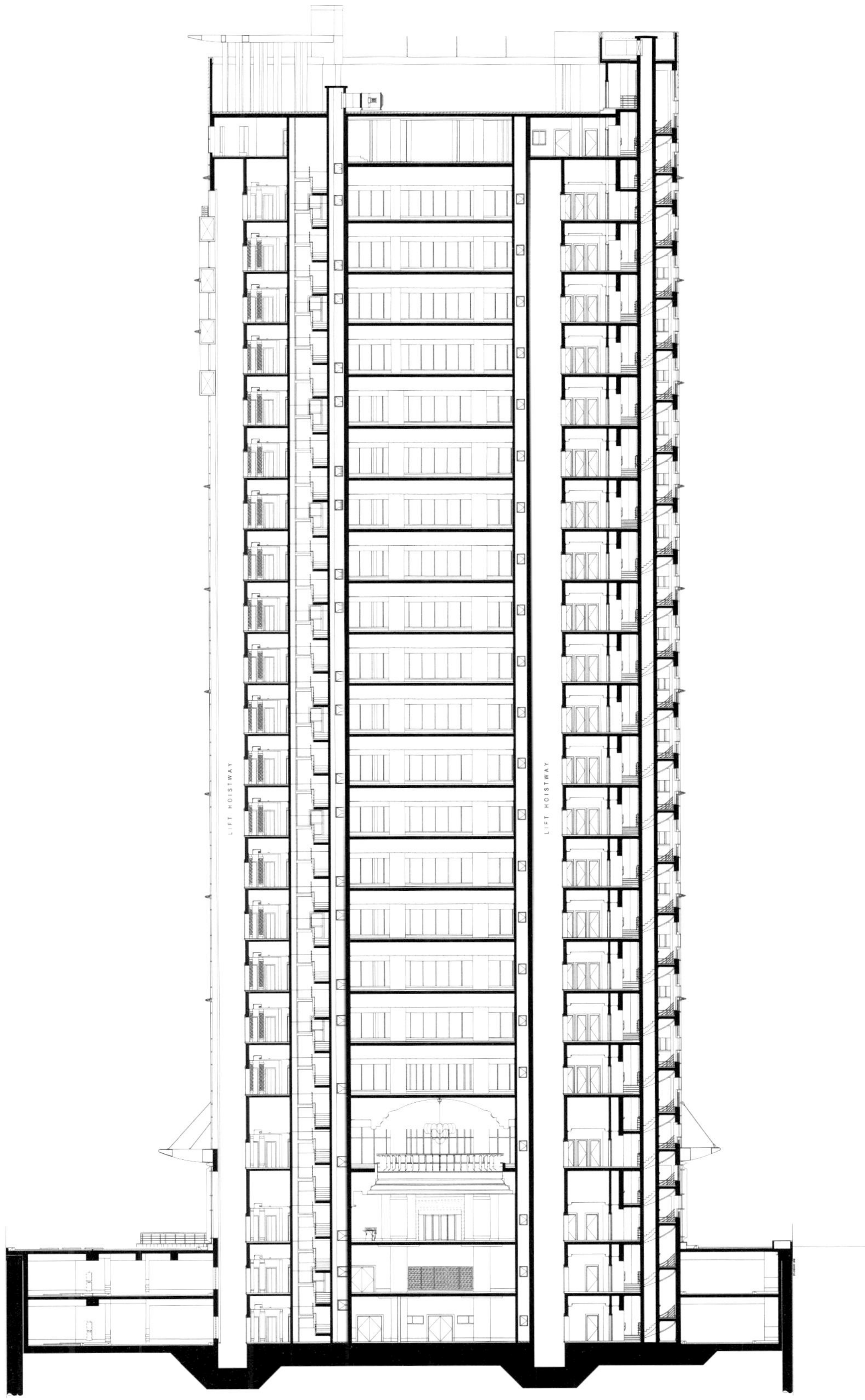

Longitudinal Section

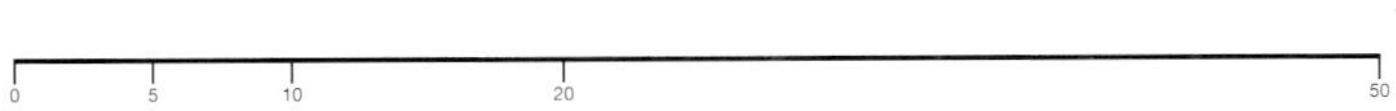

Alfardan Twin Towers

Alfardan Twin Towers

West Bay, Doha, Qatar

Completed, 2007

Client: Alfardan Real Estate Co.

The Alfardan Twin Towers are a complex architectural project made up of three main elements: a 42-storey high-rise, a 28-storey tower block, and a podium linking the two towers at ground level. The towers are among the tallest recent constructions of the West Bay area in northern Doha, and AEB designed them to function as an efficient and self-sustaining community, in tune with the new lifestyles that are emerging in Qatar today. The taller of the two towers includes luxury apartments plus a private health club and swimming pool organised on two levels, while the lower tower contains large open-space office suites.

Both towers stand on a triangular base – with sides that slightly curve towards the outside – with its geometrical centre concentrating all stairs and elevators. This core of service spaces, which is devised to perfectly offset the external walls inside the office tower, takes the shape of a more compact and squared block in the apartment tower, to allow the most functional layout for apartments.

The façades of both towers exhibit a clear hierarchy: the two sides of the triangle overlooking the bay are fully glazed, their transparent curtain wall ensuring an unobstructed view over the Gulf,

with a string-course at each slab level, and a projecting metal frame at the crown integrated with the clear layout of the fronts. For the third façade of both towers it was necessary to guarantee protection from sand storms and winds blowing from the desert, and it therefore comprises a regular grid of blind aluminium panels associated with few smaller openings. The arch-shaped podium, home to exclusive boutiques, cafés, corporate offices, and a car showroom, shows an undulating metal roof suspended over a massive glass façade, that follows the street's alignment.

All the collective spaces within the complex are cladded with premium marble and stonework, with a liberal display of patterns that evoke local tradition so as to offer a warm counterbalance to the international hi-tech style of the exterior.

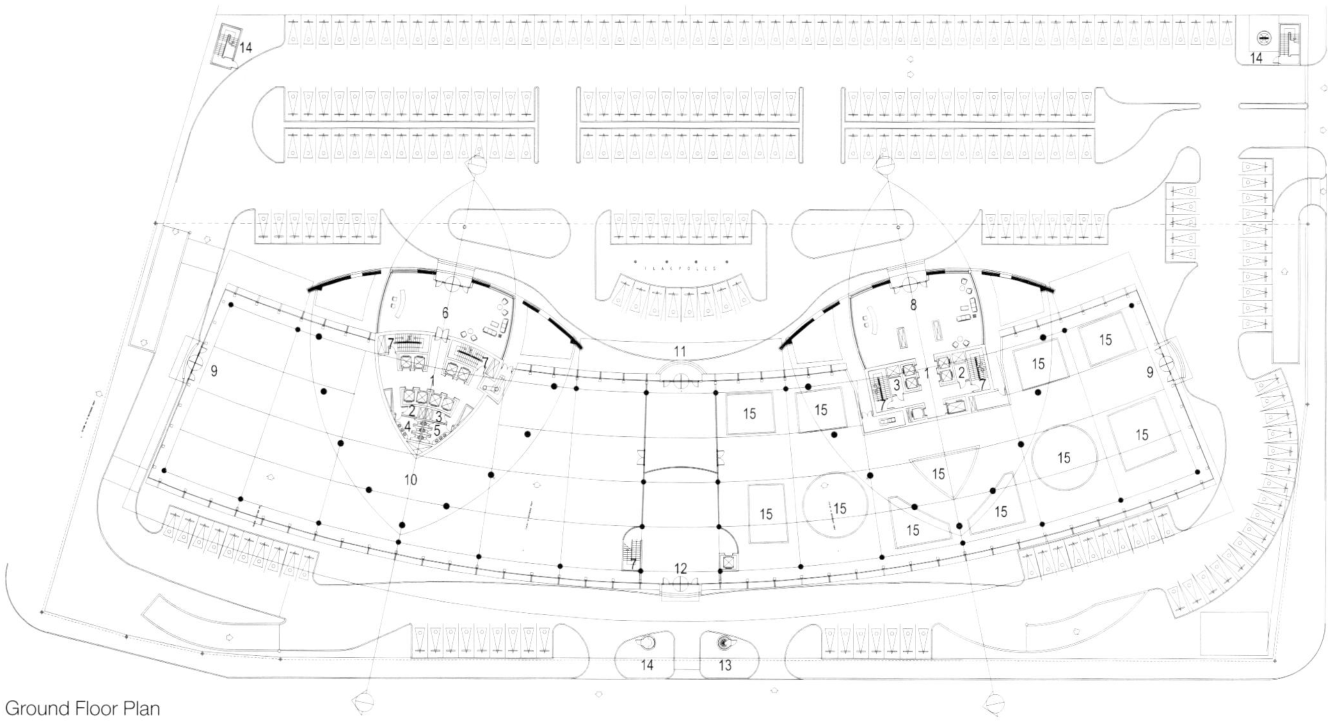

Legend

1. Elevator / Stair Lobby
2. Telephone Room
3. Electric Room
4. Male Toilets
5. Female Toilets
6. Office Entrance Lobby
7. Staircase
8. Apartment Entrance Lobby
9. VIP Car Show Room Entrance
10. Car Show Room
11. Main Podium Entrance
12. Secondary Podium Entrance
13. Fire Escape
14. Guard's Post
15. Specialist Boutique

Ground Floor Plan

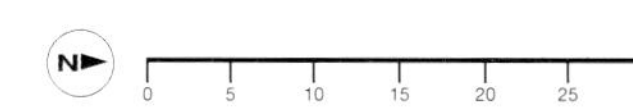

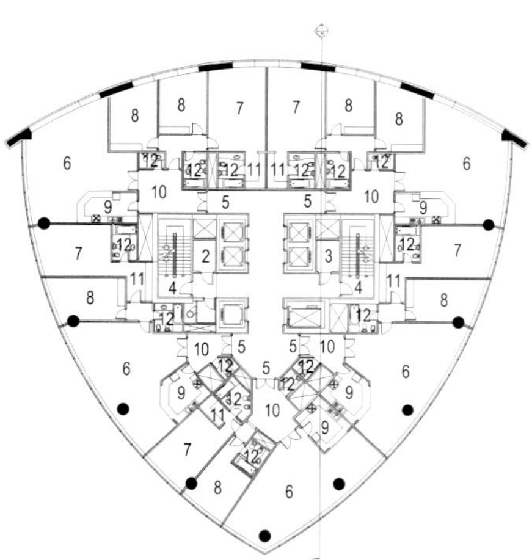

Legend

1. Stairs / Elevator Lobby
2. Telephone Room
3. Electric Room
4. Staircase
5. Entrance Hall
6. Living & Dining Room
7. Master Bedroom
8. Bedroom
9. Kitchen
10. Hall
11. Dressing Room
12. Bathroom

Typical Floor Plan (Level 2 to 24)
Apartment Tower

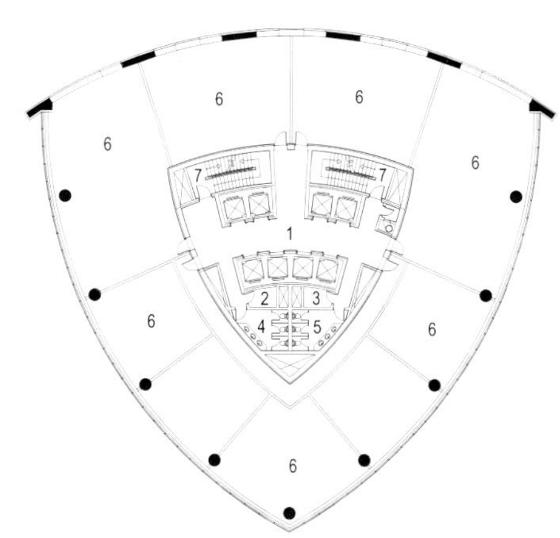

Legend

1. Stairs / Elevator Lobby
2. Telephone Room
3. Electric Room
4. Male Toilets
5. Female Toilets
6. Office Space
7. Staircase

Typical Floor Plan (Level 2 to 24)
Office Tower

Alfardan Towers

أبراج الفردان

Al Sharq Village & Spa

Al Sharq Village & Spa

Ras Abu Aboud, Doha, Qatar

Completed, 2008

Client: Qatar National Hotels

Awards

- Arab Towns Organisation Award (2008)
- Winner in Tourism and Hospitality, CityScape Qatar Awards (2012)

Located in the eastern part of Doha's city centre and directly overlooking the sea, the Al Sharq Village and Spa Resort takes advantage of its superb position to claim its title of iconic project, one which aims to further boost Qatar's reputation for superlative standards on the international tourist market.

For this commission AEB developed a lucid design concept to be applied throughout the project, from the general spatial layout, to the heights and shapes of the different volumes, and up to the tiniest details. The basic idea is to integrally reproduce a vernacular Qatari village that has grown organically over time, and by doing so offer a meaningful response to the current construction boom that is seriously threatening the traditional urban fabric of the region.

In the process of adaptation of the model to the needs of a contemporary facility, the former courtyard – around which the private living quarters used to be grouped – provides space for a large central swimming pool, which is surrounded by fourteen pavilions, shaped as traditional Qatari private *bayt* (villa) – but actually hosting a total of 174 rooms, including different type of suites. Each *bayt* has a unique layout, freely inspired by the house of a specific group of inhabitants of ancient villages – sheikhs, merchants, pearl divers, and fishermen, among others.

A network of open-air paths leads from the main pool to the guestrooms, crossing a sequence of public, semi-public and semi-private spaces, further enhancing the atmosphere of intimacy and joy in the discovery of typical spontaneous settlements. Also part of the resort are a spa – the largest in the region, spreading over more than 5,000 square metres – and a souq-like indoor mall, appointed with boutiques and shops selling antiques.

As with local traditional architecture, all the buildings display solid rough façades, enriched with rhythmic recesses, entirely painted in cool earth tones, matched with wooden doors adorned with brass details, and opening onto the richly decorated interiors, featuring a precious variety of hues and fabrics.

SIX SENSES SPA

Al Qassar Tower

Al Qassar Tower

West Bay, Doha, Qatar

Completed, 2008

Client: Alfardan Real Estate Co.

The Al Qassar Tower rises in a strategic position on West Bay's principal vehicular road, the Majlis Al Tawoon street. As one of the many corporate buildings standardised in this district of Doha, its design demands for unique aesthetic features to ensure it stands out from the neighbouring high-rise blocks.

For this building, AEB has forgone the standard solution of a totally transparent curtain wall – common to most contemporary service buildings – and has instead defined a more innovative image for the tower façades.

Thanks to the use of precast technologies, unique cladding modules were made to compose a much more complex surface, which provides the Al Qassar with a highly distinctive image while also creating a pattern between its interiors and the surrounding landscape.

The tower includes five lower levels of parking lots, two underground and three above-ground. This volume acts as a monumental square "podium", and is enveloped with finely embroidered panels influenced by traditional geometric patterns, which allow natural light to penetrate the interiors, and ensure air circulation.

Office spaces occupy the section that rises from a polygonal base, where glazed surfaces alternate with broad pilasters and cornices. The typical floor plan shows an articulated but clear layout, with the four corners rotated 45 degrees from the main square direction. Service spaces – such as elevators and restrooms – are located at the core of the building, and are surrounded by a concentric corridor providing access to all the other functions and work-spaces, most of which enjoy natural daylight.

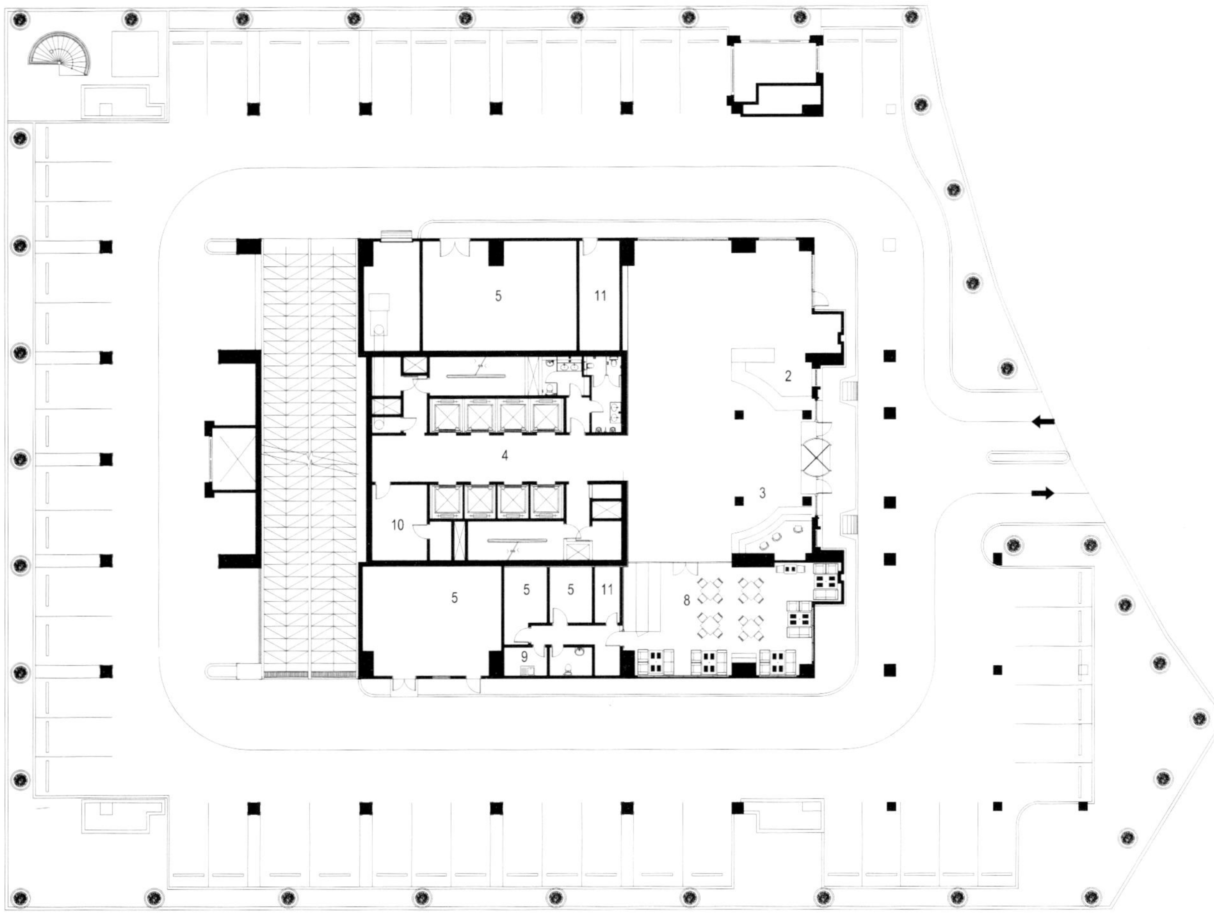

Ground Floor Plan

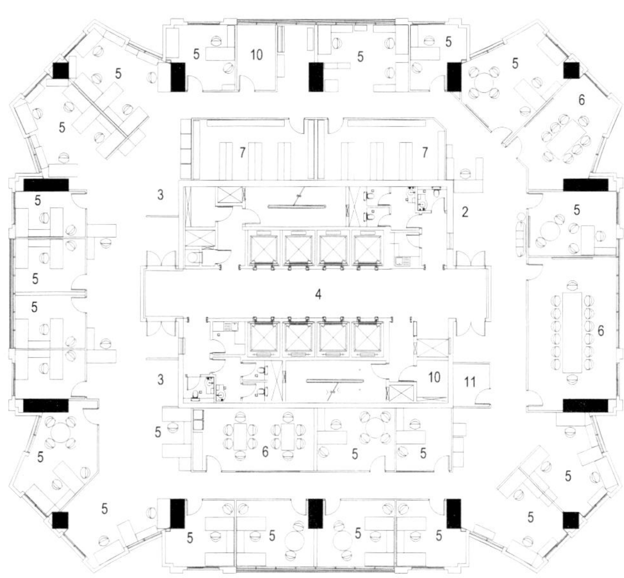

Typical Floor Plan

Legend

1. Main Vehicular Entrance
2. Reception Area
3. Waiting Area
4. Elevator Lobby
5. Office
6. Meeting Room
7. Archives
8. Coffee Shop
9. Pantry
10. Technical Room
11. Store

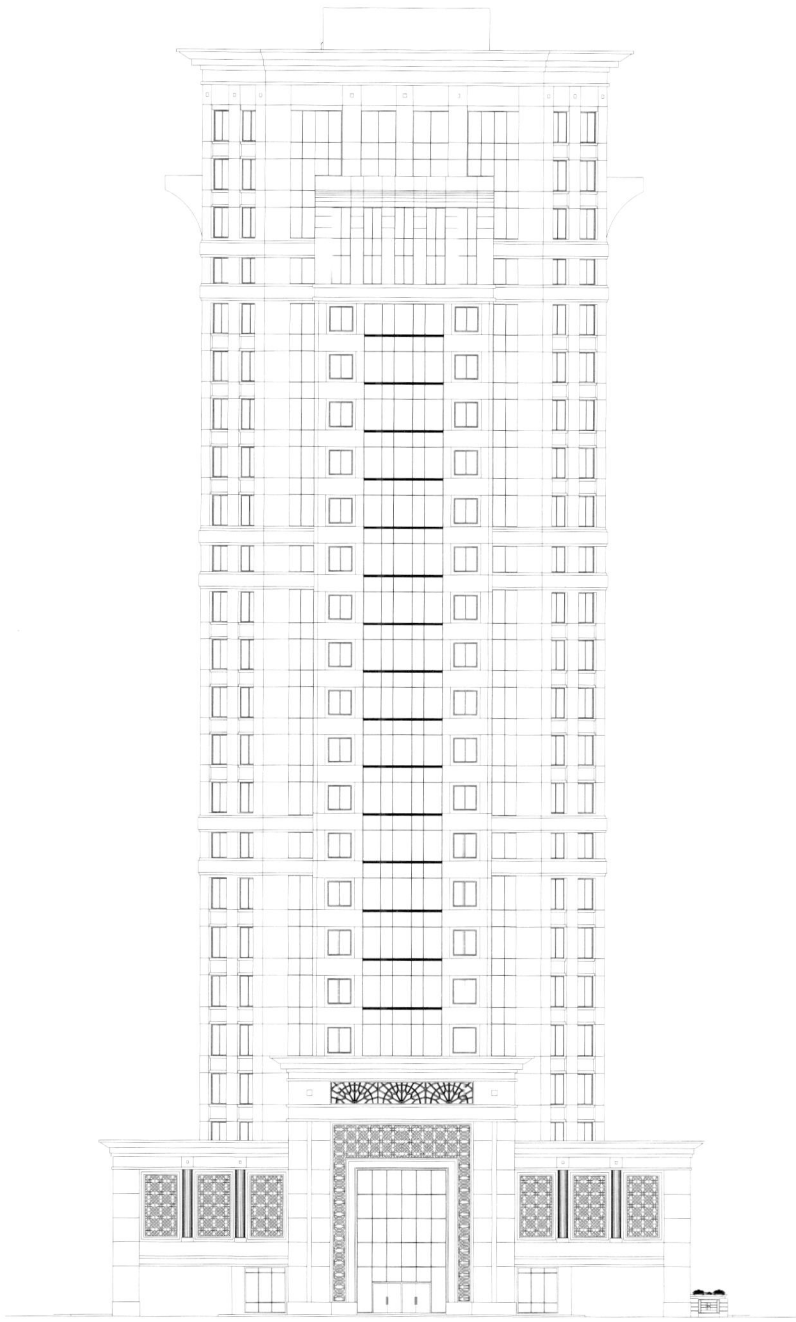

Front Elevation

Rear Elevation

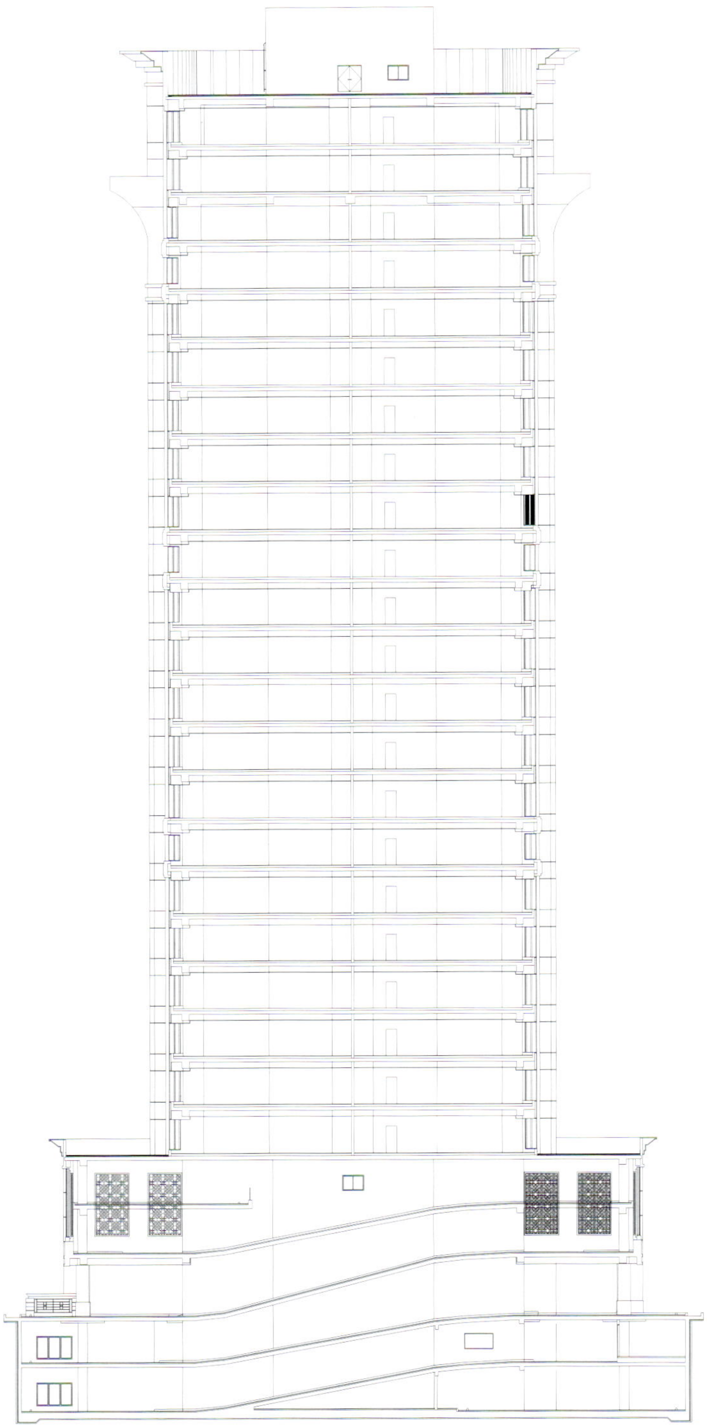

Cross Section

برج
القصار
Burj
Al Gassar

Al Dhayaan Municipality

Al Dhayaan Municipality

Al Dhayaan, Qatar

Completed, 2009

Client: Public Works Authority

Awards
- Organisation of Islamic Capitals and Cities Award (2010)
- Arab Towns Organisation Award (2013)

As a consequence of the discovery of the country's vast oil and gas reserves, Qatar experienced a huge migratory flow of the population from the interior, mostly towards its coastline, and particularly to the city of Doha.

Currently the Gulf country is striving to restore a more balanced use and development of its territory by building entirely new urban centres, while revitalising old rural villages situated in the most strategic areas of its neglected inland, thus encouraging its population to relocate to areas other than Doha. Given its proximity to the capital, the former traditional settlement of Al Dhayaan is one of the first to have been selected to boost this process of resettlement.

In this sense, one hopes that Al Dhayaan will not only provide a template for regenerating this neglected territory, but that it will also offer a challenging opportunity to rethink and harness the

way in which Doha is quickly expanding. By acting as an area in which to concentrate the main public institutions, it could slow the rapid growth of Qatar's capital and counterbalance its organic and fairly unstructured sprawl.

Here, AEB recreates a landscape reflective of the different fields of the architectural tradition of Qatar and the Gulf. At first glance, the complex stands out as a defensive citadel, with its compact volumes, massive blind walls and plentiful castellated parapets emerging from the desert; internally, the sequence of open spaces reproduces the morphology of ancient cluster-shaped civil settlements, with the buildings gathering around a central courtyard; lastly, the minaret of the local mosque rises up as a highly visible landmark. Moreover, the punctuated use of the typical *masharabiyah* windows is a further tribute to the know-how of the craftsmen of the region.

While evoking the forms of the past, Al Dhayaan aims to suggest the possibility of an alternative contemporary lifestyle, away from the congestion of the metropolis. Visitors leave their cars in parking lots in the external part of the village, whose core is only accessible to pedestrians and emergency vehicles. All the main functions – including municipality buildings, a mosque, health and emergency centres, a police station, a civil defence station and several service blocks – are within walking distance and can be reached through a system of paths and squares. Here, the use of palm trees, lotus and neems – among other plants – aims to convey a desert-like atmosphere, to further visually connect with the surrounding landscape.

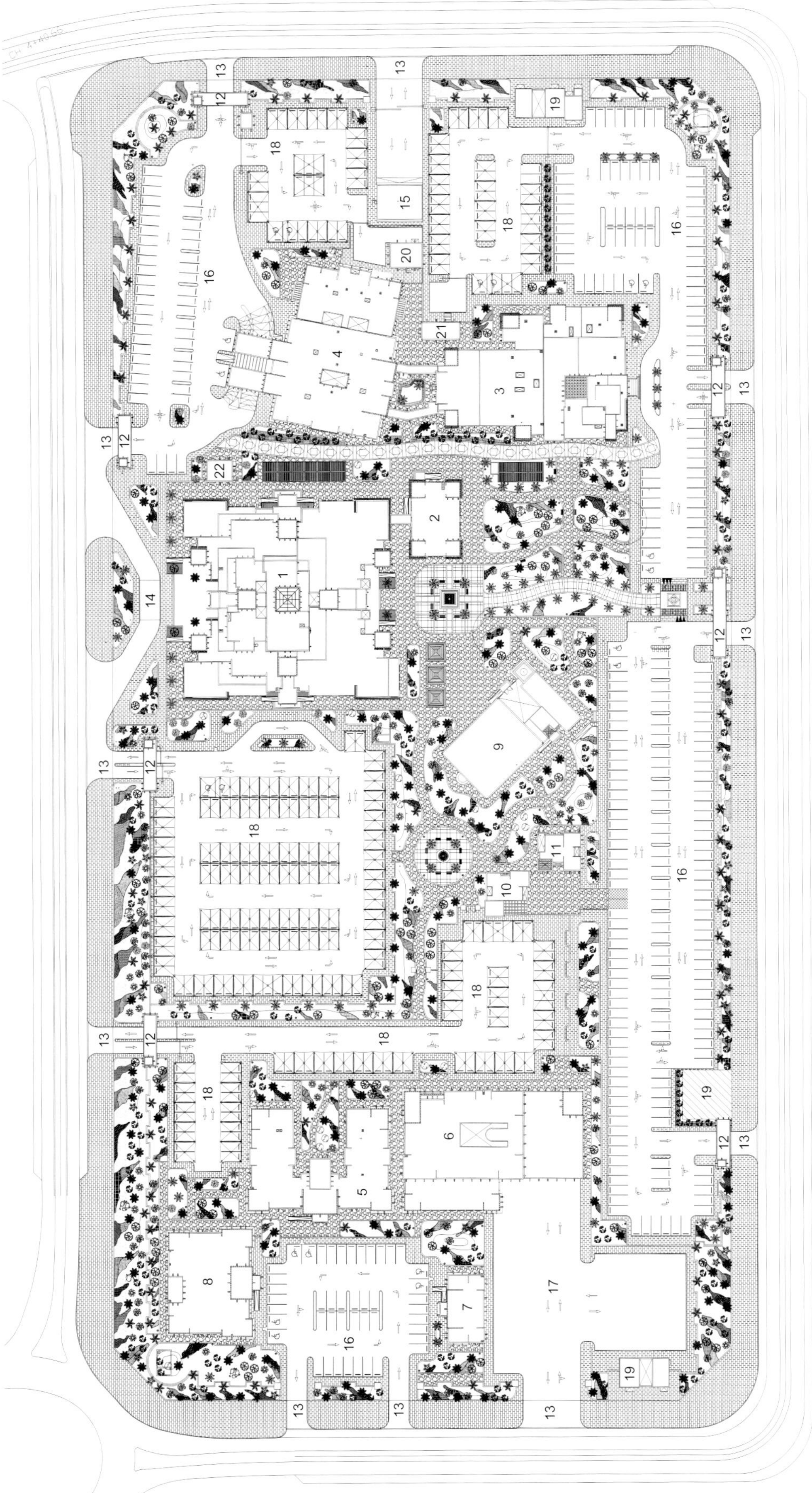

Legend

1. Main Municipality Building
2. Archive Building
3. Health Centre
4. Emergency Centre
5. Police Station
6. Civil Defence Block
7. MOI Service Block Annex
8. MOI Service Block
9. Mosque
10. Imam's House
11. Muazzin's House
12. Gateway
13. Entrance / Exit
14. Drop-off Area
15. Ambulance Parking
16. Public Parking
17. Training Yard
18. Staff Parking
19. Substations
20. Medic Gas
21. Q-Tel, Pharmacy, Store
22. Generator Room

Overall Site Plan

Municipal Building. Front Elevation

Municipal Building. Longitudinal Section

Municipal Building. Cross Section

Municipal Building. Side Elevation

Al Daayen

Health Centre. South Elevation

Health Centre. North Elevation

Health Centre. West Elevation

Health Centre. East Elevation

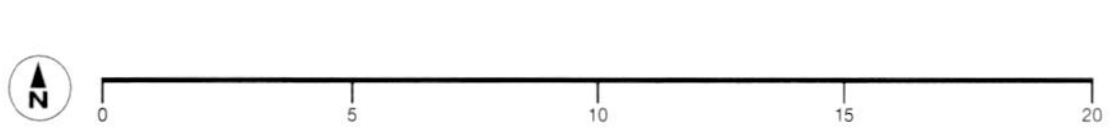

Mosque. Front Elevation

Mosque. Rear Elevation

Mosque. Right Elevation

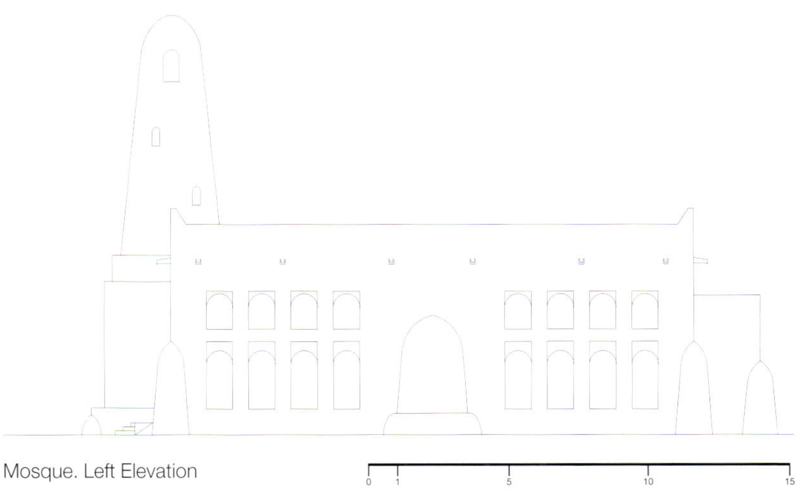

Mosque. Left Elevation

Al Rayyan Municipality

Al Rayyan Municipality
Al Rayyan, Doha, Qatar
Completed, 2009
Client: Public Works Authority

In order to optimise and coordinate the various functions of the public municipal departments, AEB designed the Al Rayyan Complex, which gathers them all together in a single location. The main municipal building – which includes the divisions of finance, administration, health, planning, and logistics – is complemented with a fully-equipped theatre and a state-of-the-art archive building to endorse the Public Works Authority's cultural investment in the facility as a whole.

The design offers a template for future Qatari institutional complexes, whereby the country's architectural tradition is explored through a set of typologies and aesthetics that are deeply rooted in the local context while masterfully addressing the complex needs of a modern service building. To achieve this, AEB's design references the ancient typology of the Qatari courtyard house with its distinctive layout of a central, empty gathering space onto which all the main rooms overlook. This traditional pattern is accordingly adapted to a larger scale, mindfully conserving a balance of voids and built volumes.

In the present case, the traditional open-air courtyard is reinterpreted as a covered central atrium that is accessible from each side of the building, and allows easy navigation to all the different agencies. The interiors of the government offices feature an intricate articulation of the individual spaces devised to facilitate interchange and easy navigation between departments. The high walls and towers surrounding the complex are garnished with the occasional insertion of parapets, *mashrabiyah* windows and other embellishments, as explicit reminders of Qatar's former fortified cities.

Here too, AEB has taken its cue from local tradition while weaving in completely original modern touches, so as to forge new references for today's young architects: for instance, the theatre building boasts a bluntly contemporary treatment of its two volumes sloping in opposite directions, the lower one entirely wrapped in a precious abstract pattern, and the upper one almost integrally plain white.

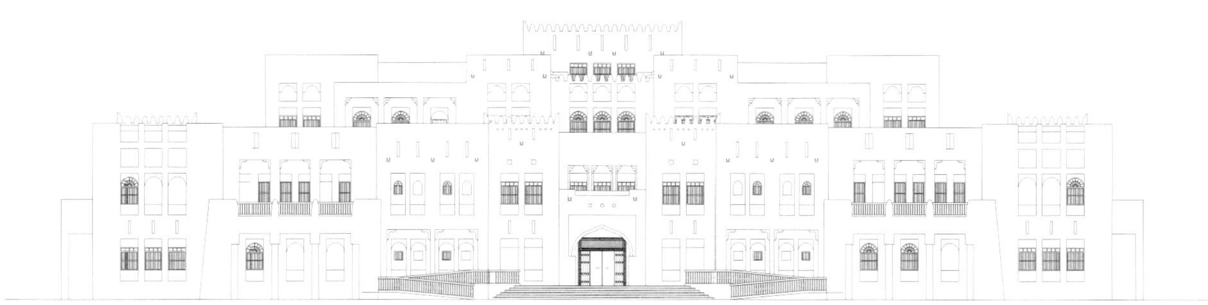

Municipality Building. Front Elevation

Municipality Building. Rear Elevation

Municipality Building. Right Elevation

Municipality Building. Left Elevation

WEST ENTRANCE

THEATER
EXIT

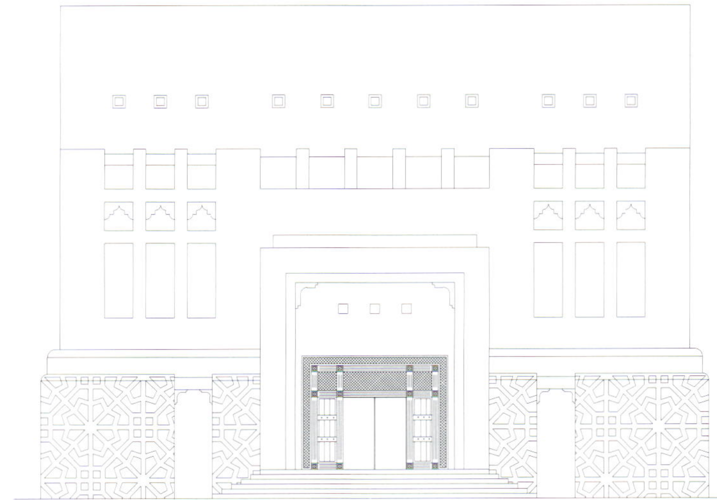

Theatre. Front Elevation

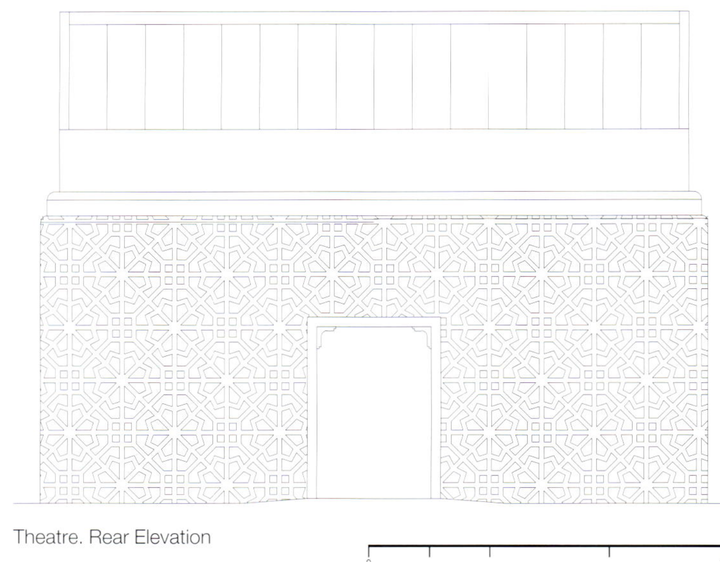

Theatre. Rear Elevation

TOYOTA
TOYOTA

TOYOTA
TOYOTA

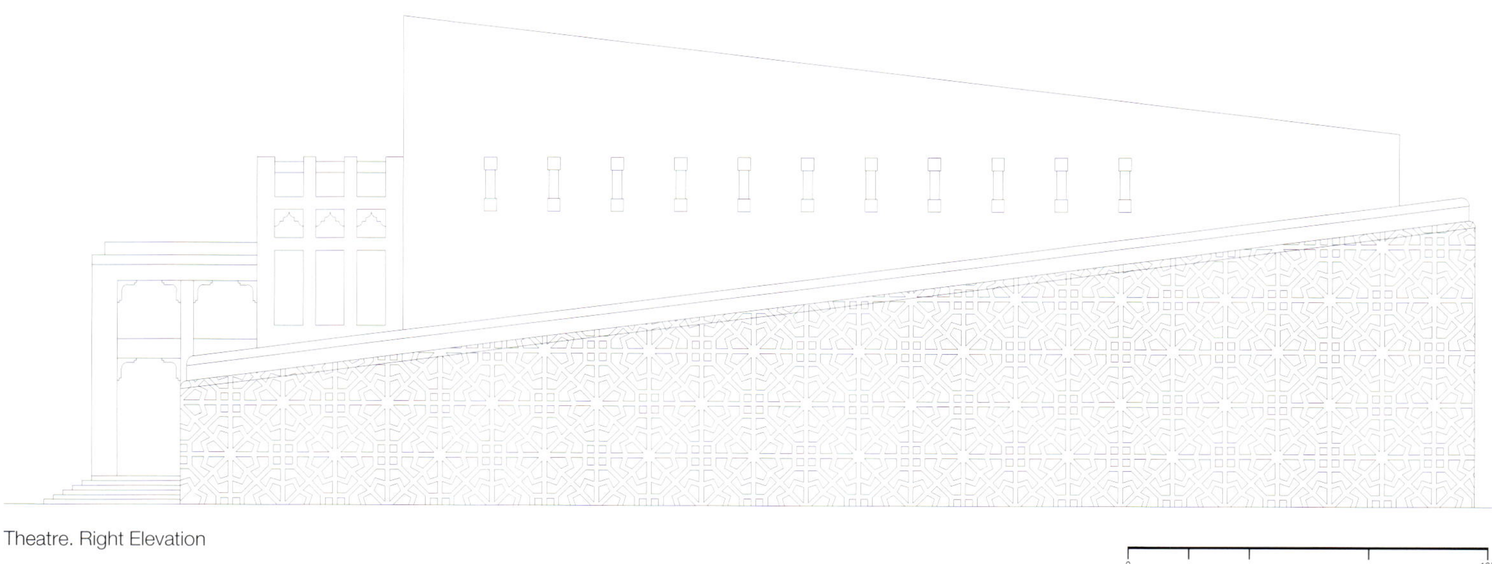

Theatre. Right Elevation

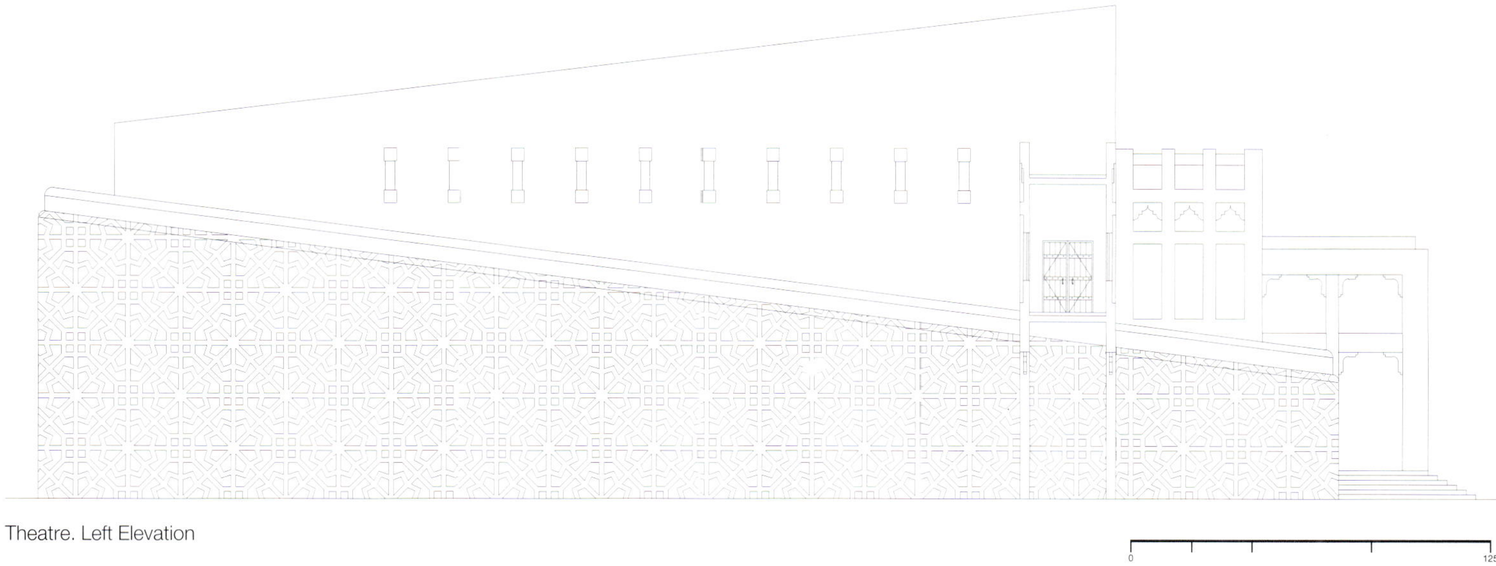

Theatre. Left Elevation

Kempinski Residences & Suites

Kempinski Residences & Suites

West Bay, Doha, Qatar

Completed, 2009

Client: Alfardan Real Estate Co.

Standing 252 metres tall, a colossal wind-tower dominating the landscape of the West Bay district is immediately noticed by passers-by when they glimpse the Kempinski Residences & Suites, one of the most emblematic of the many luxury residential high-rises designed by AEB in Doha, and currently the tallest operating building in Qatar.

To ensure that the Kempinski complex would stand out from its neighbouring towers, a great deal of inspiration was drawn from the simplest and once most common typology of the Gulf region's architecture, namely a type of hollow tower known as a *barjeel*, whose design ensured the constant circulation of air – a typical cooling system used in older buildings.

Although on a much larger scale, the Kempinski complex boasts the typical wind-tower's square plan, while the arrangement of its façades recalls its predecessor's geometrical decoration through alternating broad glazed surfaces and pilasters cladded in aluminium.

The geometry of the square is also reproduced at the base of the building – where four smaller tower-like structures surround it and draw attention to its entrance – and at mid-height of the four fronts – as bi-dimensional decorations.

The décor of the interiors confirm the VIP status of the complex through the widespread use of marble surfaces and backlit recesses covered with geometrical patterned lattices, these too directly taken from Qatari tradition.

Occupying most of the building's 62 floors are 370 fully furnished apartments in a wide variety of available typologies – from 65-square-metre studios to the 1,050-square-metre "sky villas", six-bedroom duplex units located at the very top of the tower.

The Kempinski complex might well be considered a self-sufficient community, providing its inhabitants with every type of facility and amenity, including two indoor swimming pools, a gym, two restaurants, a lounge bar area, and a business centre with a boardroom for executive meetings.

GOURMET

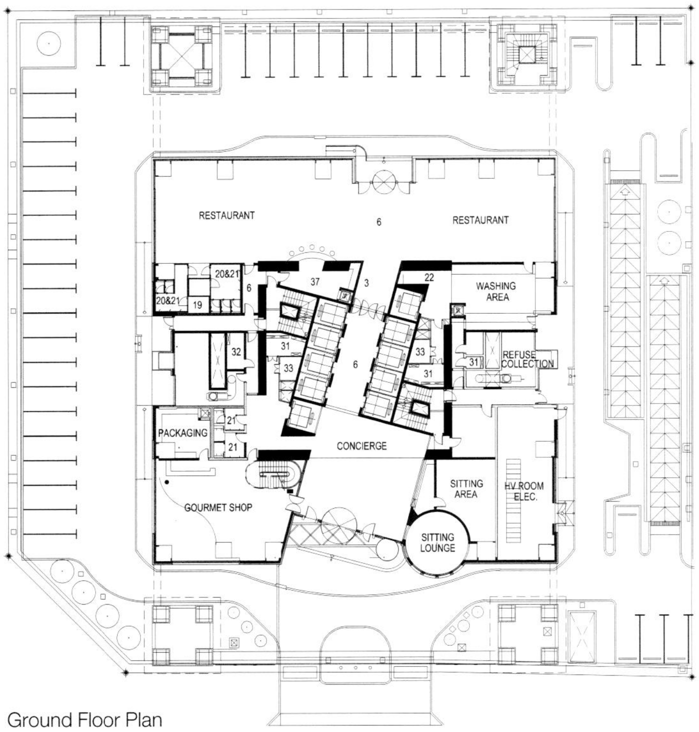

Ground Floor Plan

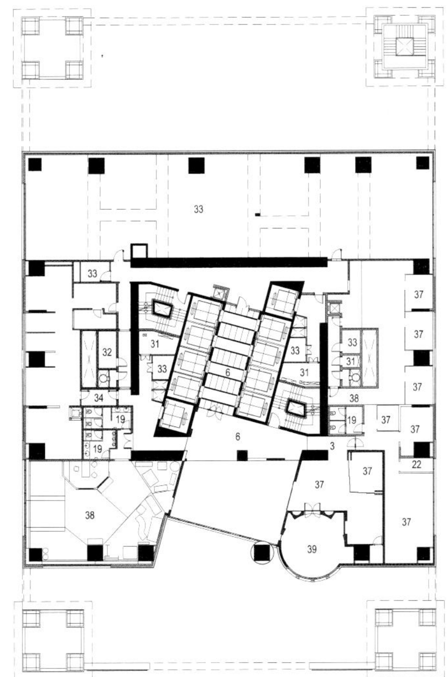

Mezzanine Floor Plan

Legend

1. Entrance
2. Reception
3. Hallway
4. Corridor
5. Vestibule
6. Elevator Lobby
7. IPOD Lounge
8. Bar
9. Pool Bar
10. Linen Counter
11. Gym Area
12. Treatment Room
13. Steam Room
14. Cardio Area
15. Wet Area
16. Herbal Bath
17. Colour Therapy
18. Locker Room
19. Toilet
20. Toilet & Bath
21. Shower
22. Store
23. Tambour
24. Majlis
25. Bedroom
26. Dressing
27. Dining
28. Kitchen
29. Maid's Room
30. Laundry
31. Electrical Room
32. Q-Tel Room
33. Service Area
34. Refuse Store
35. Home Theatre
36. Living Room
37. Office
38. Nursery
39. Conference Room

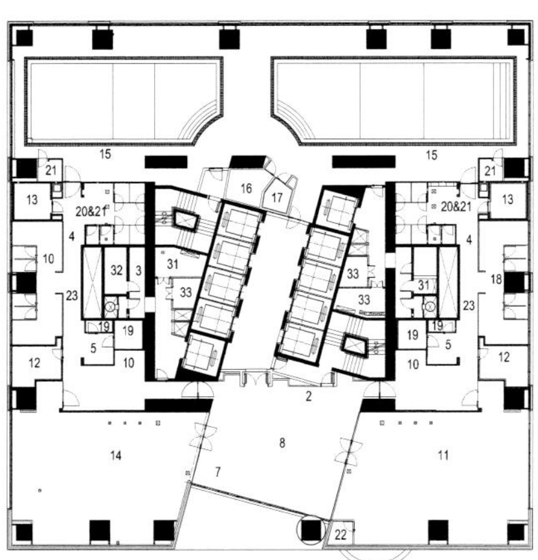

First Floor Plan

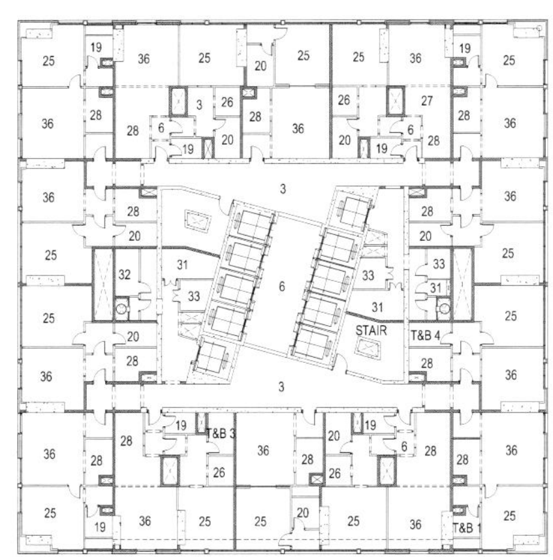

Second Floor Plan

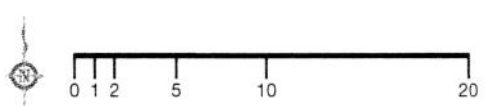

Typical 3rd–5th Floor Plan

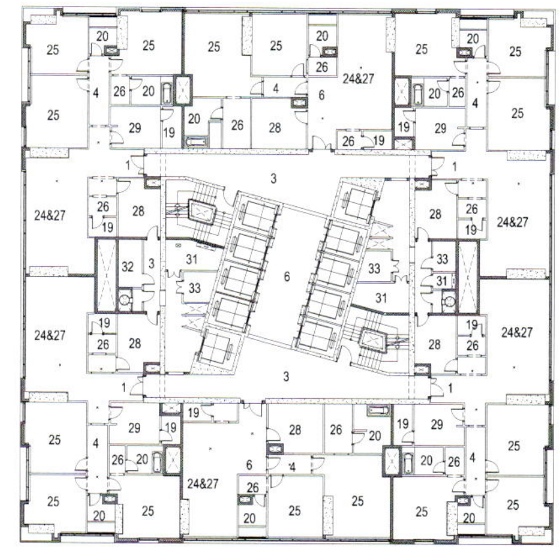

Typical Floor Plan

QIT
QIT

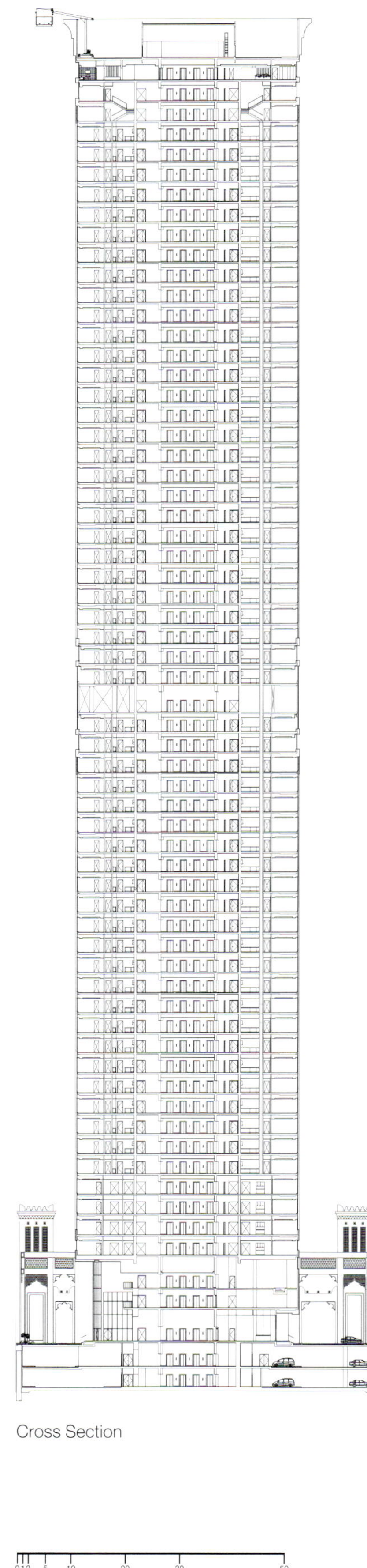

Cross Section

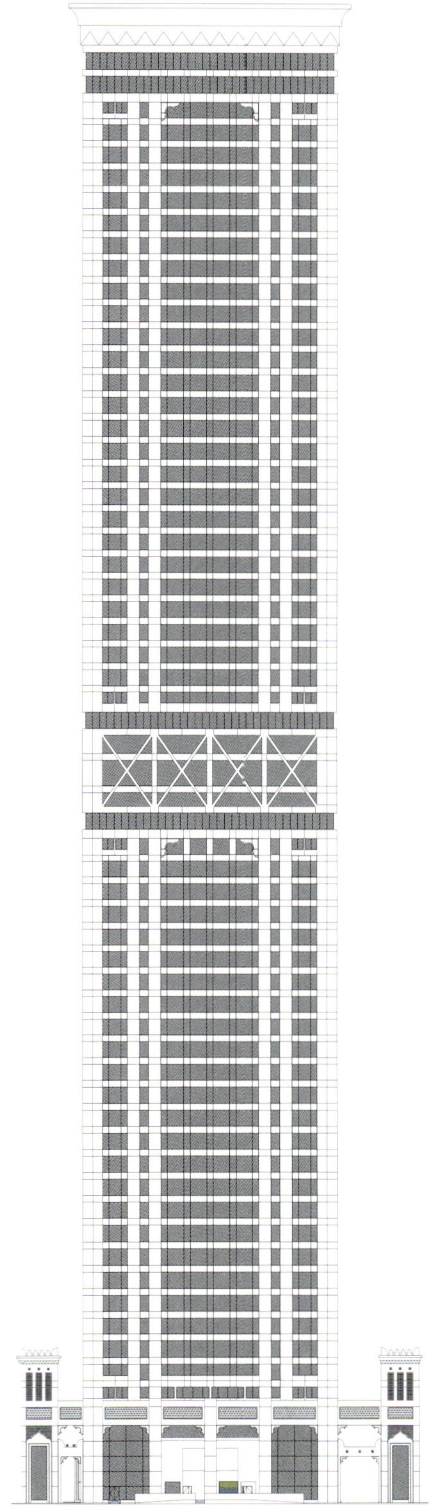

Right Elevation

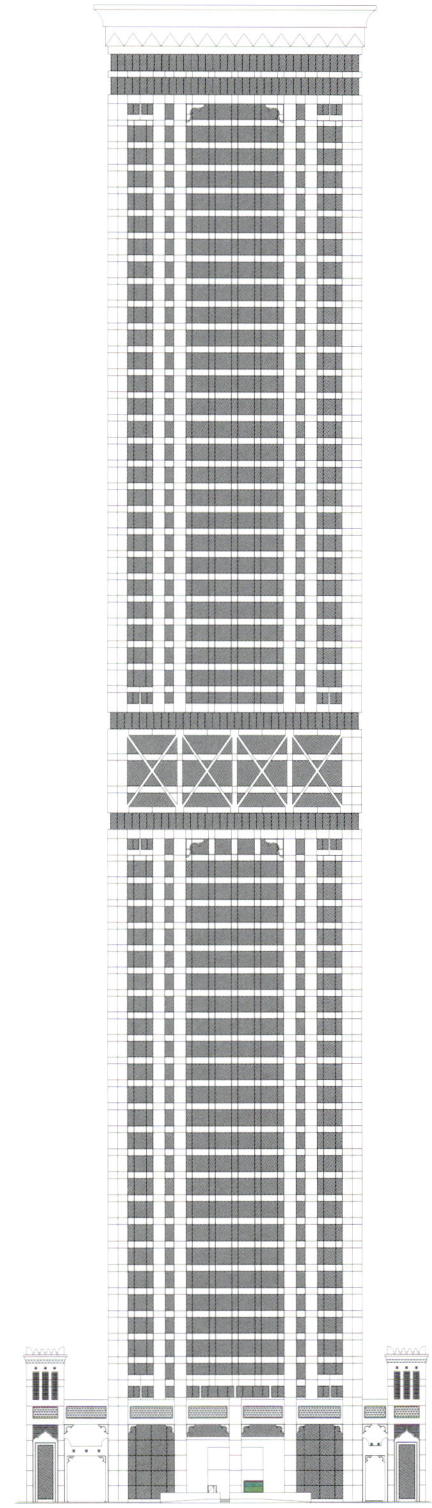

Left Elevation

Kempinski
K

Awqaf Mosques

Awqaf Mosques

Design

Client: Ministry of Awqaf

As confirmation of its active role in fostering Qatar's identity through its public and private architecture, while restoring and rehabilitating its cultural heritage, AEB was approached by the Ministry of Endowments and Islamic Affairs in 2011 to develop the design of typological mosques that would serve as a reference and building model.

The 18 Awqaf mosque prototypes are precisely designed to answer and respect religious practices and the typical building standards of Islamic places of worship.

Providing different sizes and capacities – from 150 to 5000 worshippers – the prototypes offer a range of functional two-storey plans that allow potential donors to conceive and build future mosques that comply with the most correct and sustainable features in spatial distribution and worshippers' access and use.

The projects all manifest the elegant simplicity of the classic Qatari flat-roofed mosque. It comprises a massive perimeter wall and a main praying hall suited to serve the community – prayer being both a private and a communal practice. All other spaces are conceived to ease the respect of the religious dictates of Islam. These include the correct orientation of *Ṣalāt* prayer repeated five times a day gazing in the direction of *Qibla*; the ablution spaces before the main prayer hall; the separate entrances and circulation paths for men and women; and the clear distinction between *taher* and *non-taher* areas (where the wearing of shoes is either allowed or forbidden).

A single minaret, set on a typical Syrian square base, rises on the front side, and all designs boast a central uncovered area, the square *sahn* (courtyard) which for smaller mosques (planned for 300 and 400 worshippers) takes a rectangular shape.

Ground Floor Plan

Legend

1. Main Prayer Hall
2. Courtyard
3. Main Entrance
4. Guest Room
5. Minaret
6. Imam's Residence Entrance
7. Toilet and Ablution
8. Side Entrance
9. Female Prayer Hall

Front Elevation

Right Elevation

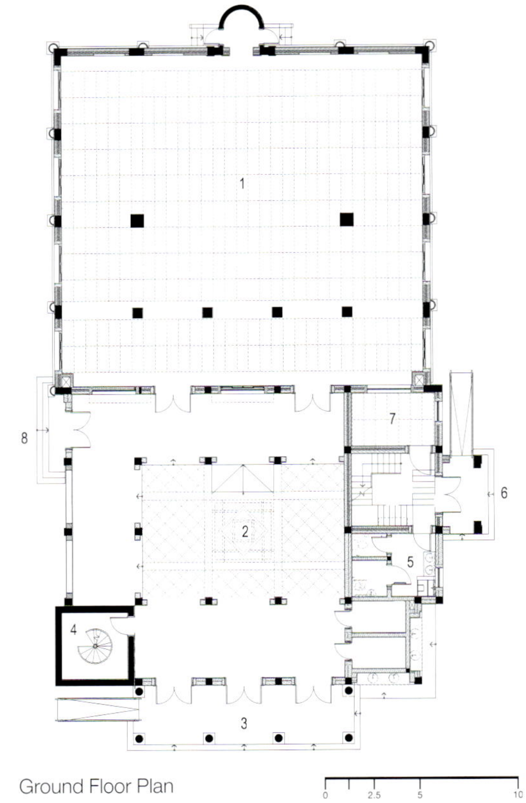

Ground Floor Plan

Legend

1. Main Prayer Hall
2. Courtyard
3. Main Entrance
4. Minaret
5. Ablution and Toilets
6. Female Entrance
7. Female Prayer Hall
8. Side Entrance

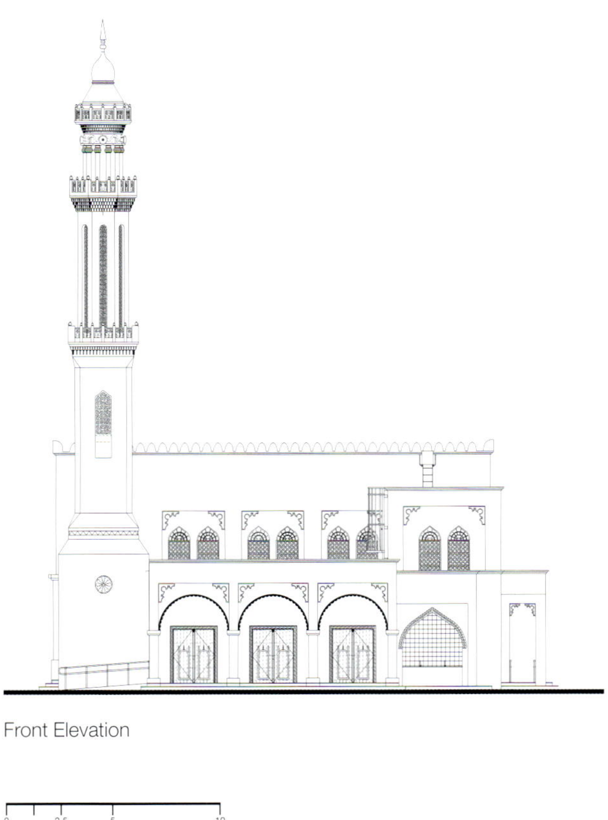

Front Elevation

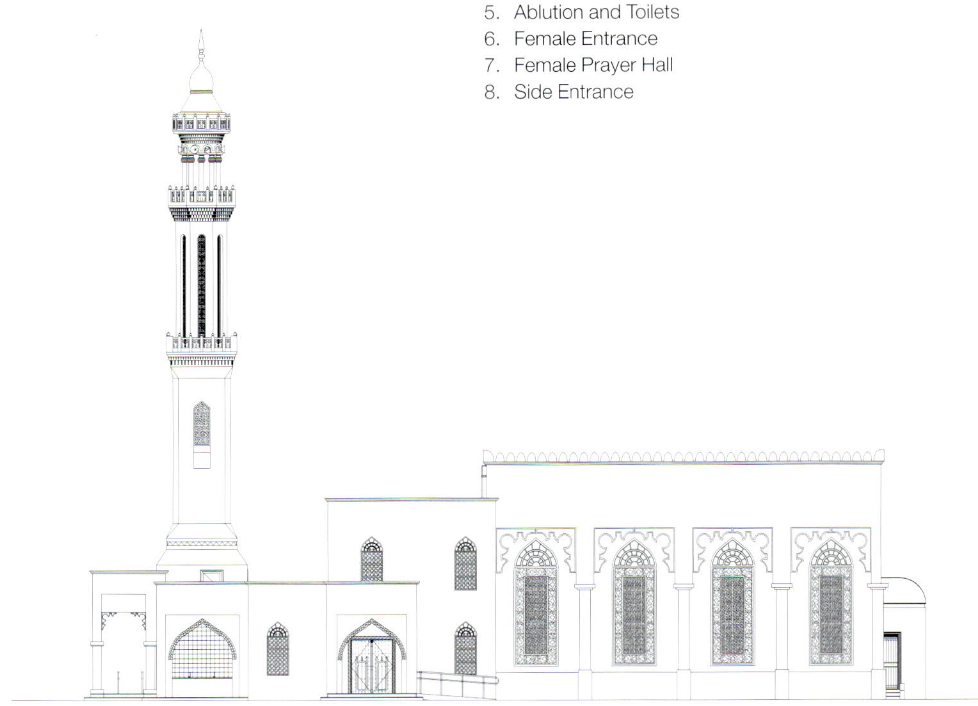

Right Elevation

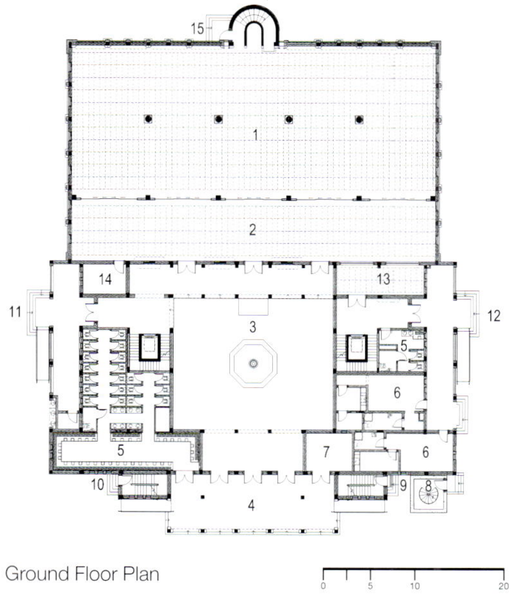

Ground Floor Plan

Front Elevation

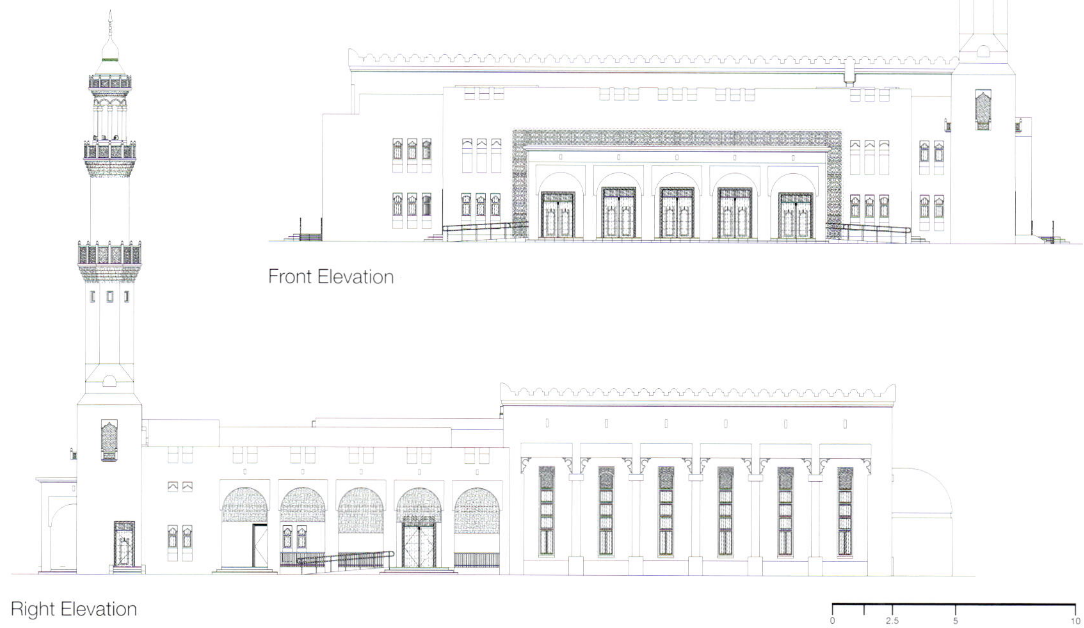

Right Elevation

Legend

1. Main Prayer Hall
2. Daily Prayer Hall
3. Courtyard
4. Main Entrance
5. Ablution and Toilets
6. Guest Room
7. Services
8. Minaret
9. Imam's Residence Entrance
10. Muazzin's Residence Entrance
11. Side Entrance
12. Female Entrance
13. Female Prayer Hall
14. Library
15. Imam's Entrance

Front Elevation

Right Elevation

Legend

1. Main Prayer Hall
2. Daily Prayer Hall
3. Courtyard
4. Main Entrance
5. Ablution and Toilets
6. Guest Room
7. Minaret
8. Imam's Residence Entrance
9. Muazzin's Residence Entrance
10. Side Entrance
11. Mezzanine Entrance
12. Imam's Entrance

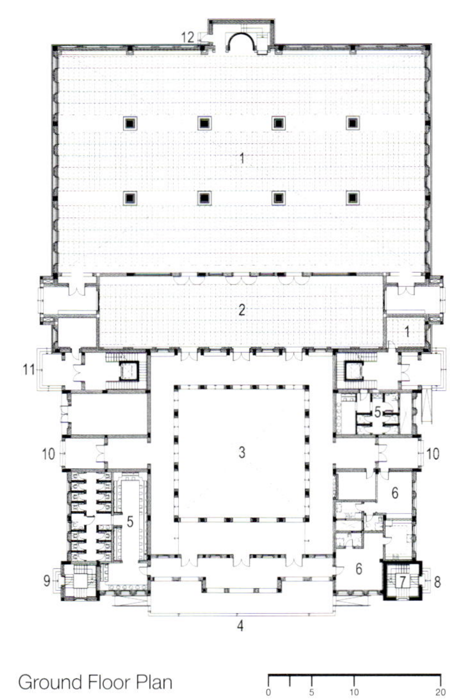

Ground Floor Plan

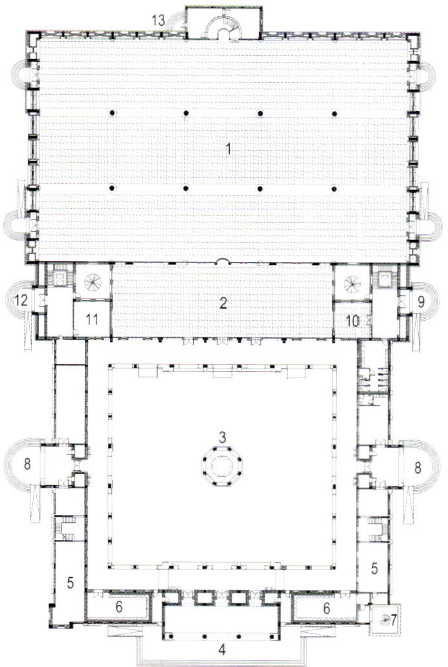

Ground Floor Plan

Legend

1. Main Prayer Hall
2. Daily Prayer Hall
3. Courtyard
4. Main Entrance
5. Quran Study
6. Ablution
7. Minaret
8. Side Entrance
9. Female Entrance
10. Female Prayer Hall
11. Library
12. Mezzanine Entrance
13. Imam Entrance

Front Elevation

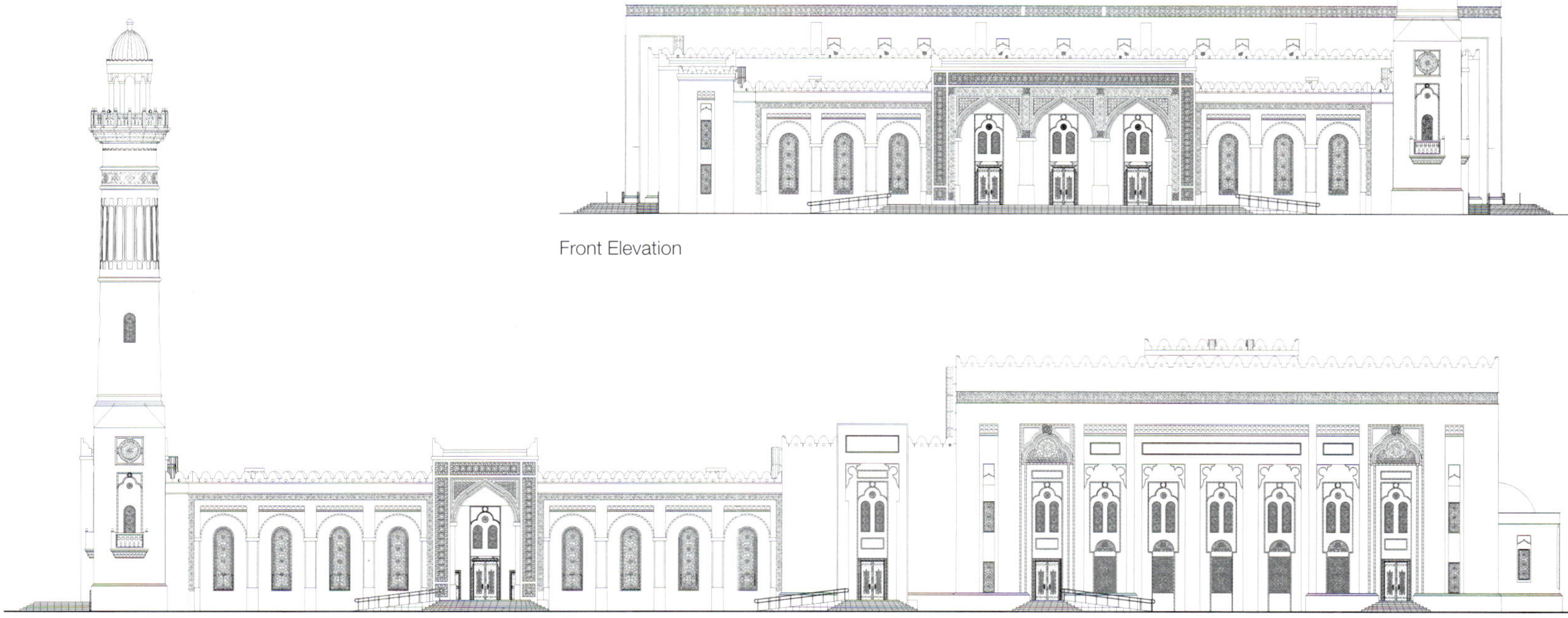

Right Elevation

Barwa Al Sadd

Barwa Al Sadd

C-Ring Road, Al Sadd, Doha, Qatar

Completed, 2011

Client: Barwa

The epitome of state-of-the-art, mixed-use self-sustaining development, the Barwa Al Sadd earned first place in the international competition launched by the Barwa corporation, which allowed architects complete freedom to develop the most innovative solutions they could muster.

The main challenge was the integration of the various functions, along with how to handle the separate car and pedestrian fluxes leading to each building, and ultimately what the aesthetics might be for such an ambitious programme.

Given this challenge, AEB split the complex into two clearly identifiable areas. Its front part, overlooking C-Ring Road, a major axis for vehicle traffic in Doha, encompasses a system of four high-rise buildings arranged in a crescent-like layout.

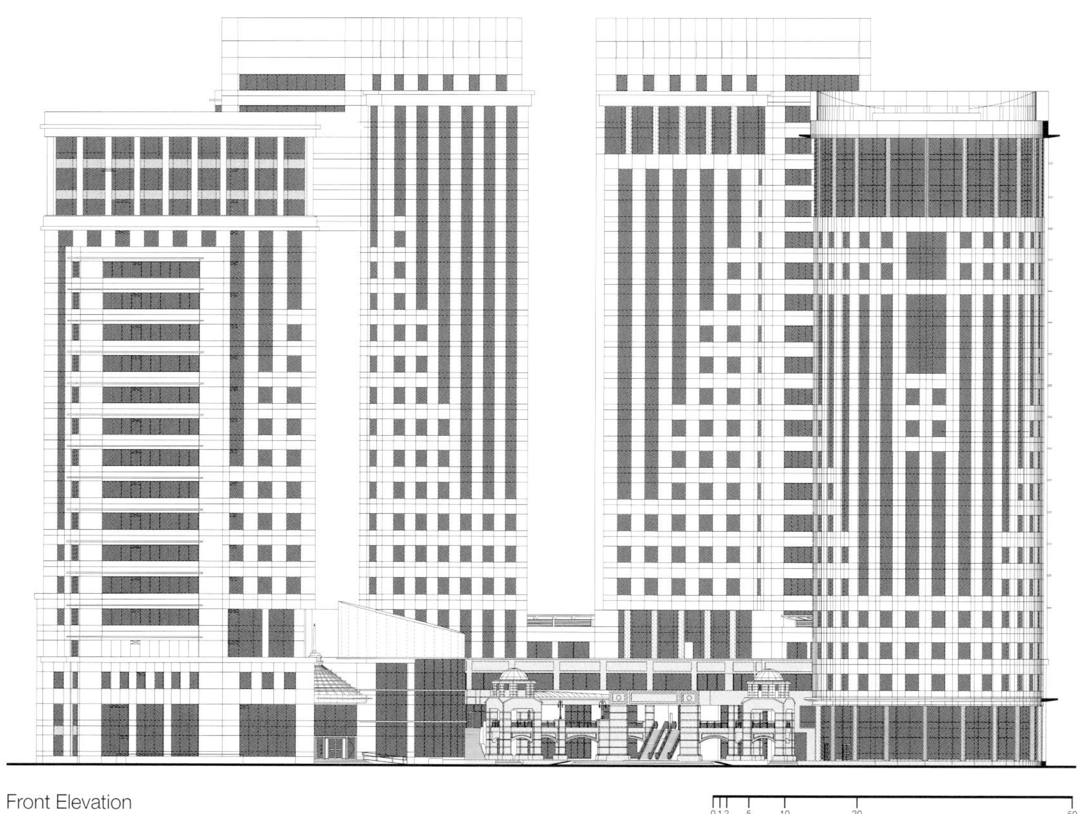

Front Elevation

The semi-circular shape avoids the frequent overcrowded atmosphere of high-density interventions, and ensures an unimpeded panoramic view for the majority of the interior spaces. A podium level containing restaurants, boutiques and shops connects all of the buildings up to the third floor, and alleviates the effect of massing overhead, informing the complex with a more human scale.

Meanwhile, the residential section located behind the towers comprises five low-rise apartment buildings, a spacious children's play area, and a recreation unit with modern facilities to cater to the needs of the community.

Visitors access the Barwa Al Sadd from the south, entering the impressively designed circular plaza, with its polished decorative paving, and assorted pools and fountains.

Overlooking the crescent, the entry plaza forms a monumental gateway into the complex, while coordinating the pedestrian walkways connecting the residential area.

Ground Floor Plan

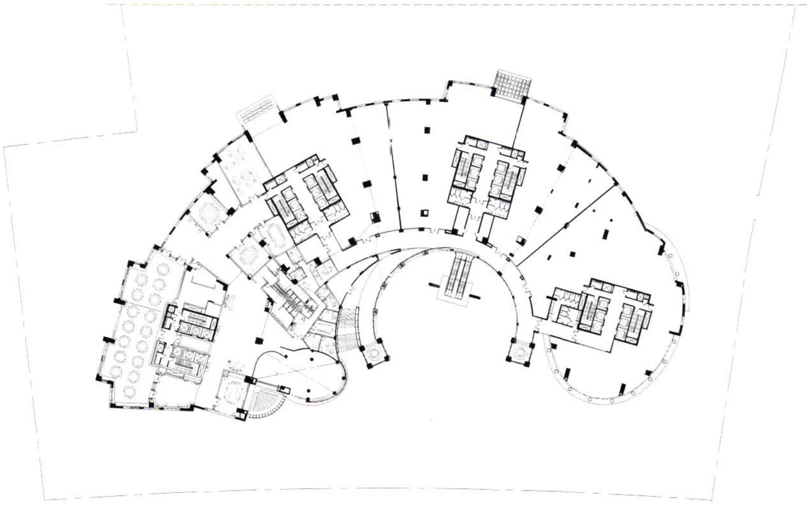

First Floor Plan

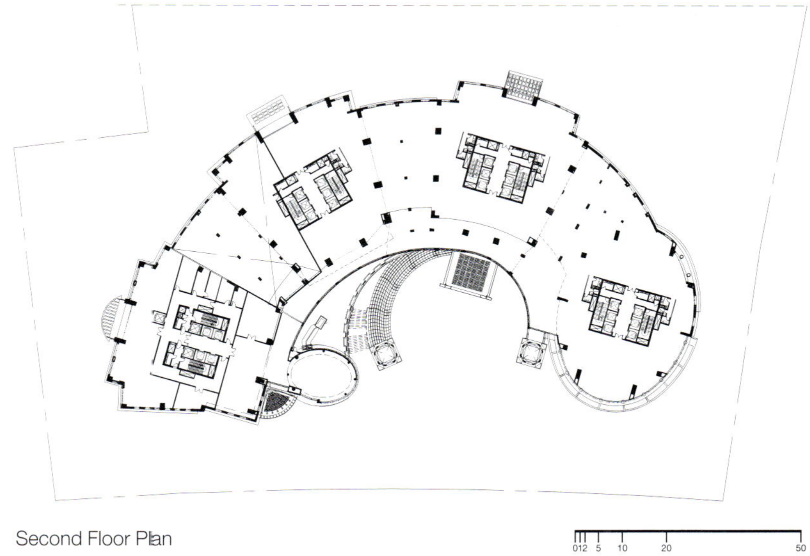

Second Floor Plan

Business Park & Hotel

Business Park & Hotel

Airport Road, Najma, Doha, Qatar

Completed, 2011

Client: H.E. Sh. Mohamed bin Hamad Al Thani

The Business Park & Hotel is a mixed-use development occupying a plot of more than 23,000 square metres, which provides a handsome complement to a mainly low-rise neighbourhood in south-east Doha. The complex's distinctive organic outline rises alongside the Al Matar motorway, a major axis leading to the city centre from the southern outskirts.

The intriguing oval nucleus hosts the conference and exhibition centre, providing the pivotal feature of a concentric cluster of elements that include six office buildings, a C-shaped hotel slab connecting two of them, and a separate showroom pavilion.

The event centre is appointed with cutting-edge technological features, such as digital signage, video-conferencing facilities, recording cameras, and wireless touch command screens. The hotel provides top-drawer international hospitality and includes a boardroom, six meeting rooms, 378 guest rooms, an all-day dining restaurant, a lobby lounge, a Brazilian lounge, a Churrascaria restaurant, and an exclusive rooftop swimming pool. Moreover, a noteworthy addition to most of the bedrooms is a transparent glass partition that allows natural light to filter through to the bathroom.

All the buildings display the same architectural language, with aluminium and glass cladding and strips of LED lights wrapping them at every slab's level, which contribute to convey the image of a boldly contemporary urban complex. The same atmosphere can be found in the interiors, where curved corridors reproduce the dynamic layout of the external spaces, skylights allow the sun to penetrate the full-height entrance halls, and a selection of high-tech cladding materials match the sophisticated carpet designs to emphasise cohesive décor.

All open areas enclosed by the pavilions are restricted to pedestrians only, who can enjoy a pleasant gathering space thanks to the carefully studied landscape design – including a COR-TEN steel sculpture, benches, and strategically located potted palms.

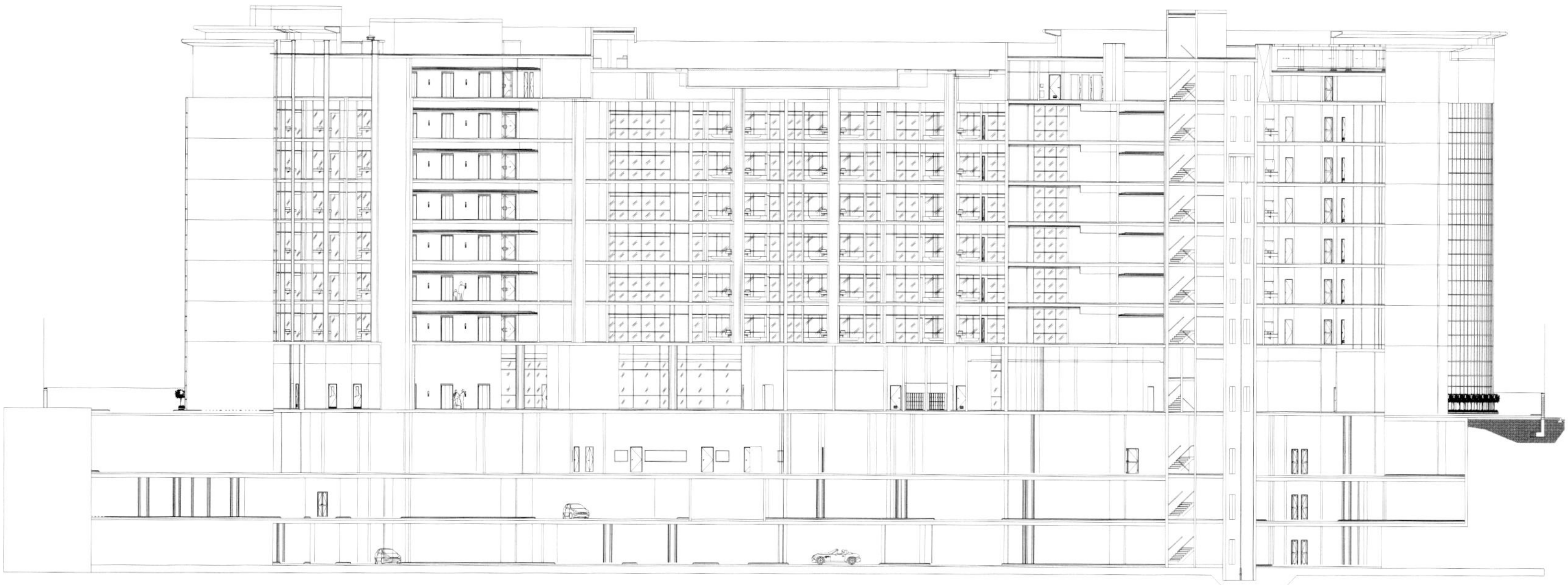

Hotel-Apartment. Longitudinal Section

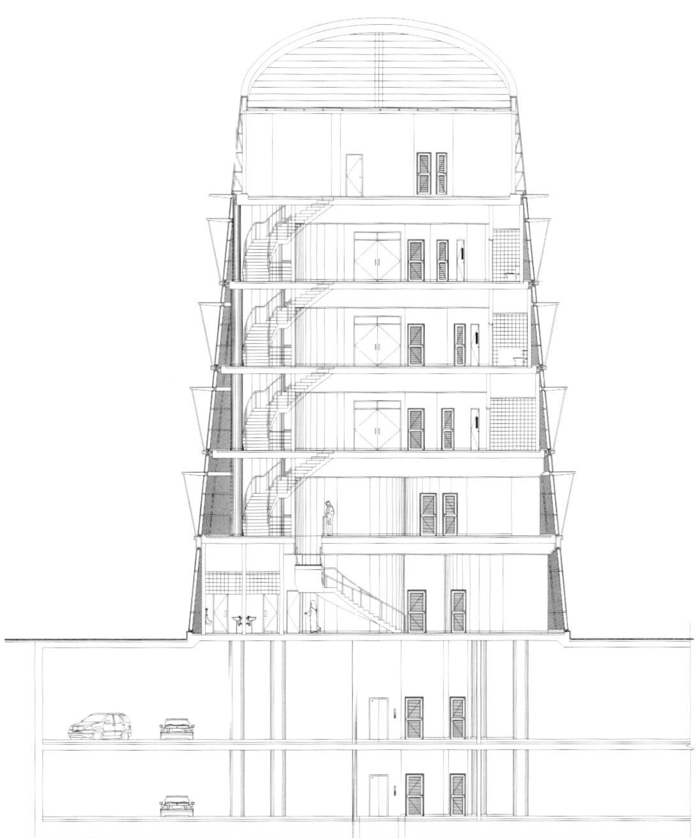

Showroom. Longitudinal Section

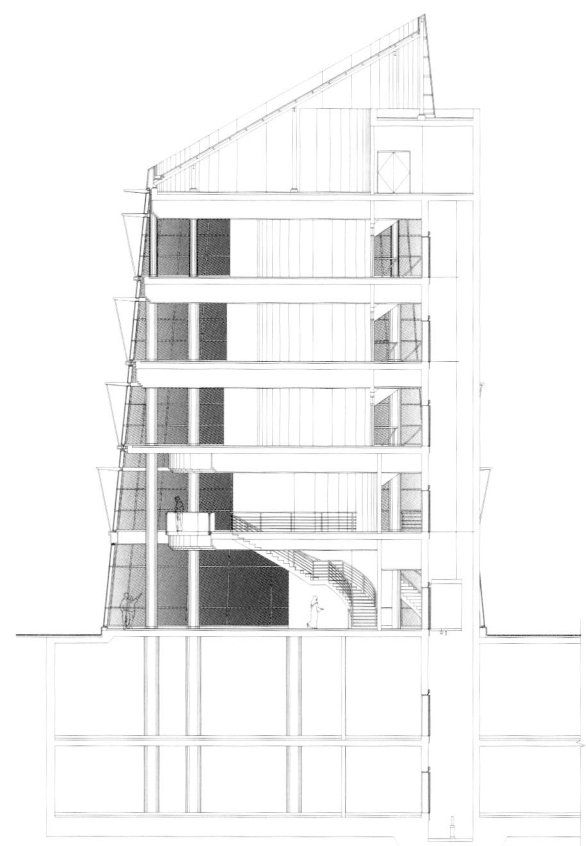

Showroom. Cross Section

ICON MEDICAL CENTER
مركز أيكون الطبي
واحة الأعمال

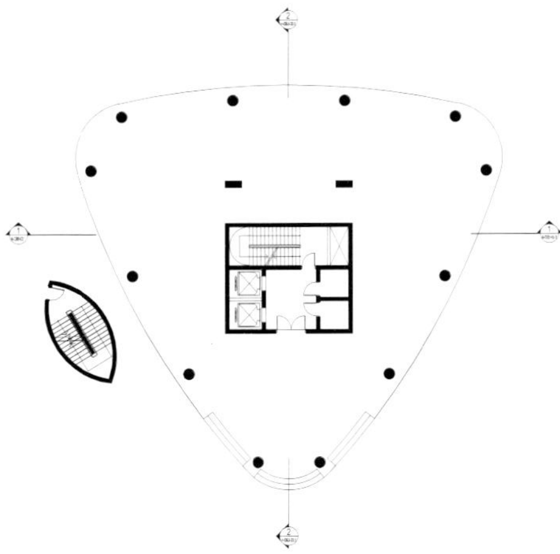

Office Building. Basement Floor Plan – Level 2

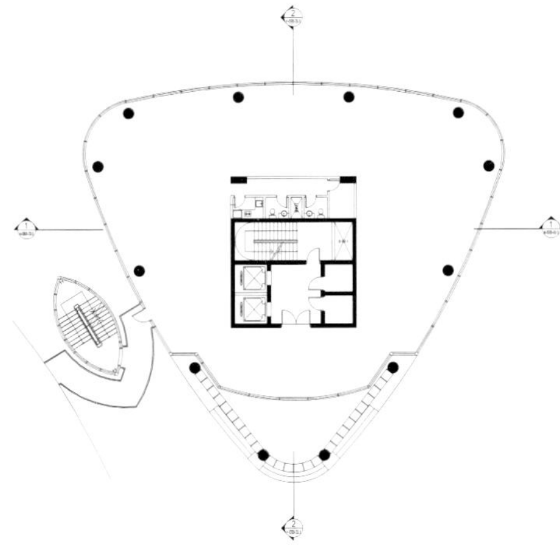

Office Building. First Floor Plan

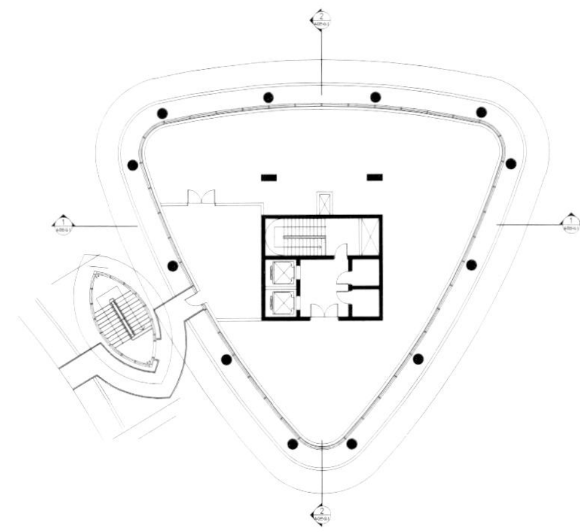

Office Building. Service Floor Plan

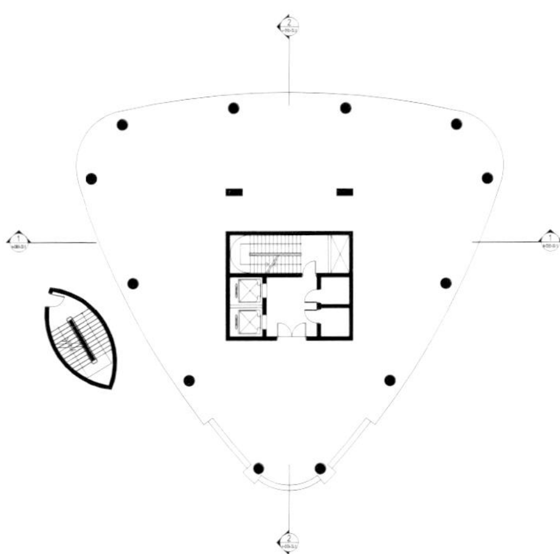

Office Building. Basement Floor Plan – Level 1

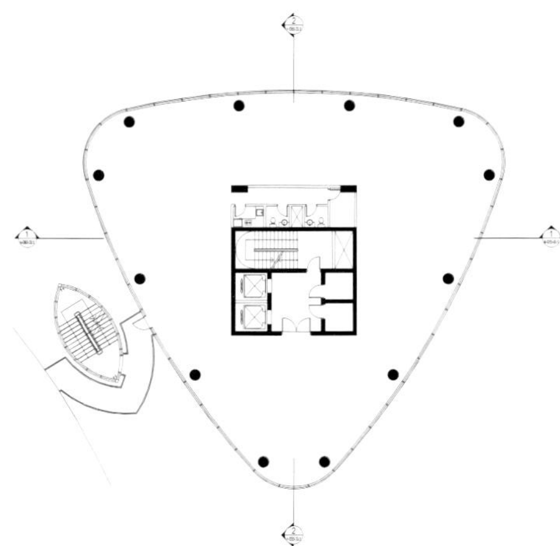

Office Building. Typical 2nd-4th Floor Plan

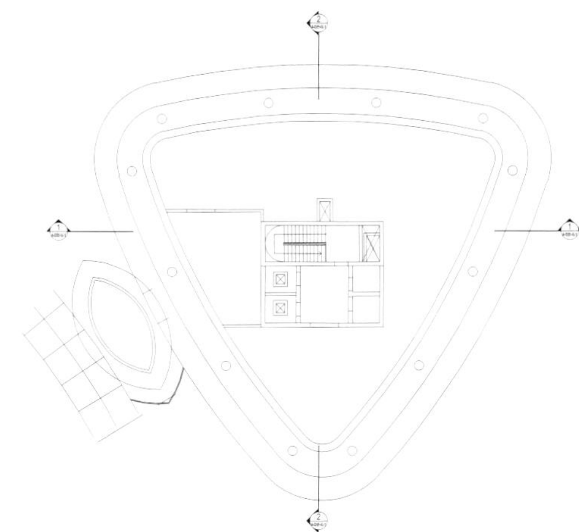

Office Building. Main Roof Plan

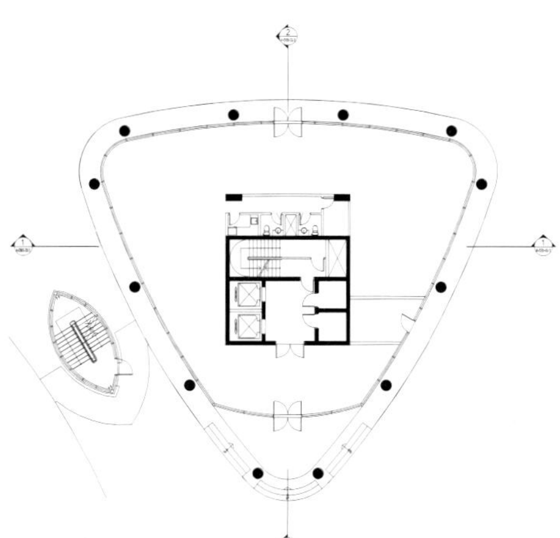

Office Building. Ground Floor Plan

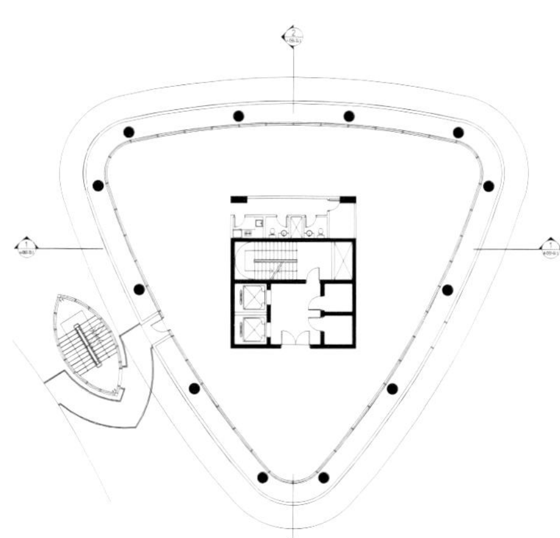

Office Building. 5th Floor Plan

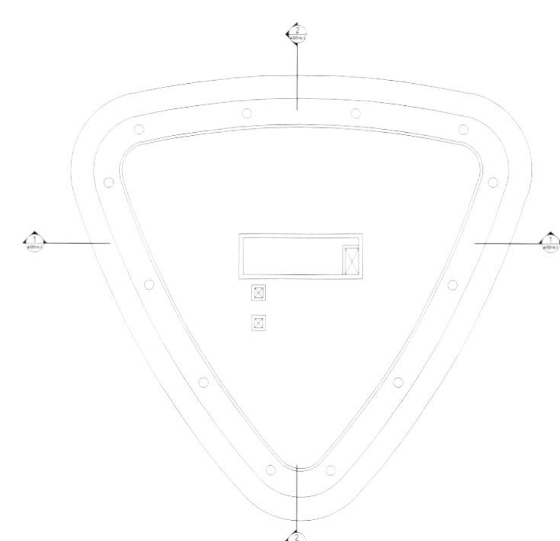

Office Building. APEX Roof Plan

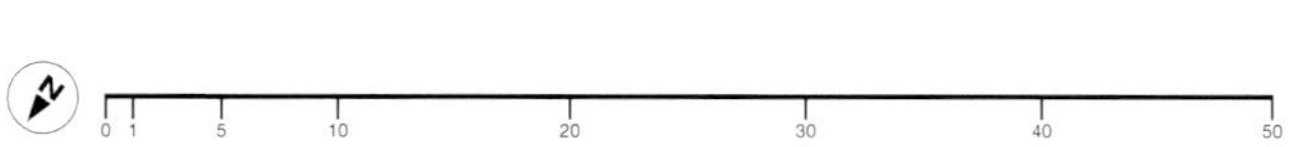

Oman Embassy in Qatar

Oman Embassy in Qatar

West Bay, Doha, Qatar

Completed, 2011

Client: Oman Ministry of Foreign Affairs

In spite of both being Gulf countries, and therefore facing similar climatic conditions, and – to a certain extent – sharing a common cultural and historical background, Oman and Qatar's traditional architectural features differ slightly. This is why, when commissioned to design the Oman Embassy in Qatar, AEB investigated the specificities of Oman's heritage and aimed to integrate elements of the two cultures into a single building, which would represent the embassy's role of an institutional space in which cultural and political exchanges between the two nations take place.

The use of simple pointed arches and white stone cladding defines a clear Omani atmosphere, which is elegantly combined with parapets and decorative wall recesses, both referencing Qatari style, thus conveying a unified but complex overall image of the embassy. The dark wood lattice of the many *mashrabiyah* windows of varying shapes and dimensions represents state-of-the-art Qatari craftsmanship, and distinctly contrasts with the brightness of the plain façades.

Situated at the very heart of the diplomatic district in West Bay, the embassy relates to the surrounding low-rise buildings by reproducing their height and scale, while at the same time standing out thanks to its distinctive layout. The complex is made up of three main masses: the embassy itself, which comprises all the public functions; the ambassador's residence; and the guardroom, which signal's the building's main entrance. High walls surround the building lot, and not only ensure maximum privacy and security, but also envelop a lavish garden, crossed by shaded walkways and planted with local flora, with several fountains and an octagonal pavilion enhancing the calmness and serenity of this oasis.

Embassy Building. Front Elevation

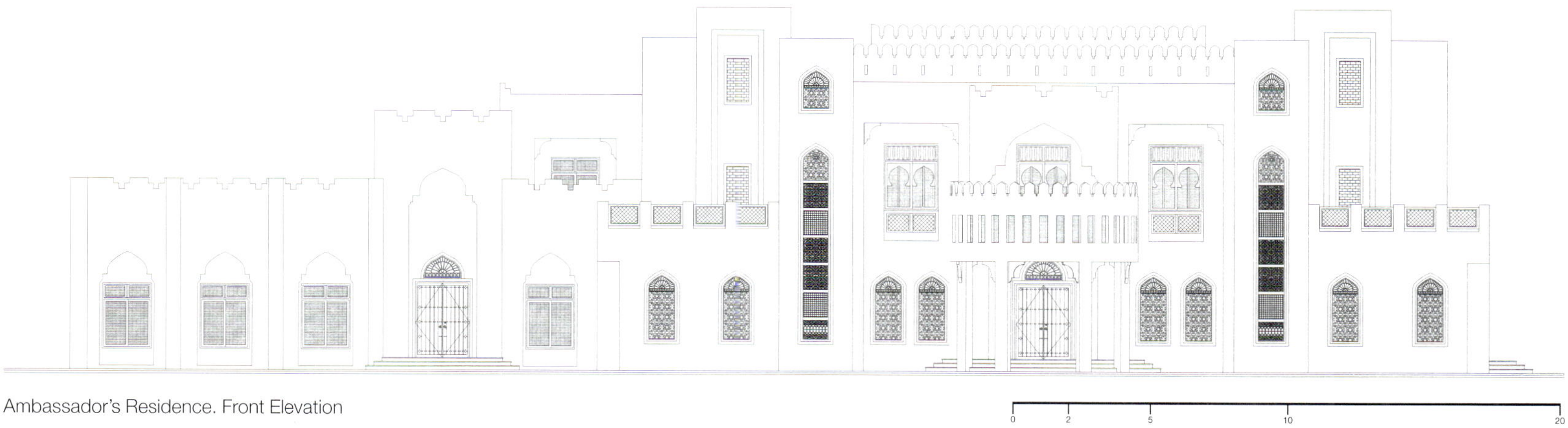

Ambassador's Residence. Front Elevation

Al Mirqab Souq Waqif Boutique Hotel & Amphitheatre

Al Mirqab Souq Waqif Boutique Hotel & Amphitheatre

Souq Waqif, Doha, Qatar

Completed, 2011

Client: Private Engineering Office

Designing Doha's cityscape today not only means defining a contemporary aesthetic for its most recent districts – one that taps into local tradition but is fully in line with evolving international styles – but also entails relating closely with the city's historical neighbourhoods.

This awareness of context was one of the main challenges AEB had to deal with while developing the Al Mirqab Souq Waqif Boutique Hotel and Amphitheatre, located at the south-east edge of Souq Waqif, on the corner of Bank Street. In fact, a part of the souq's historical urban fabric – highly compact and criss-crossed by narrow, irregular paths – is still preserved, and presents a very delicate context for any contemporary development to really belong to.

In addition to adapting to the limited and varying general heights of the existing buildings, the new complex aims to reproduce the intricacy of its historical stratification, which progressively resulted in the concentration and juxtaposition of several structures and volumes. The hotel thus integrates masses of different dimensions and orientation, with the clock tower overlooking the crossroad, and assorted other elements emerging from the building's average G+1 level.

As a tribute to Qatari traditional architecture, the building's elevations present multiple layers projecting or receding from the principal plane of the façade: recesses, finely embroidered frames, multi-layered parapets, verandas, arcades, and shaded walkways give the complex a very strong urban presence, and generate a delicate and ever-changing chiaroscuro of lights and shadows over its plain white plastered walls.

In contrast, the design of the interiors combines pure white surfaces with wooden cladding, decorated fabrics, carpets, and multi-coloured marble, to convey a sophisticated atmosphere reminiscent of Qatari decorative tradition.

التراس
Al Terrace
Lebanese Cuisine

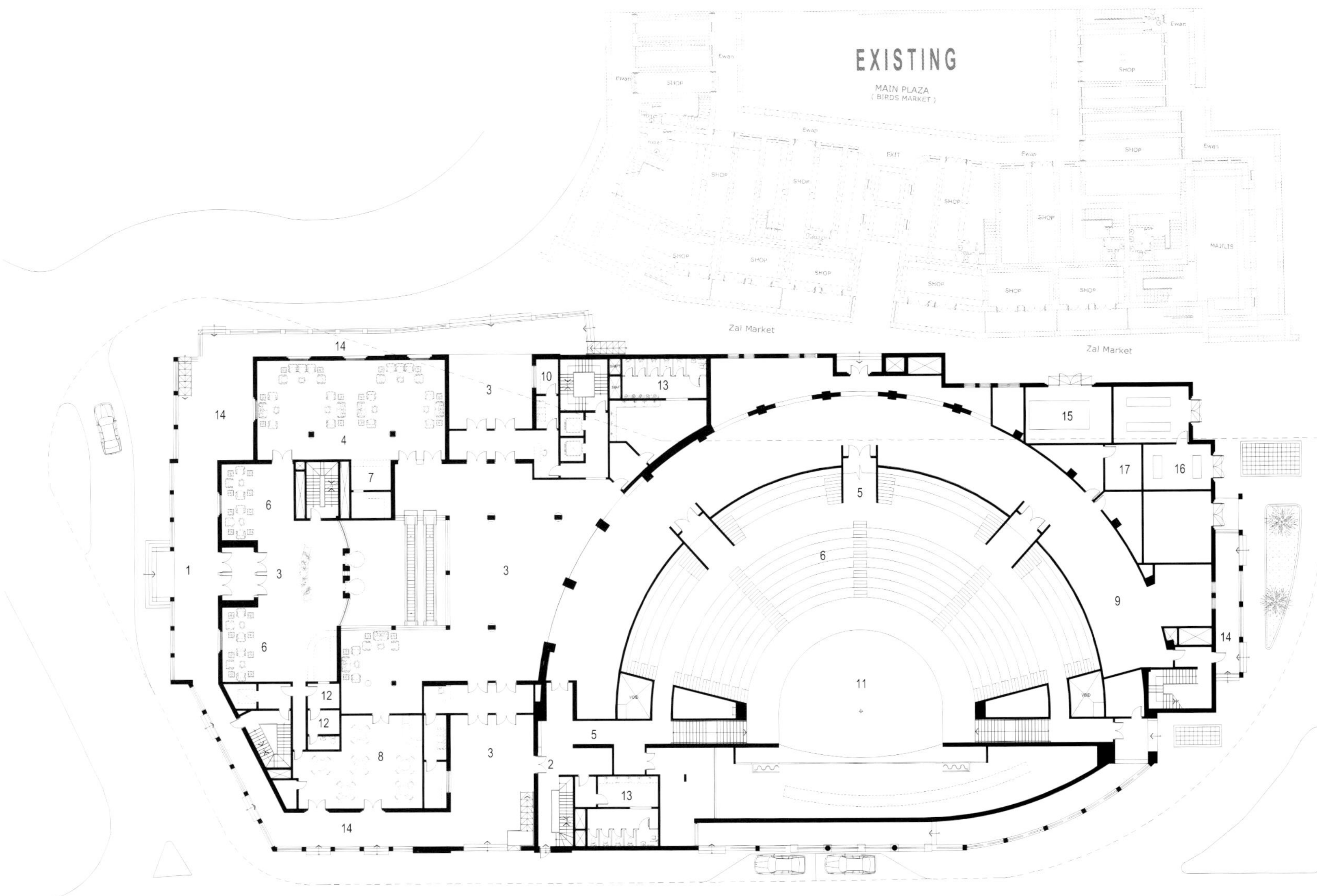

Ground Floor Plan

Legend

1. Main Entrance
2. Staff Entrance
3. Lobby
4. Lounge
5. Hallway
6. Sitting Area
7. Counter
8. Coffee Area
9. Snack Area
10. Ticket Room
11. Platform / Stage
12. Office
13. Toilets
14. Arcade
15. Genset Room
16. Transformer Room
17. Fuel Room

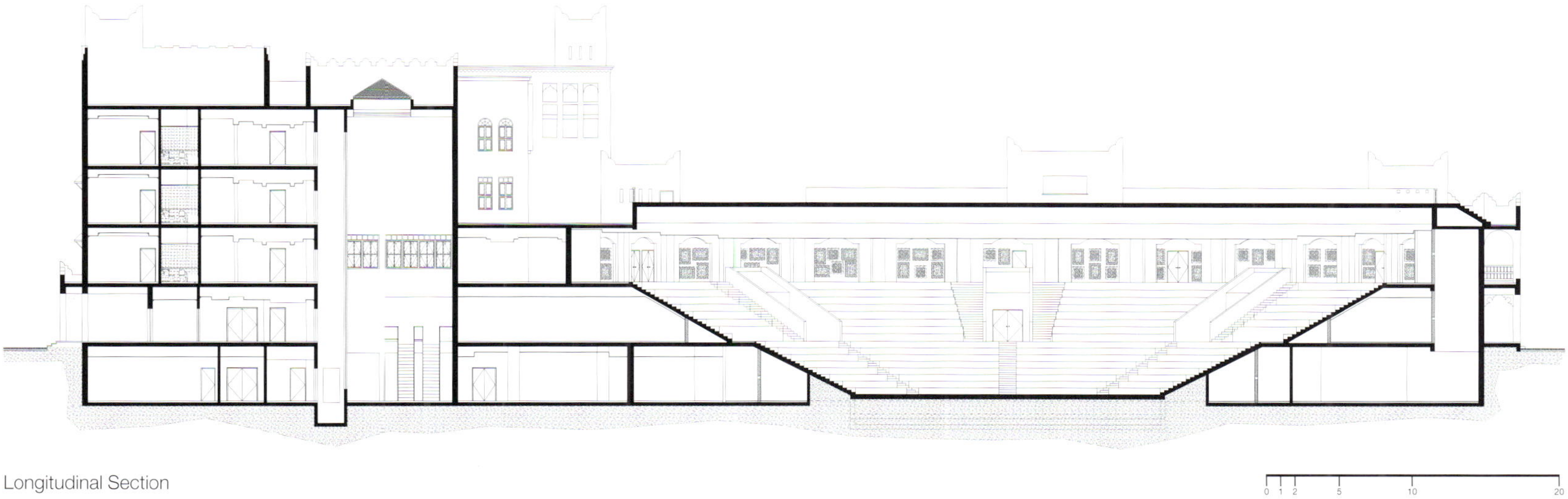

Longitudinal Section

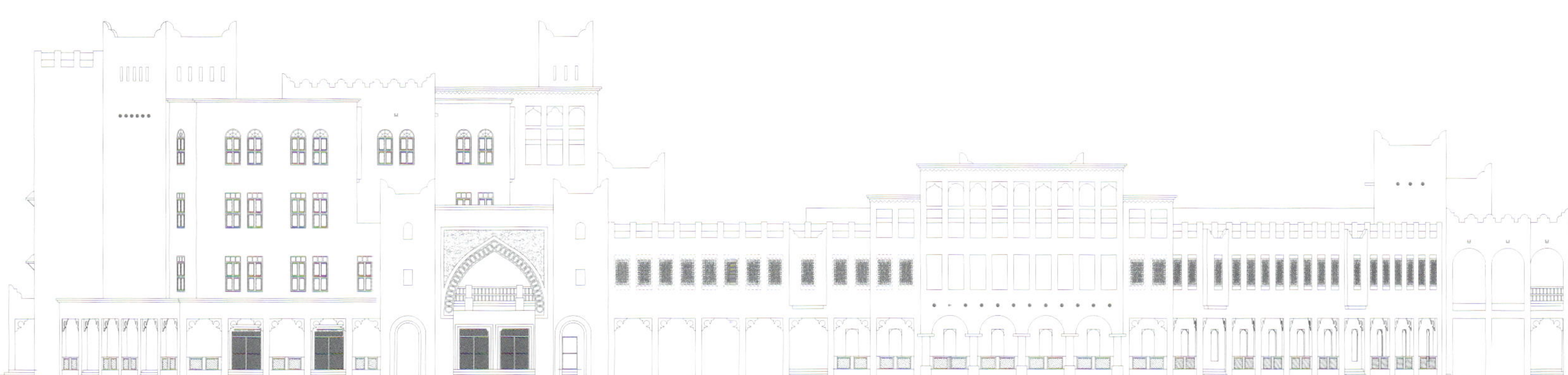

Front Elevation

شارع حمد الكبير
Grand Hamad Street

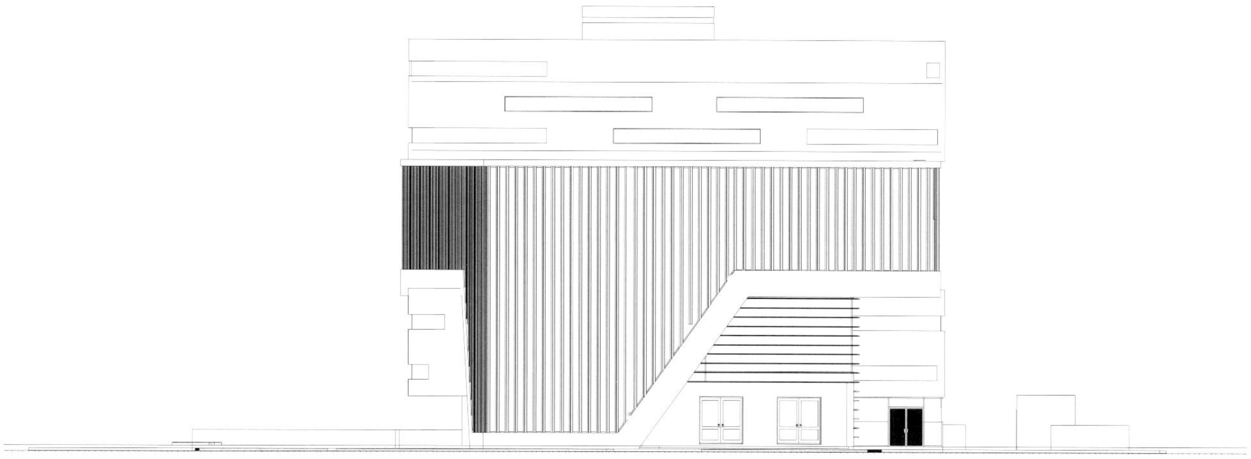

Right Elevation

Front Elevation

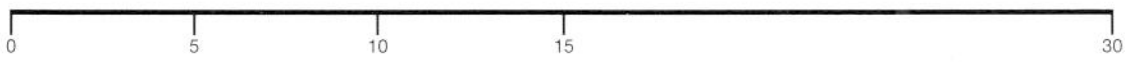

The New Modern

An Emerging Cultural Environment

Luca Molinari
in conversation with
Ibrahim Jaidah

Luca Molinari: I'd like to focus now on innovation and contemporary architecture, which basically means 90% of your work for clients, private investors, and corporate architecture. The issue is a delicate one, because it questions what is considered "contemporary" or "modern" in this part of the world. It no longer involves the classic "glass box" type of modernism, but a subtler reassessment of what it means to think modern and build modern in this region. It seems to me that your studio offers a complex profile: on one hand you are a typical professional firm that addresses the requests and needs of your clients, while on the other hand you are trying to shift the demand from the standard high-rise toward something which re-interprets the sense of modernity and contemporary in this challenging and highly distinct part of the world. What sort of "modern" architecture do you believe can apply to this region today, and how has your idea of modernity evolved since the early 1990s?

Ibrahim Mohamed Jaidah: Well, in Qatar in particular the term "modernity" has transitioned through various phases. I mean, the modern stuff that appeared very early on in the 1960s and 1970s was somewhat influenced by international schools, but it showed a great awareness of the environment – as you can see in the Doha Fire Station. On the whole, the glare of the sun has always been screened, and there were some positive responses until the big tower boom of the 1990s, which heralded a brief period in which architects ignored the contextual environmental issues. Although, admittedly, plenty of new buildings of that period show a complete disregard for the "glass box".

Fortunately, this situation did not last long, because as soon as these all-glass buildings went up, the authorities quickly realised that a city built like that was not a viable option, and they enacted a very simple and straightforward law that ruled out fully glazed façades in favour of a 50/50 composition. Now the law is enforced, and architects are very often asked to mathematically prove that their proposed designs are 50% solid and 50% glazed openings. This simple law – which arrived, I think, in early 2000 – put a halt to this type of all-glass architecture.

At AEB we avoid designing buildings where glass dominates the western façades, choosing instead to reduce windows and openings here because, of course, this is where the heat is. In corporate architecture you have to make good use of the sea and downtown views, so as not to deprive those inside of such features. So this is what we tend to do, and I think it's had an influence on recent architecture and projects still under construction. Now, with top-drawer international architects practising locally, the country's new modernists are developing a new perspective whereby Doha's skyline is evidently influenced by international architecture. There is still a tendency to do unconventionally shaped buildings – for example towers twisting on their own axis. This has almost become a typical feature of architecture in the Middle East, perhaps more than anywhere else, since this region is a bit like laboratory. A practitioner's playground, if you like.

LM: Yes, there's a boom going on over here.
IMJ: Yes, there is a boom under way – and architecture has become a critical commodity. Fortunately, Doha itself has not "suffered" as much as the other cities where even more construction is taking place. Here we've kept a bit more control over what's being developed.

LM: Less of the "Dubai effect", then…
IMJ: Precisely, though I wouldn't say that Dubai is a bad example. Dubai is a phenomenon by itself, and also unique as a setting. Basically, a modern Qatari movement has been created, but with all the commercial aspects of global architecture. Most notably, there is a big set of projects that are driven by what I call the "Msheireb effect", which is more sensitive to the environment and more sensitive to the place and the specifics of the setting. This is where I hope the seeds of the local vernacular will blossom. Now what we really need is for the new generations of young architects to actually start practising their profession. So many of them come out of universities, but unfortunately very few end up with a job in a studio, and the majority opt to work for the government – which is only natural – and in fact the government absorbs a lot of them.

LM: Sure, but working in the government might be useful, too.
IMJ: Most of the young graduates end up emulating other people's work. They don't operate creatively, doing their own stuff. In the early stages of my career I worked in the design department where projects were created, and later on I was asked to take a higher position. I was young, so I turned to my mentor for advice; he later became a minister. At the time he

was overseas, so I called him and said: "What should I do? I've been asked to move to the higher position, which is quite challenging for someone two years out of college…"
He simply asked me: "Do you want to actually work, or just tell people what to do?"
I replied: "I want to work."
So in the end I respectfully declined the offer.
A lot of young architects are now assessors and state employees, and this is good because they are not only decision-makers, they're also designers at heart. The positive thing is that they have become more sensitive about their local identity. This is the outcome of a sort of local awakening that has been taking place in the past 15 years – and not only in architecture, but also in poetry, costumes, music… It's a sort of Middle Eastern Renaissance.

* * *

LM: Let's talk about the emerging cultural environment which you say is producing alternative conditions that will inspire the next generation. To your mind, what does it mean to be a contemporary modern architect in this area? Assuming the so-called "era of glass" is coming to an end and we are entering a completely new phase of architecture in its different typologies, in what ways do you think retail and hospitality architecture have changed over time? For example, the traditional malls are now been designed in a completely different way. I would like to discuss these changes with you in more depth in relation to your work and experience.
IMJ: As in any other fast-developing city, here in Doha hospitality and retail have become the driving features of the local economy. This is a proven fact in different cities around the world. With this type of architecture, you adapt the building more to a theme, to a lifestyle. The mall is essentially a box, but then you give it a theme, whether it's an Italian or French

style, or an international fancy box entertainment sort of style. So here all the elements of identity and architectural approach get dissolved, and to some degree silenced.
Because of this, commercial or thematic approaches are increasingly adopted. For example, in the case of the Kempinski Marsa Malaz hotel, which is built in a Venetian-like setting, a blend of Venetian spirit with a touch of Arabian flavour is used to transmit this lifestyle. This thematic approach has become a global tendency in architecture. In each case, you try to create the mood suited for the commercial setting. You can even do a leisure resort with a "minimalist" feeling, or a "Maldives" atmosphere…

LM: I guess that's the "Las Vegas effect", right?
IMJ: Yes, this patterning of space is perfectly represented by Las Vegas – or Disney World, for instance. This phenomenon is becoming a big trend. But there have been some cases where we have managed to convince the client to "go back to basics" and include traditional or purer elements within commercial projects, and the results were unique.
A good example would be Al Sharq Hotel, in which we injected the ingredients of the typical old Qatari village to endow the place with a touch of intimacy. Since this was a government-driven project, the directive was to give it a very vernacular look. But even if you were not able to visually experience such development, if I took you around Al Sharq you'd feel the shading and the shadows of the density; or stepping into the courtyard, you'd feel that sense of the *local*. This is a strong marketing strategy, even with the thematisation (the Arabian flavour and so on…), and here in Qatar we should invest in it. I think anyone coming from the West – or from the East as well – who hopes to experience this Arabian-flavoured lifestyle would far prefer it than a standard mall in the typical international style.

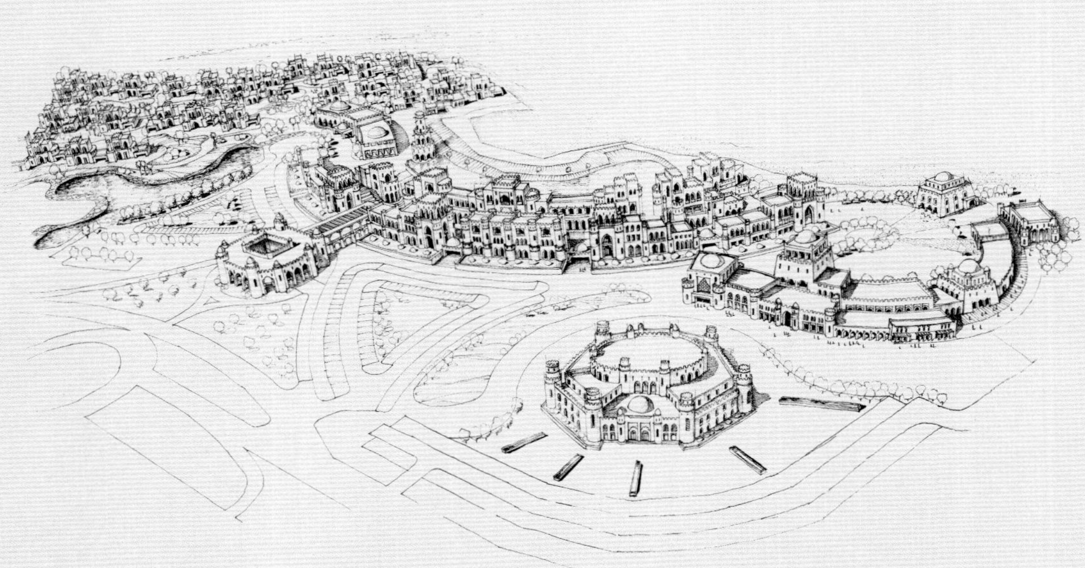

So even within the limits of the thematisation drive, I think we can sense a locally influenced trend taking place. I can say that here at AEB we are leading it. Not long ago we were commissioned by government subsidiaries to carry out some studies, which showed that this form of thematic architecture driven by our own traditions and culture could produce magnificent results.

LM: So what you are saying is that, ultimately – as happened with corporate building – the ideas and interventions of the government can be a huge contribution, as long as the government pushes proper examples. Basically, public policies can affect the choices of the private sector, right?

IMJ: Quite so. It's always the case. I remember early in my career when I was working for the government, I once said: "Let's do something using our local vernacular," and my colleagues replied: "You mean like a museum? Ahahah! No."

And that was the mood until the mid-late 1990s, when HH The Father Emir Sheikh Hamad, who was the ruler at the time, shifted his interest toward local identity. At that point, the private sector started paying attention and rode the trend. History has recorded such tidal shifts in style. After all, the Renaissance spirit was driven by the royalty, and logically the merchants followed the royal whims. The arts too have always been levers of change… even the arts of Leonardo da Vinci's period were very much influenced by the Church, and artists performed on recurring themes and techniques.

LM: So you think that Nouvel's addition to the National Museum will have a lasting effect?

IMJ: It surely will. The old building is surrounded by Jean Nouvel's new work, and it has become a point of reference: it's the largest building in the neighbourhood, and expresses

elements that are pure and original to Qatar. I would call it an authentic yardstick of what is widely considered "Qatari architecture". Even though there are many similarities in the architecture around the Gulf, the combination of features incorporated within this single building make it utterly unique to Qatar.

LM: Let's move on now to your thoughts on workspace architecture. Nowadays people tend to work all massed together, and as we know it's not easy to build workplaces that offer proper environmental qualities. How are working spaces changing? Assuming they are in fact changing…

IMJ: Well, yes, at the beginning we had the classic tin of sardines and little else, but that's not so any more. For over decade now we've been creating much more pleasant working places. Take for example the Commercial Bank. It employs an "active façade" – that is, cutting-edge glazing technology that enables its users to adjust the environment inside to suit their needs. And now in Lusail we are doing similarly interesting projects that pivot on the conditions of the working environment inside. Another project worth mentioning is Alfardan Twin Towers in the West Bay. It might seem quite straightforward, but actually the building's orientation became hugely significant. The plot of land allowed for a pattern

of small square openings coupled with long vertical window gullies on the building's west face, where we have also placed all the internal circulation routes – stairways and elevators – which are accessed via a ground-floor atrium on a triangular, fully glazed open plan. Because of the way we've designed the inside environment, it is pleasant because even when curtains are open, you don't have that relentless glare typical of our Gulf sunshine. I have been in some offices facing west in which you literally need sunglasses! It just doesn't work without some form of protection. So building orientation has become paramount in all our projects in Lusail.

LM: True, and proper planning means energy saving and lower maintenance costs. Companies that invest in energy-efficient architecture also save money.
IMJ: Exactly. Right now we're working on a new project, the Alfardan complex in Lusail. The client happens to want a huge showroom, and the only access to the main road is on the west side. After plenty of in-depth research we decided to use German glazing technology that incorporates electronic diming in the glass itself. It still allows maximum visual exposure, but reflection and glare are significantly lower. So now we are using advanced technology to harmonise with the environment. I feel that as long as we take careful note of our environment and context – and respect it – we will always be able to find appropriate technological solutions. Unfortunately, in some cases the environment is still being ignored, and you see full curtain-walls facing the wrong way in a museum, let's say, even where the main displays are, which means that curtains need to be drawn to screen out the sunlight. Sometimes the city master plans themselves are not sensitive to the environment, and so when you face these limits, you are forced to be innovative and incorporate other challenging elements into your designs. These go back to the planners, and unfortunately the city planners often show no respect for the environment.

LM: Indeed, and this brings me to my last question. We seem to be shifting from the idea that the city is built only of architectural bodies, toward a more aware conception of planning. Central to this shift is designing new environments and new forms of landscape, therefore a shift from buildings *per se* to the settings they occupy. Or, to put it another way: during the past 20 years the focus was mainly on buildings, overlooking the in-between space, the so-called "pedestrian area", the "ground zero area", which in the Gulf region is not an easy feature to manage. And yet if you look back to the traditional Middle Eastern city, you can see that these "diaphragm" spaces were fundamental to the quality of the urban environment. Which are the most important challenges for the coming years in relation to the definition of a new urban environment?
IMJ: Yes, you are quite right. Fortunately the regional planning department has begun to realise this fact, and have started to study how to integrate walkways, bicycle paths and the best, healthiest and safest types of pedestrian crossing. We're really working hard on it.

LM: What is your idea of a good environment to live in? It seems to be a recurring theme in your work.
IMJ: There are many features essential for improving the living environment. For a start, using local types of trees as a shading device is the best way to create an urban landscape that offers the required protection. Also playing with vertical levels has become more important, to allow for overhead pedestrian walkways, for instance. Note that people tend to take shortcuts when crossing the street. That's a basic cultural thing. So patterns of behaviour and street

mentality must be studied on the ground, as it were, before forcing outside theories on the public environment, otherwise it simply will not work. You can't successfully implement any theory unless you have really considered social behaviour patterns.

And when referring to social behaviour, I am not talking only about the mentality of native Qataris, but of the many different nationalities residing in our country. I think it's worthwhile studying and challenging assumptions – and maybe even doing a prototype to test the reactions of the locals, before you impose something upon them that works somewhere else. Many standard pedestrian solutions simply do not work here in Qatar. The climate is different, people's behaviour is different, the discipline is different. The same thing applies to the streets themselves. Streets are streets, but people like to cross from one sidewalk to the other, just as they wish. That's a cultural trait. Therefore, urban features should be designed to suit the host mentalities.

Private Villa at The Pearl

Private Villa at The Pearl

The Pearl, Qatar

Completed, 2013

Client: Private

When it comes to designing private houses, AEB's expertise relies both on the research carried out by Ibrahim Mohamed Jaidah on Qatari vernacular settlements, and on the firm's awareness of the urgent need to develop entirely new housing typologies that respond to the evolving needs of the varied population of contemporary Qatar.

Pearl Villa shows the firm's ability to integrate a straightforward modern design that reworks contemporary models of the single-family home, mostly drawn from western culture, yet with a great deal of inspiration directly taken from local custom. In traditional Qatari residential architecture, the relationship between inside and outside was manifestly polarized. Blank walls flanked the narrow alleys (*sikkas*) cutting through villages, while all the windows opened on the internal courtyards, where most of the family life unfolded. Pearl Villa reinterprets this dichotomy by adding the brand new element of landscape, and particularly a breath-taking sea view. A precise hierarchy is established between the façade overlooking the entrance road, which has very few openings, including the full-height glass wall flanking the stairwell, and the elevation overlooking the beach, which is almost entirely glazed to ensure a pervasive permeability between architecture

and nature. The simplicity that informs the entire design clearly emerges in the floorplan, with its straight walls rotating to follow the plot's shape, and the two side volumes projected towards the sea to embrace the external terrace. The latter is the most representative space of the house, and it can be accessed through a folding glazed wall that links it to the main living room at the ground floor. A swimming pool clad in blue tiles softens the threshold between the paved surface and the sand dunes. A sequence of shaded terraces provides a variety of open spaces at each floor of Pearl Villa, which is topped by an unexpected isolated volume. AEB has honoured the artistic needs of the owner by creating a transparent rooftop studio suspended over the building, where he can work undisturbed, while enjoying the stunning views of the sea.

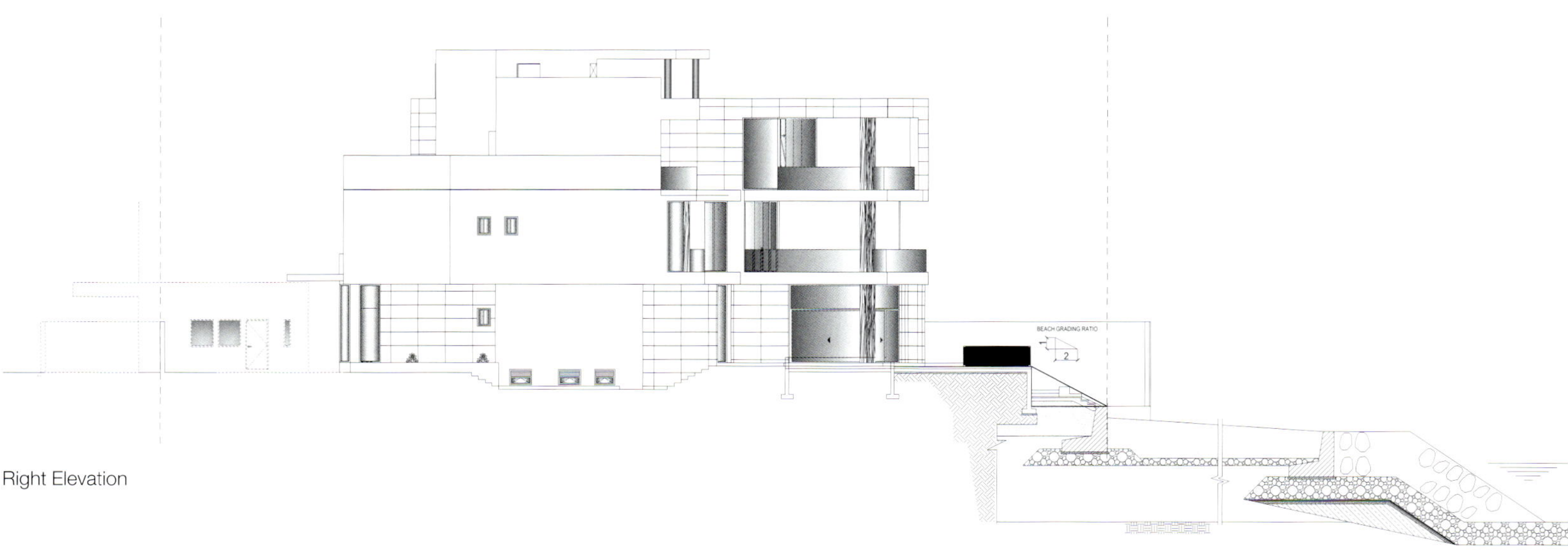

Right Elevation

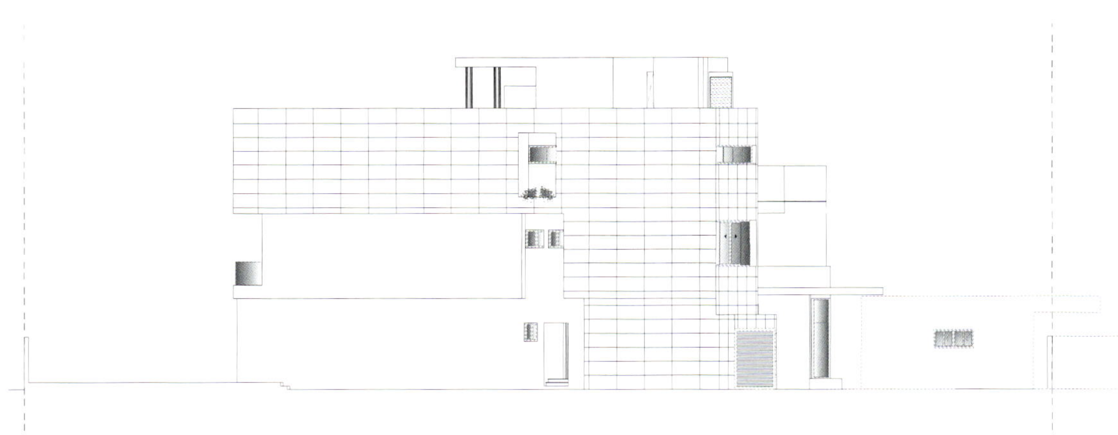

Left Elevation

Fire Station Artists in Residence

Fire Station Artists in Residence

Wadi Al Sail, Doha, Qatar

Completed, 2014

Client: Qatar Museums

The refurbishment of the former Civil Defense Building and its transformation into a gallery and artists residency is a milestone project both for AEB's design philosophy, and for the urban history of Doha, as it showcases the will and capability of the firm to re-invent the most important elements of the city's built heritage, and turn this legacy into high-quality contemporary facilities. The project on the former Fire Station takes on a big relevance in this context, as it belongs to a distinctive architectural movement of modern Doha, along with the Sheraton Hotel and Post Office, among others.

AEB's design preserves the Fire Station's original tower and elegantly clads it in stainless-steel mesh and LED lighting modules, while carefully restoring its façades, with a particular focus on their most iconic feature – the bronze honeycomb grid shading the upper floors. On the other hand, the interiors are completely re-invented: most of the internal walls were removed and the structural elements stripped back, in order to create a highly functional and sophisticated open space.

The original station is now flanked by a brand new U-shape annex containing a wide range of facilities for artists and the public: workshops, a foundry, and a small cinema operate alongside a restaurant, an art supplies shop, a bookstore, and a café. Giving onto the plaza, the cafeteria has folding glass doors, which in winter months open the interior to the outside. The restaurant above the café also has operable glass doors on three sides, which open to a terrace seating area, shaded under the overhanging roof.

Entirely paved with granite and furnished with seats, the plaza is designed as a comfortable meeting place and mediates the relationship between the existing station and the annex, while at the same time acting as the head of the system of public spaces inside the future Grand Park, one of the most important in Doha. Meanwhile a shallow basin can be filled with a thin layer of water, thus generating unexpected reflections that further enhance the poetic atmosphere of this space.

The Fire Station gallery is home to a rich and unique programme of events, which both promotes the local and regional contemporary art scene and fosters international cultural exchange.

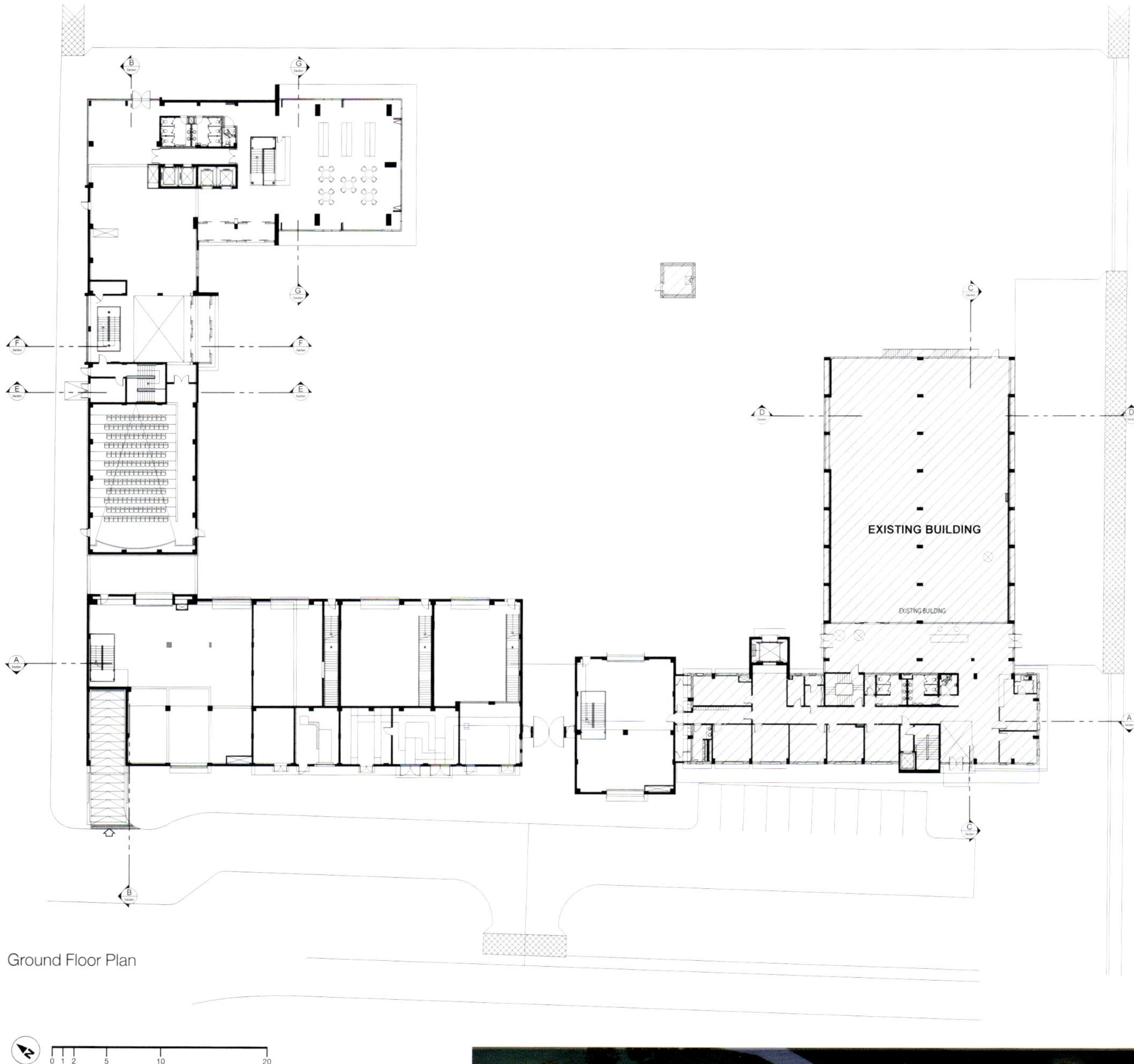

Ground Floor Plan

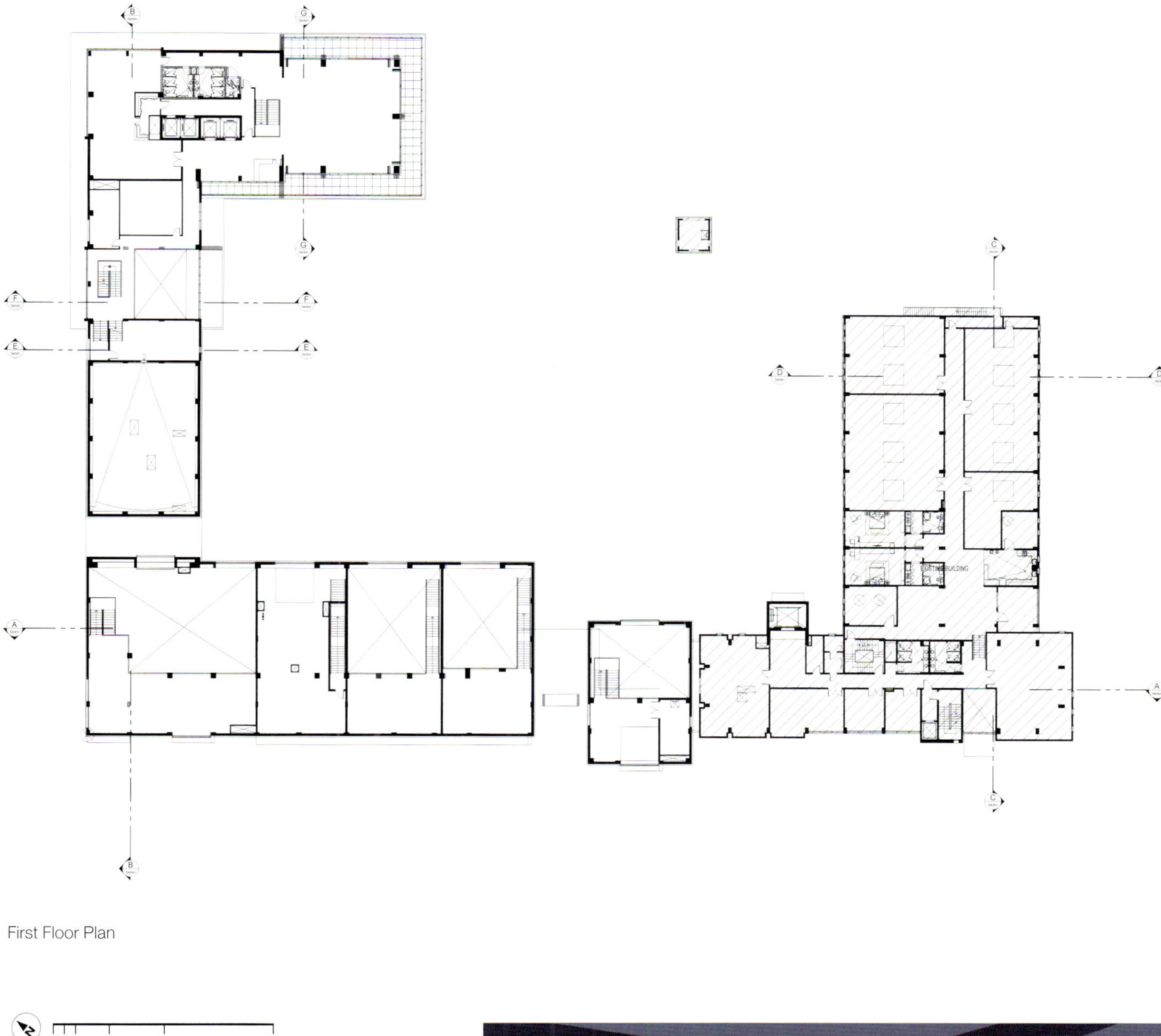

First Floor Plan

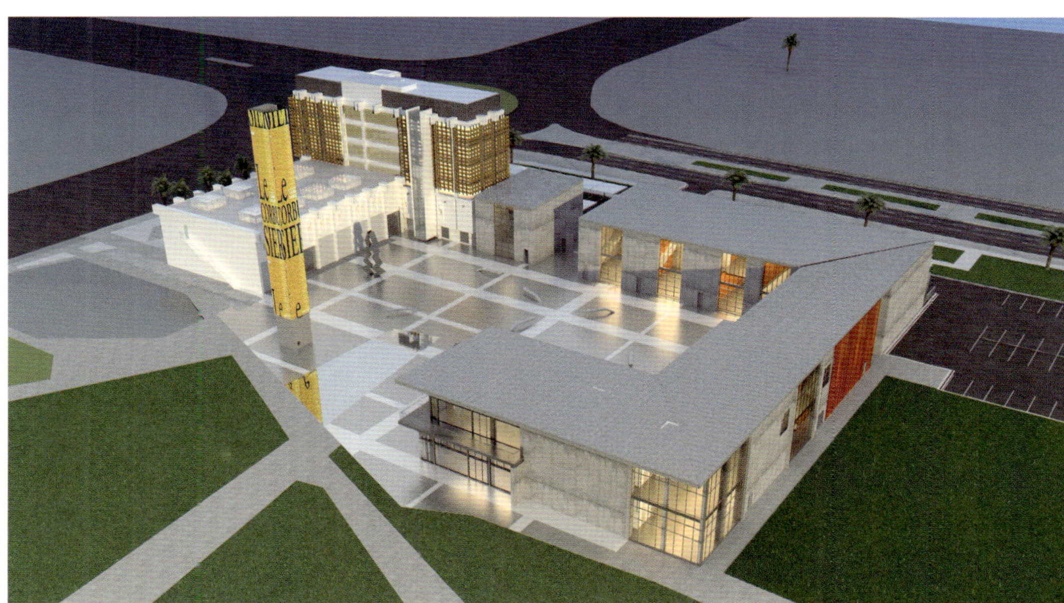

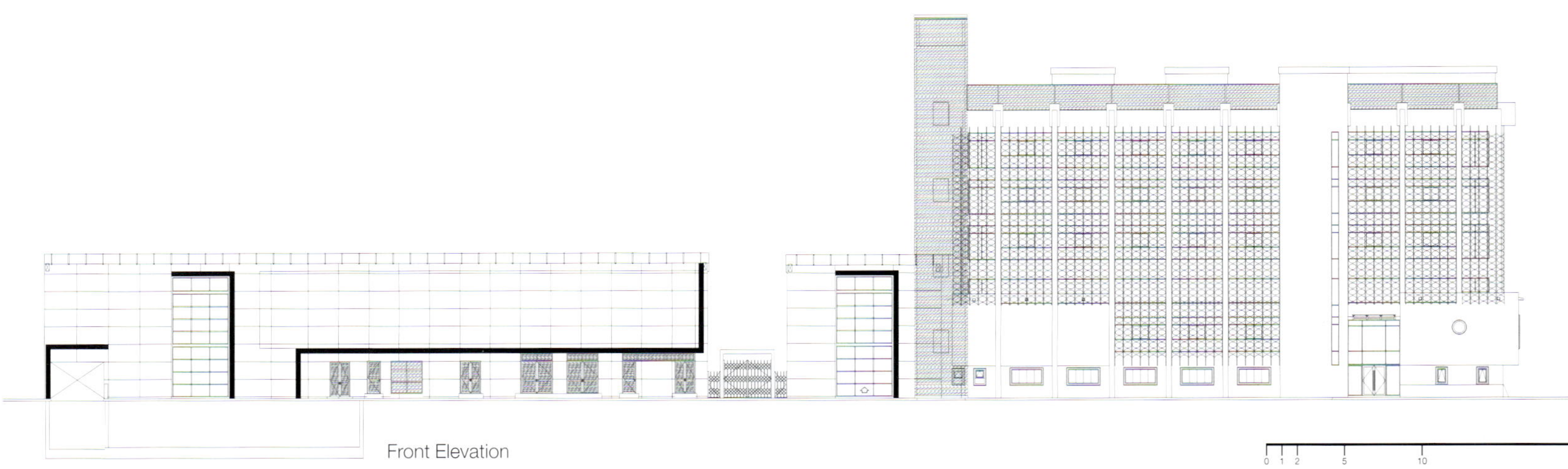

Front Elevation

Right Elevation

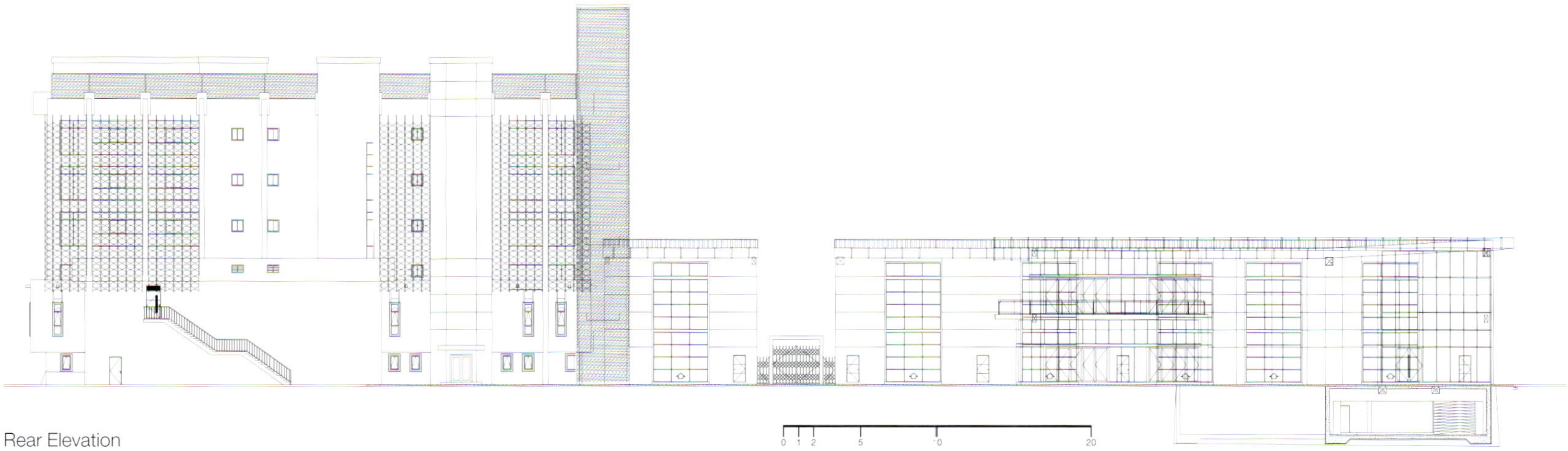

Rear Elevation

Left Elevation

FIRE STATION

State of Qatar Embassy in the Kingdom of Bahrain

State of Qatar Embassy in the Kingdom of Bahrain

Manama, Bahrain

Completed, 2014

Client: Ministry of Foreign Affairs

AEB won the competition promoted by the Ministry of Foreign Affairs to design the main representation of the State of Qatar in the Kingdom of Bahrain, by proposing a building that would be mindful of Qatar's architectural tradition, but also up-to-date with the most advanced technical and construction standards.

Completed on site in 2014, the complex of the Qatar Embassy in Al Saif covers a surface area of more than 9,000 square metres, surrounded by three vehicular roads, and flanked by a neighbouring lot on its south edge.

The design of the development reproduces the articulated landscape of a Qatari village: a sequence of volumes of different heights and orientation join together in a compact block and, by doing so, superpose several layers of parapets, geometrical decorations, *mashrabiyah* windows, and domes.

The intricacy of the composition results from the functional setup of the building's layout, which was carefully studied to ensure maximum accessibility to visitors, while respecting strict security requirements.

While the consulate pavilion overlooks the street and can be directly accessed from it, the embassy proper is set back to leave space for a guardroom and a car drop-off bay. From here governmental employees and guests enter the main multi-purpose room, and are channelled off either to the offices or to the *majlis*, which functions as a waiting room serving the ambassador's chamber on the first floor.

The ambassador's residence stands in a more private position and is provided with a separate guardroom and driveway. Its main living areas give onto a terrace that leads to a lush garden with a shaded walkway, a circular pavilion, and a V-shaped swimming pool.

Front Elevation

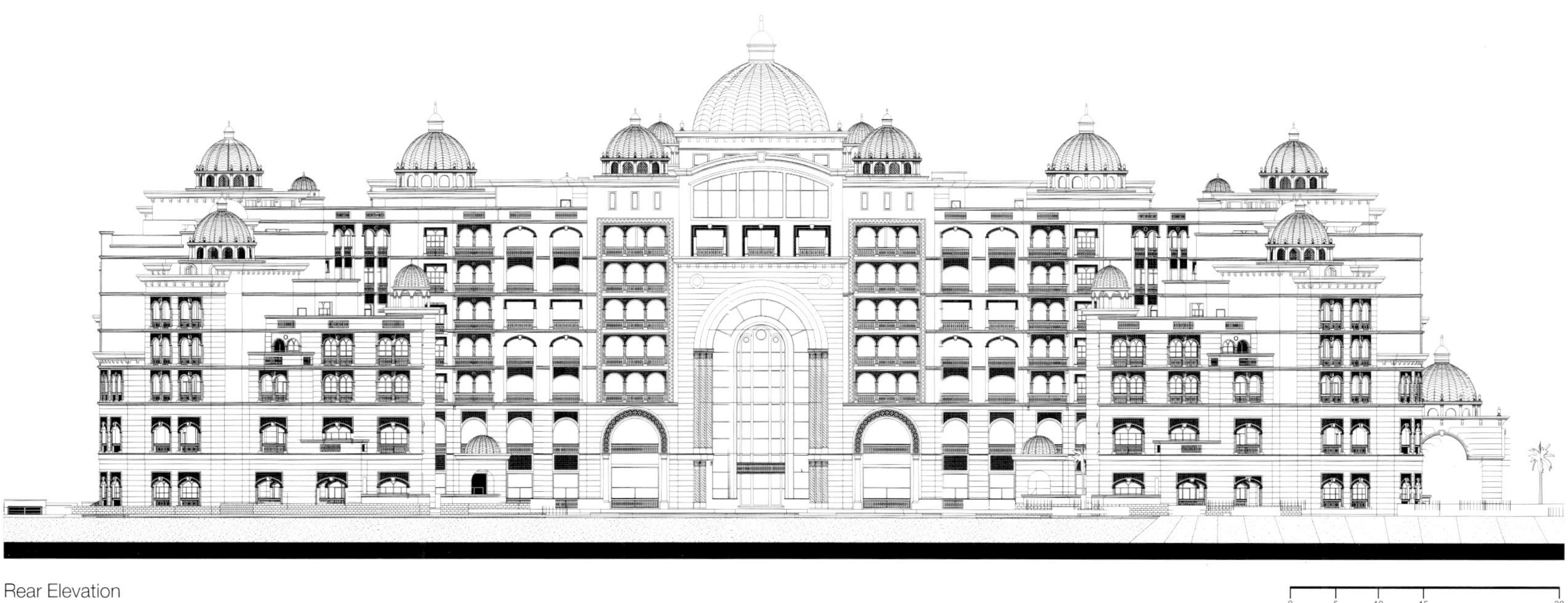

Rear Elevation

Ghanem Holdings Headquarters

Ghanem Holdings Headquarters

Salwa Road, Doha, Qatar

Completed, 2015

Client: Ghanem Real Estate Investment and Development Co.

Qatar has always had a profound relationship with the natural characteristics of the Gulf region, particularly with its immeasurable deserts and crystalline seas.

This is why, when Ghanem Holdings, one of the largest business groups in Qatar, commissioned AEB to design its headquarters, strategically located just 100 metres east of Ramada Junction, the firm's architects drew their inspiration from the extraordinary natural features of the local environment.

As a result, the distinctive plan and elevation of the building directly recall the intriguing shape of the typical mushroom coral that can be found all along Qatar's coastline, translating into a lean circular layout, with several hollow concrete slabs superimposed to define a full-height courtyard.

With two levels of retail outlets at the base, and seven levels of offices, AEB's design merges the traditional features of Arabic planning with the functional needs of a contemporary corporate building.

The retail section is accessible from the inner courtyard via the main entrance. Illuminated predominantly by natural light from a skylight eight storeys above, this courtyard is devised to serve as a public plaza appointed with seating areas. The filtered glow from the skylight playing across a seven-story *mashrabiyah* screen forms that dramatic layer of separation between the building's public/semi-public (retail and courtyard) and private/semi-private (office and walkway) spaces.

Cutting-edge integrated energy-saving devices turn Ghanem Holdings headquarters into a fully sustainable building: the building's external surfaces are protected from solar glare by a unique system of fan-shaped mesh screens that shield the direct sun whilst allowing daylight to filter into the interiors; meanwhile the courtyard emulates traditional Qatari systems to generate steady air convection, with cooler air circulating at the lower levels and warmer air trapped under the skylight.

Rising alongside one of the busiest intersections in Doha, the Ghanem eco-tower enjoys a high level of visibility during both day and night, thanks to the computer-programmed "rings" of illumination built into the building's string-courses.

قف
STOP

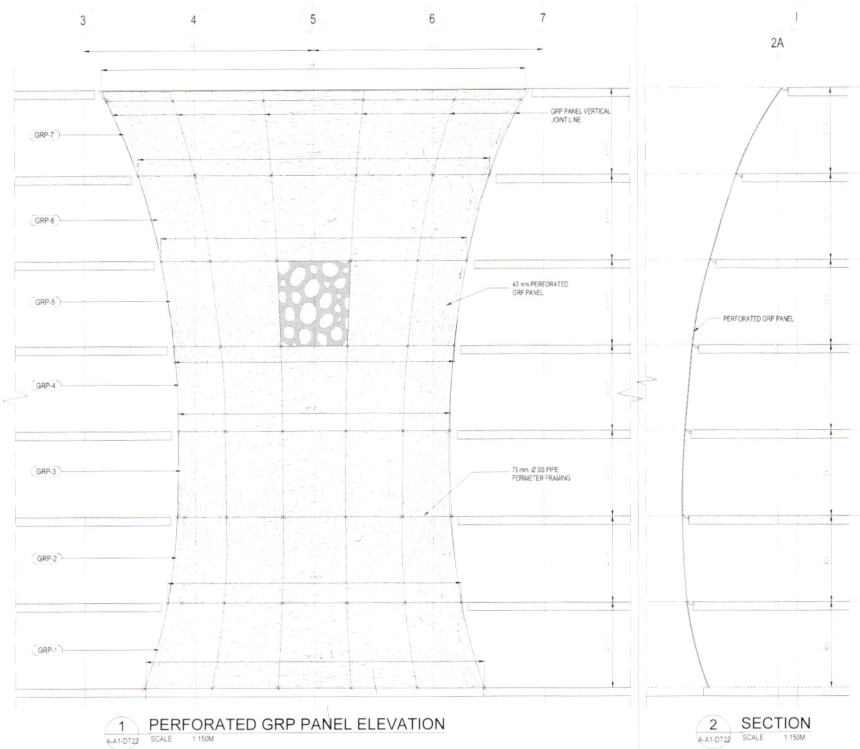

1 PERFORATED GRP PANEL ELEVATION
2 SECTION

EXOTIC CARS
اكزوتيك كارز

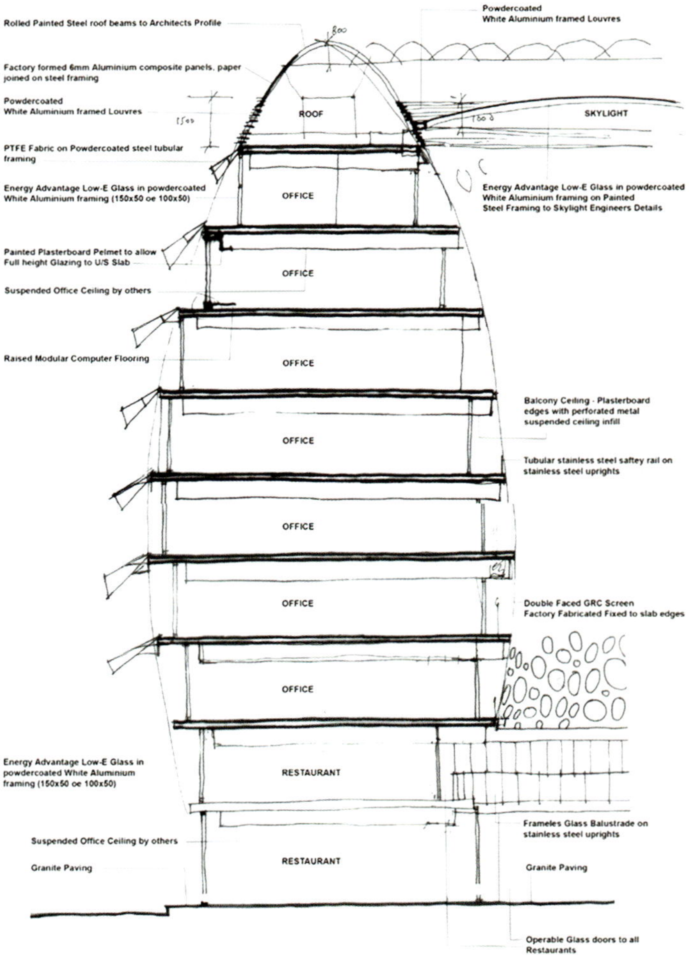

Rolled Painted Steel roof beams to Architects Profile
Powdercoated White Aluminium framed Louvres
Factory formed 6mm Aluminium composite panels, paper joined on steel framing
Powdercoated White Aluminium framed Louvres
ROOF
SKYLIGHT
PTFE Fabric on Powdercoated steel tubular framing
Energy Advantage Low-E Glass in powdercoated White Aluminium framing (150x50 oe 100x50)
Energy Advantage Low-E Glass in powdercoated White Aluminium framing on Painted Steel Framing to Skylight Engineers Details
OFFICE
Painted Plasterboard Pelmet to allow Full height Glazing to U/S Slab
Suspended Office Ceiling by others
OFFICE
Raised Modular Computer Flooring
OFFICE
Balcony Ceiling - Plasterboard edges with perforated metal suspended ceiling infill
OFFICE
Tubular stainless steel saftey rail on stainless steel uprights
OFFICE
OFFICE
Double Faced GRC Screen Factory Fabricated Fixed to slab edges
OFFICE
Energy Advantage Low-E Glass in powdercoated White Aluminium framing (150x50 oe 100x50)
RESTAURANT
Frameles Glass Balustrade on stainless steel uprights
Suspended Office Ceiling by others
RESTAURANT
Granite Paving
Granite Paving
Operable Glass doors to all Restaurants

Gulf Mall

Gulf Mall

Al Gharafa, Doha, Qatar

Completed, 2015

Client: Sh. Nasser Bin Abdullah Al Thani

Throughout history, the commercial core of any Arab town is the souq, where most of the daily trading takes place. In spite of its density and complexity, the layout of a souq always follows an extremely precise set of rules, which are approved by the numerous guilds that trade inside the market. Starting from a concentric plan, a strict form of zoning clusters merchants selling the same type of goods together, and arranges the different activities hierarchically, outward from the souq's centre – where the most profitable merchandise is to be found – to its periphery – where perishable goods are located.

Albeit with substantial variations, a contemporary mall can take inspiration from this ancient form of spatial and functional organisation, as in the case of the Gulf Mall, located in northern Doha. Covering a surface of almost 90,000 square metres, this two-storey shopping arcade is made

up of four main areas which, despite forgoing the ancient souq's thematic connotations, stand out thanks to their unique aesthetics, which draw on four different tendencies of the Gulf region's architecture.

The local traditions of Kuwait, Oman, Saudi Arabia, the Emirates, Yemen, Bahrain, and Qatar itself are among the main sources of inspiration for the Gulf Mall's design, which makes extensive use of wooden frames, water spouts, gargoyles, projections, and pergolas, wind towers, fortified towers, and decorative arches and recesses. Decorative motives are used extensively around the "gates", which serve both as entrances to the mall and as a focus of interest, while showcasing the splendour of the mall's interiors to approaching visitors.

GULF MALL

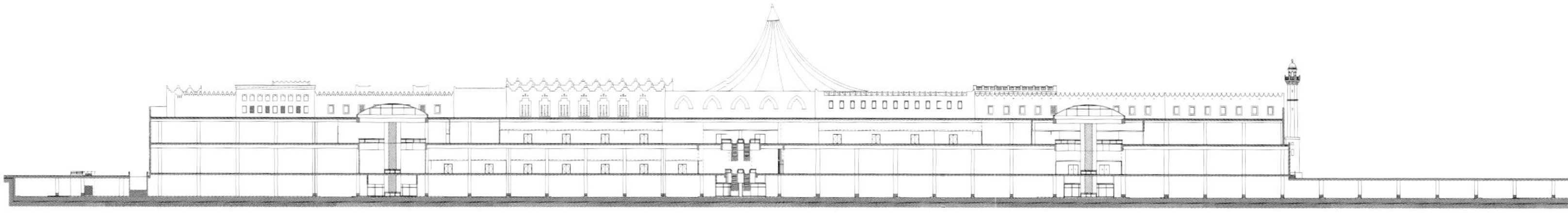

Longitudinal Section

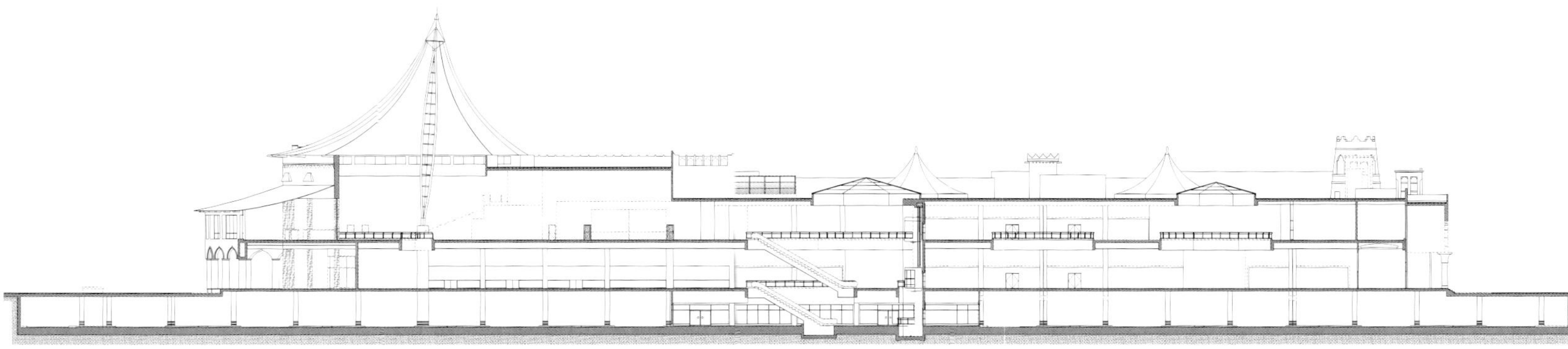

Cross Section

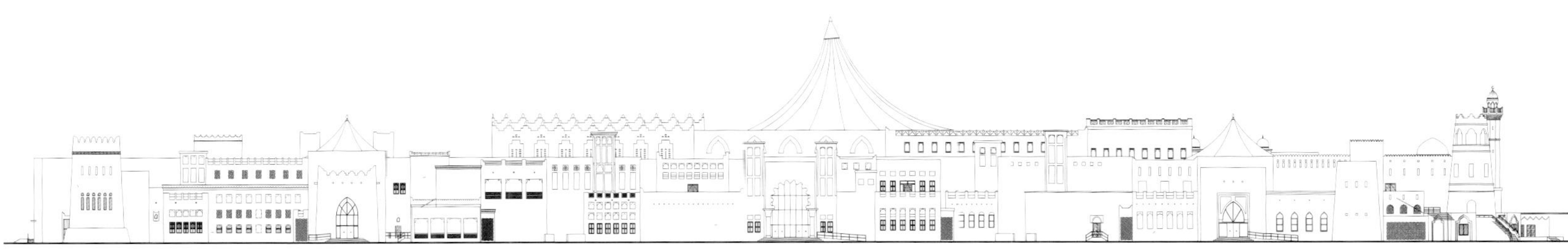

Front Elevation

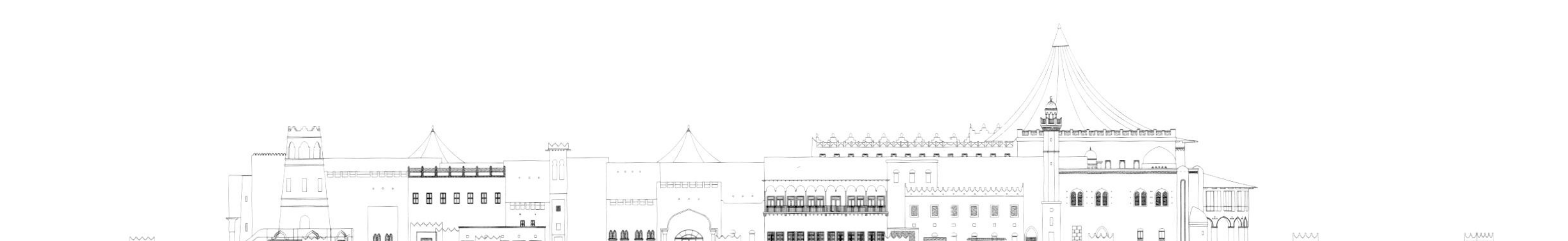

Right Elevation

State of Qatar Embassy in Lebanon

State of Qatar Embassy in Lebanon

Beirut, Lebanon

Completed, 2015

Client: Ministry of Foreign Affairs

Designed by AEB, the new embassy for the State of Qatar will soon be added to the many international representations of the diplomatic district of Beirut.

As the main physical presence of Qatar in Lebanon, the new embassy building assumes a fundamental institutional role, and through its form reflects the vision and role of Qatar as a state. For this reason, its façades are richly decorated with motifs of Qatari traditional architecture, such as the small and narrow windows, most of which are fitted with traditional carved gypsum screens, and the numerous arched wall recesses cut into sheer stone surfaces.

In addition to referencing these specific features of Qatari culture, in order to make the building distinctive, easily recognisable and emphasise its structure, AEB has chosen the classic Islamic symbol of the square, which is multiplied and applied to all the structure's masses.

Indeed, the various blocks of the complex share a similar square plan – reproduced at different scales – and rotated by 45 degrees to align their edges on the main east–west axis, running from the principal road to the back of the lot.

Its ground floor features an impressive enfilade of rooms, including the foyer, the hall, and a full-height multi-purpose room, directly lit from above through a large skylight.

Despite its rich décor, the overall image of the building remains that of a compact and muscular fortress, while also recalling the layout of traditional villages and thus conveying at first sight the complexity of its interior spaces.

As a result of a slight shift of the different volumes, large terraces are created on top of each other – a tribute to traditional Lebanese architecture – which offer admirable views of both the mountainous landscape to the east, and the Mediterranean coast to the west.

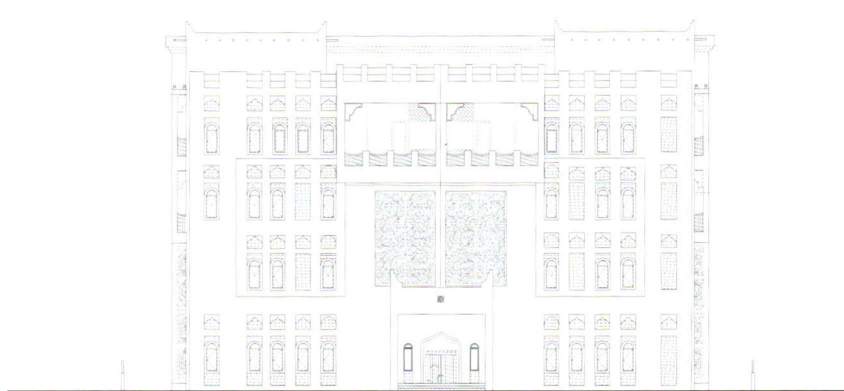

Front Elevation

Right Elevation

Ministry of Interior Headquarters (MoI HQ)

Ministry of Interior Headquarters (MoI HQ)

Wadi Al Sail, Doha, Qatar

Completed, 2016

Client: Private Engineering Office

In accordance with Private Office Engineering's vision of building on the national identity, the project for the Ministry of Interior is realised as an imposing monument to the state of Qatar.

The design of an architectural complex of such public importance required careful research into the architectural typologies and aesthetics that best represent the values and goals of the country.

In response to this commission, AEB drew a great deal of inspiration from the local and regional vernacular, critically adapting the idiom to define a layout which effectively responds to the functional needs of a contemporary institution of this nature.

Consequently, the design of the Ministry building closely follows the varied complexity of its many functions.

The main building is composed of two volumes that host the governmental offices and their service spaces, along with a wide array of accessory functions, such as prayer rooms, a gym, a lecture hall, a squash court, a lounge and a snooker room – among others.

Rows of palm trees announce the entry into a large courtyard appointed with a central sunken water wall with cascades as the main focal point; this courtyard is enclosed by the two buildings, and can be accessed through the full height entrance hall.

The complex also integrates a separate volume hosting a multi-storey car park.

All the buildings share the same aesthetics, inspired by both the fortified structures of central Doha and the fort of Umm Slal Mohammad, a small historical settlement in the heart of Qatar – one of the few to be still preserved – laying some 10 kilometres from the coast and 15 kilometres north of the city.

The overall impression of mass is enhanced by the use of tilted walls and cylindrical watchtowers, standing at the four corners of each building.

Their circular appearance is a further tribute to the vernacular art of construction: in the past, when forts where built out of desert stones – often small and irregular – perimeter corners were rounded to make them thicker and more resistant.

The few small openings typical of ancient fortifications have been reinvented in the shape of full-height narrow glazed surfaces, which allow light to reach the interiors, while producing a distinctive chiaroscuro on the polished surface of the plastered outer walls

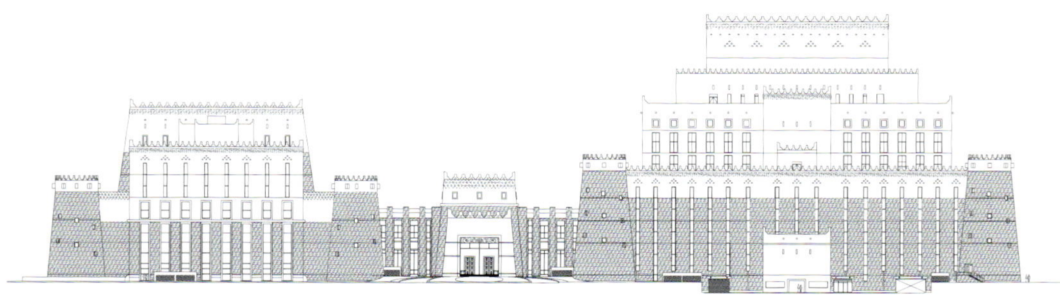

Left Elevation

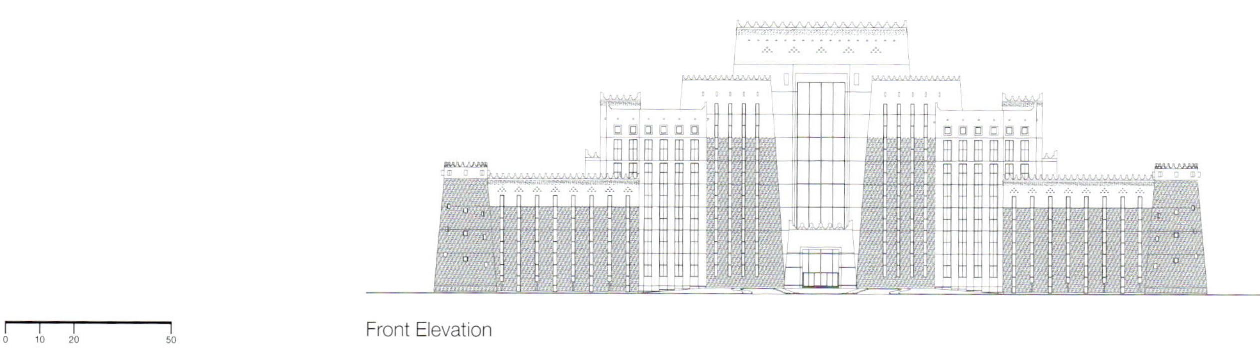

Front Elevation

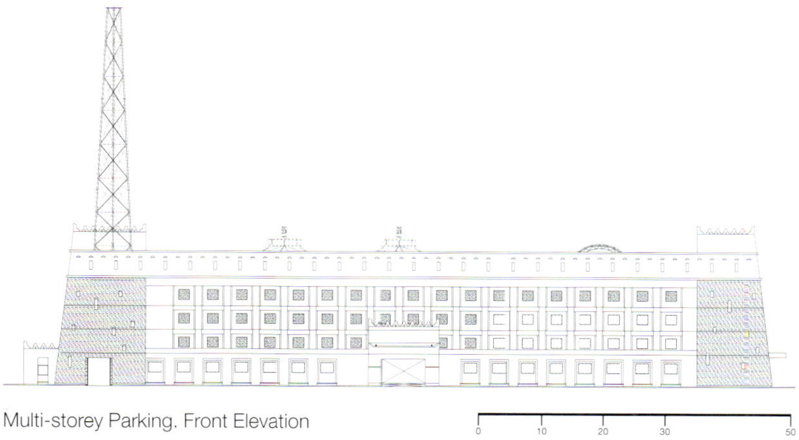

Multi-storey Parking. Front Elevation

Fraser Suites

Fraser Suites

West Bay, Doha, Qatar

Expected completion date: end of 2016

Client: Al Sarh Real Estate (Member of Al Rabban Holding)

One of the latest additions to Doha's burgeoning West Bay district, Fraser Suites encapsulates AEB's long-term research on the typology and aesthetics of high-rise buildings.

For this archetype of cutting-edge residential architecture, AEB was also commissioned to supervise the construction of the tower. This enabled the firm to oversee the entire process, from the general concept to the tiniest details, and fully express its specific know-how.

The striking western Art Deco style served as the template for the tower's decorations, providing the ideal inspiration for the requisite finesse of this high-end apartment building.

With their eclectic style and distinctive geometrical features – such as polygons, rectangles, zigzags, chevrons and sunburst motifs – the towers' striking façades stand proud among the West Bay's clustered skyscrapers.

Typically for a modern skyscraper, the decorations are concentrated on the lower levels and around the main entrance to the tower, whose columns and architraves are clad with granite, etched in a vibrating pattern of zigzag recesses.

The delicate shades of stones combine with the gold-toned bronze of the window frames and the grilles of the sun-screens, whose patterns evoke a desert palm tree.

Compact rows of thin pilasters rise from the ground level, tapering towards the top of the building, where they emerge from the profile, projecting towards the sky.

In this way, the four façades offer a rich chiaroscuro effect, transforming the simple volume of the tower into an elaborate multifaceted surface, reacting to its context and to the ever-changing effects of Qatari sunlight.

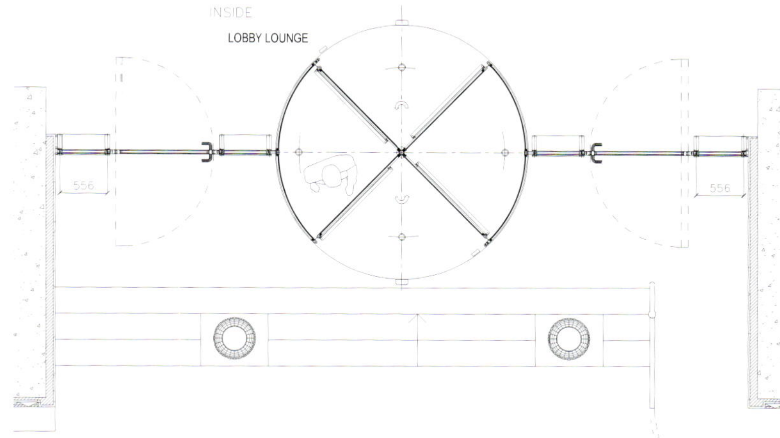

Main Entrance. Art Déco Pattern Detail

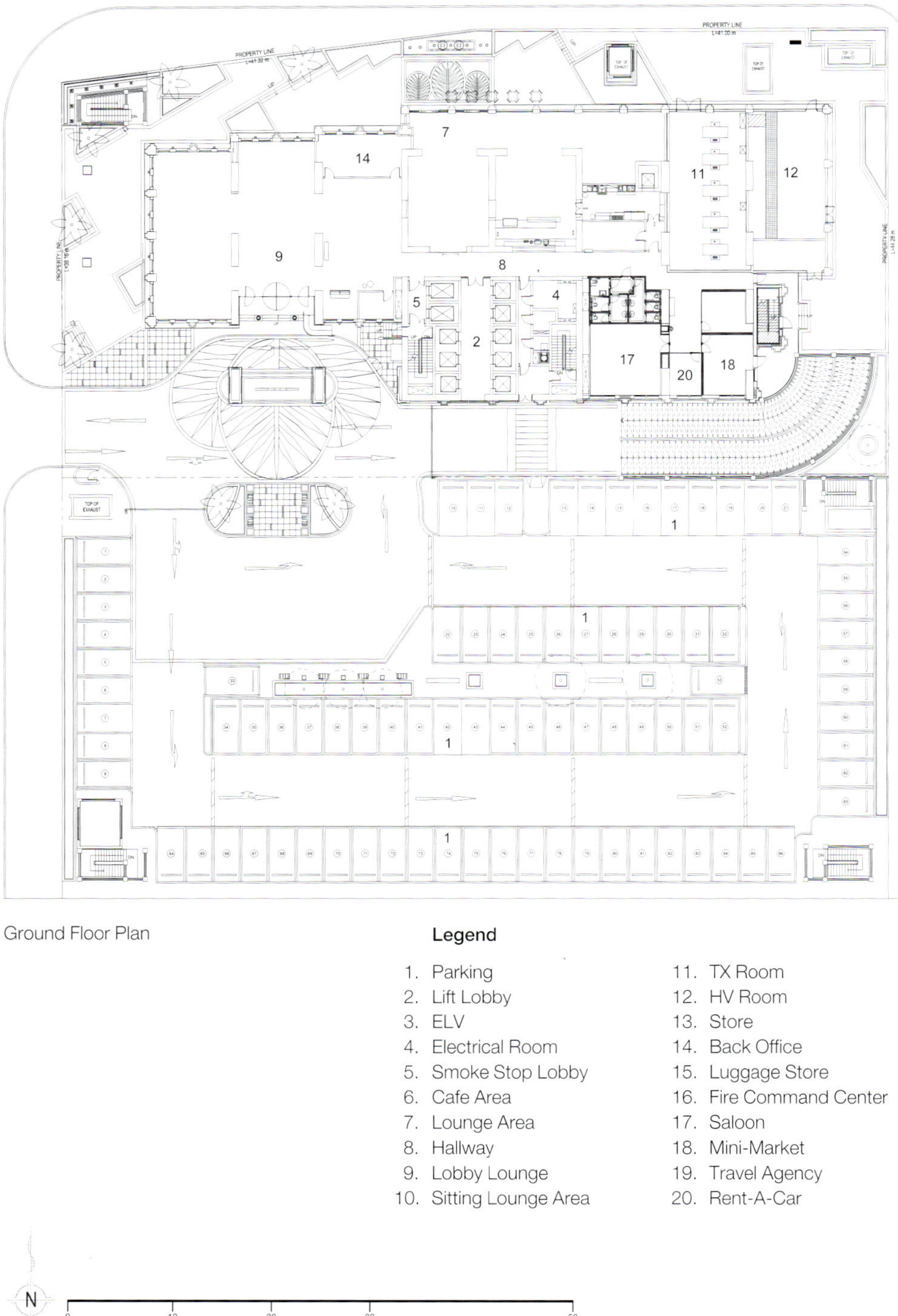

Ground Floor Plan

Legend

1. Parking
2. Lift Lobby
3. ELV
4. Electrical Room
5. Smoke Stop Lobby
6. Cafe Area
7. Lounge Area
8. Hallway
9. Lobby Lounge
10. Sitting Lounge Area
11. TX Room
12. HV Room
13. Store
14. Back Office
15. Luggage Store
16. Fire Command Center
17. Saloon
18. Mini-Market
19. Travel Agency
20. Rent-A-Car

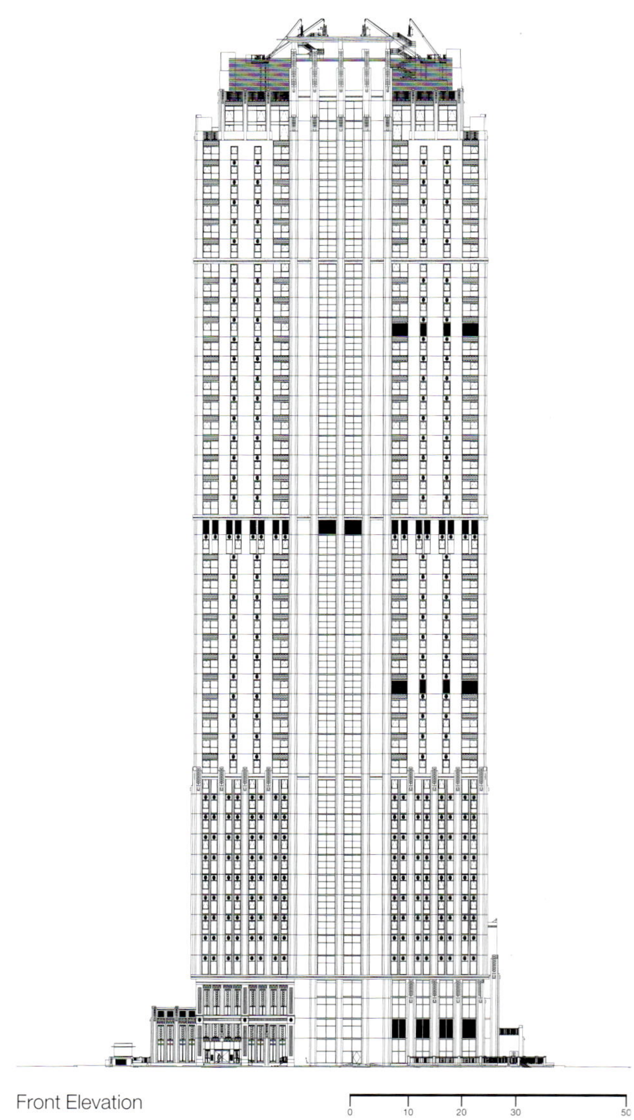

Front Elevation

FRASERSUITES

Sidra Musalla

Sidra Musalla

Education City, Doha, Qatar

Expected completion date: end of 2016

Client: OHL Contrack

Sidra Musalla is conveniently located at the intersection of the three principal buildings that compose the Sidra Medical and Research Center. This flagship project covers over 139,000 square metres, combining education facilities in partnership with Weill Cornell Medical College in Qatar, and a health care centre for women and children.

On the functional side, Sidra Musalla is easily accessed by both hospital staff and visitors, and respects the basic features of religious architecture through its careful spatial distribution, which enables it to host more than 300 worshippers at a time.

In addition to the main prayer hall, the ground floor includes ablution rooms for men and women, and separate prayer lobbies and service rooms located in the semi-circular area of its plan.

The paths to the Sidra Musalla open onto a humble sanctuary of peace and prayer, which contrasts with the rich complex surrounding it, and appears to be "lifted" off the ground, hovering over the water feature.

Composed of two main connected bodies on a circular base, the mosque is characterised by an absolute formal purity and stylised composition, with the straight prevailing lines and neutral colours of concrete and stone reinforcing its monumentality.

The minaret is conceived on a minimalist square base, a monolithic tower vigorously rising out of water with a longitudinal gash of light and – in the only symbolic reference to Islamic decoration – a crescent on the top.

Two large skylights and longitudinal and transversal slits at the bottom of the prayer hall and in the *mihrab* apse allow natural light to create shadows as a natural decoration for the interior, underlining the sacred functionality of the building as a whole.

Frameless glass represents a further element of the elegant simplicity introduced by AEB.

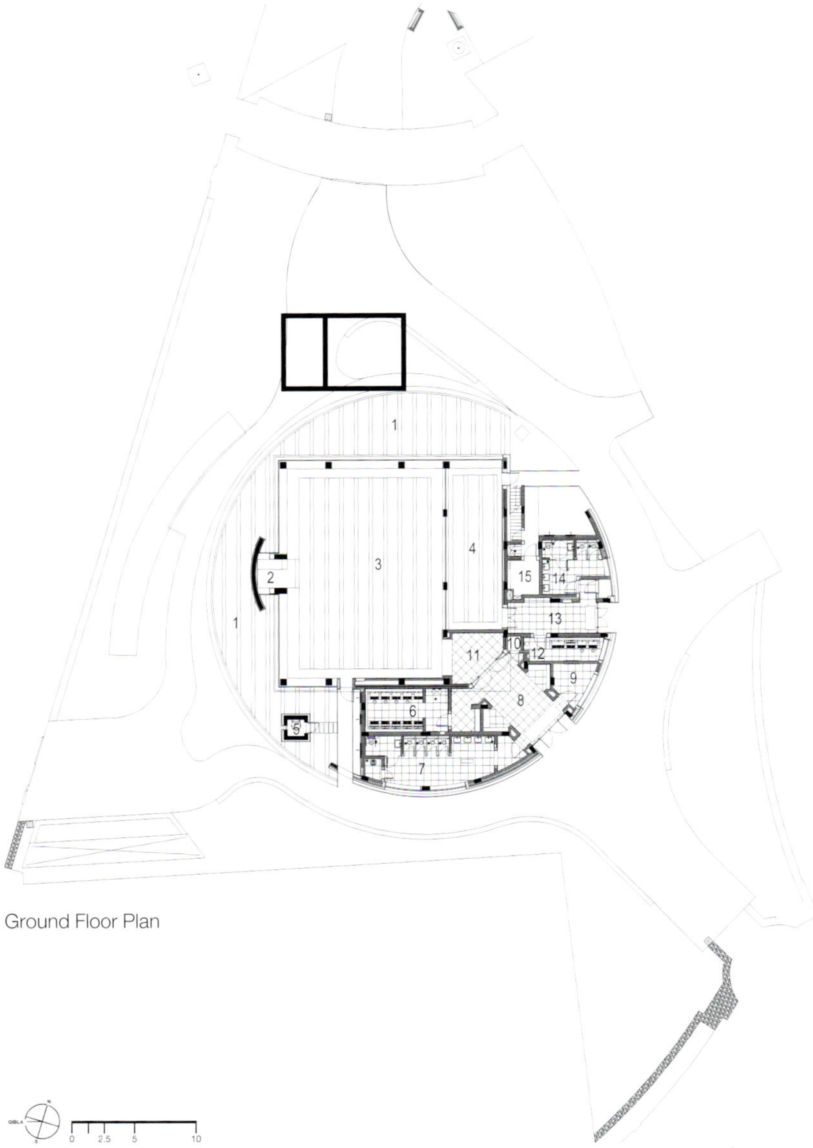

Ground Floor Plan

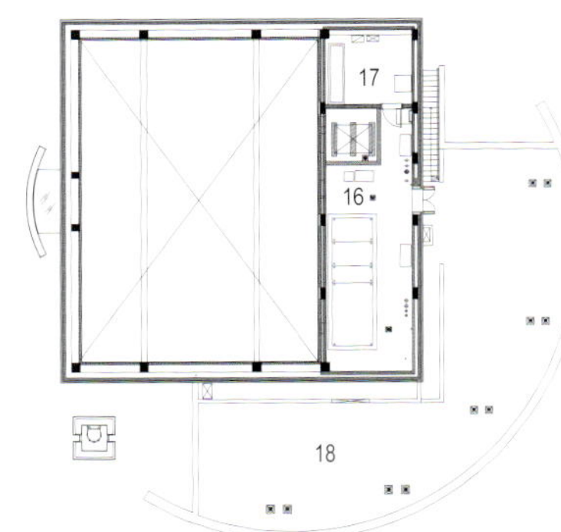

Mezzanine Floor Plan

Legend

1. Water Feature
2. Mihrab
3. Male Prayer Hall
4. Female Prayer Hall
5. Minaret
6. Male Ablution
7. Male Toilets
8. Male Prayer Lobby
9. Office
10. Closet
11. Vestibule
12. Female Ablution
13. Female Prayer Lobby
14. Female Toilets
15. Store
16. Mechanical Plant
17. Electrical Plant
18. Lower Roof

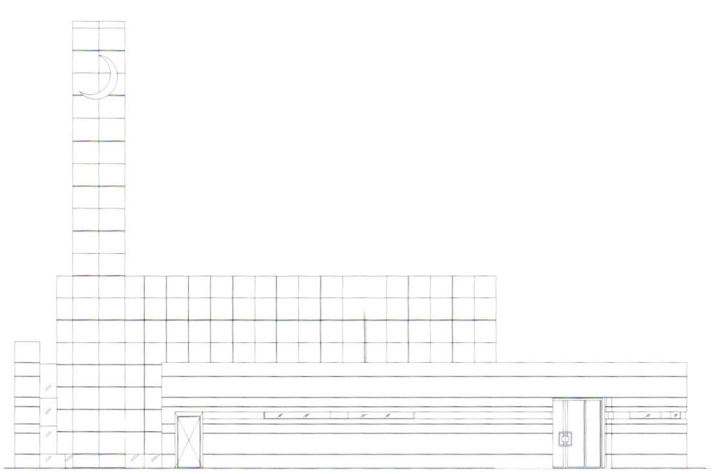

Front Elevation

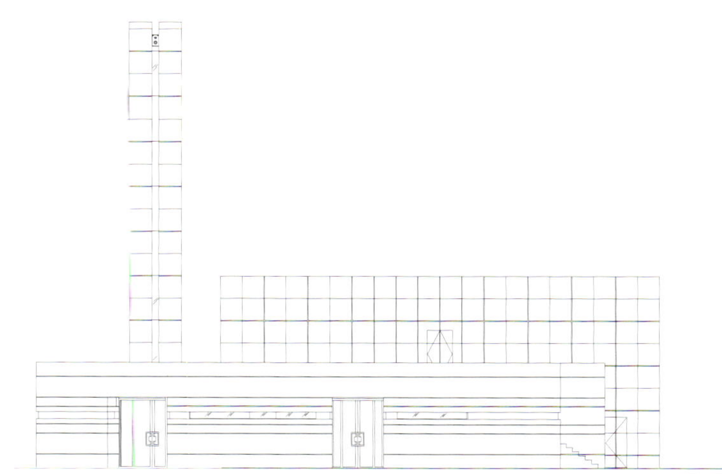

Right Elevation

Abu Sidra Masterplan

Abu Sidra Masterplan

Al Rayyan, Qatar

Status: Ongoing

Client: H.E. Sheikh Mohamed bin Hamad Al Thani

The Abu Sidra Masterplan is AEB's proposal for a suburban residential and mixed-use development on a former plot of cultivated land situated in the municipality of Al Rayyan, 13 kilometres from Doha's city centre.

In addition to taking advantage of its strategic location – along the main highways and access corridors to the capital, and close to the future connective junction between Abu Samra and the industrial area of Al Waab Street – Abu Sidra relates with high sensitivity to the gently sloping rural landscape of the area, which has been preserved and redesigned as the quality background scenery for the new settlement.

Different housing typologies – such as apartment buildings and villas of different kinds – combine to offer a wide range of possible lifestyles.

Moreover, as Abu Sidra aims to work as a self-sustaining community, all requisite services are provided, including retail outlets, leisure, education, hospitality, recreation, civic, along with medical and religious facilities.

Among other features, the "Arabian ranch" stands out as the most distinctive portion of Abu Sidra. With stables and horses alongside, locals and visitors can experience the history and culture of the site through demonstrations of the location's former agricultural activities, which keep the memory of the previous land-use alive.

Traffic and pedestrian circulation has been carefully devised to minimise the use of private cars, and to foster alternative forms of mobility. Hence, a pedestrian and cycle path runs all along the main ring-road, with access to all green spaces.

The latter are located within a walking distance for all residents, and are conceived as the main gathering places for Abu Sidra's communities.

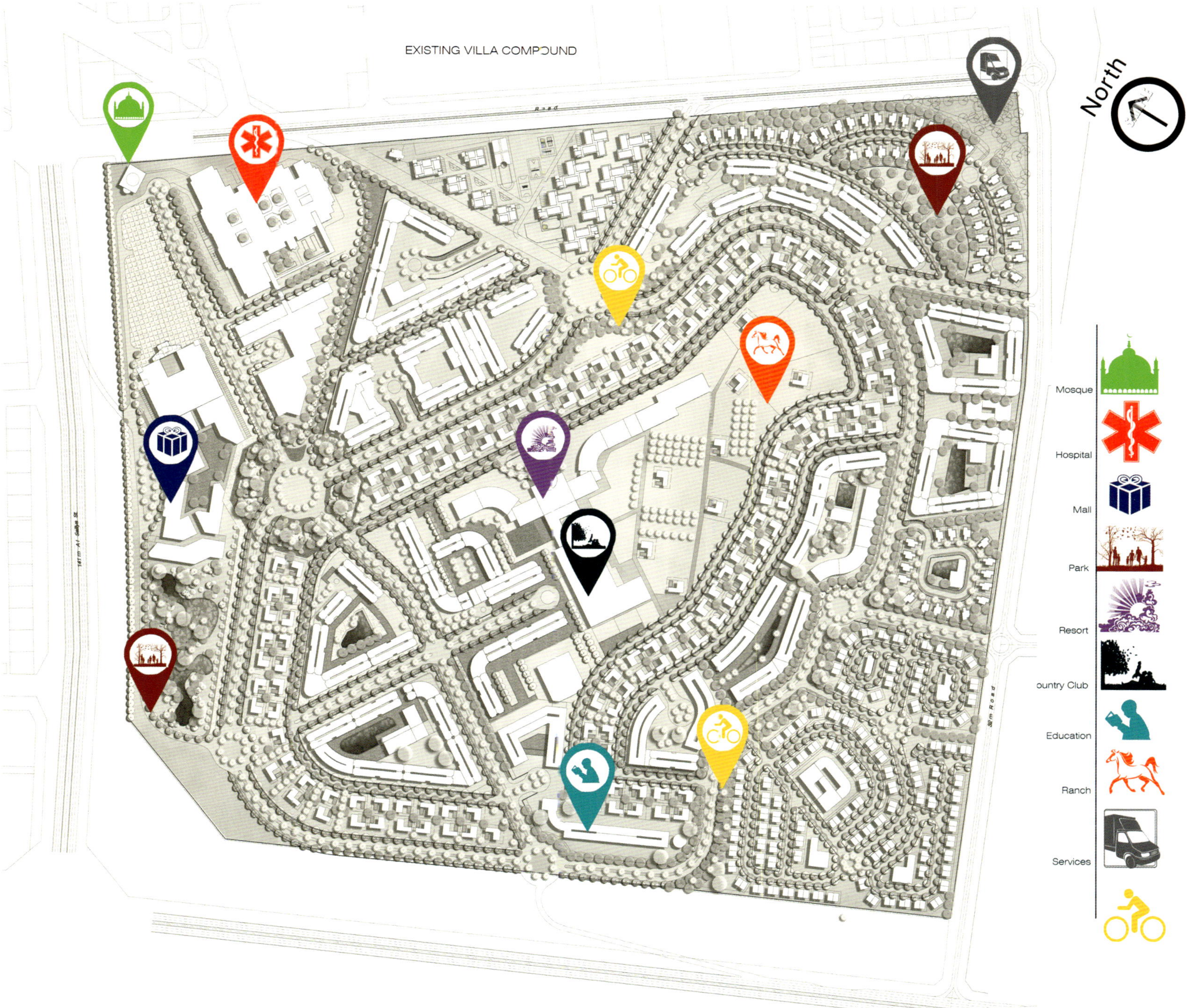
EXISTING VILLA COMPOUND
North
Mosque
Hospital
Mall
Park
Resort
ountry Club
Education
Ranch
Services

ABU SIDRA MASTERPLAN

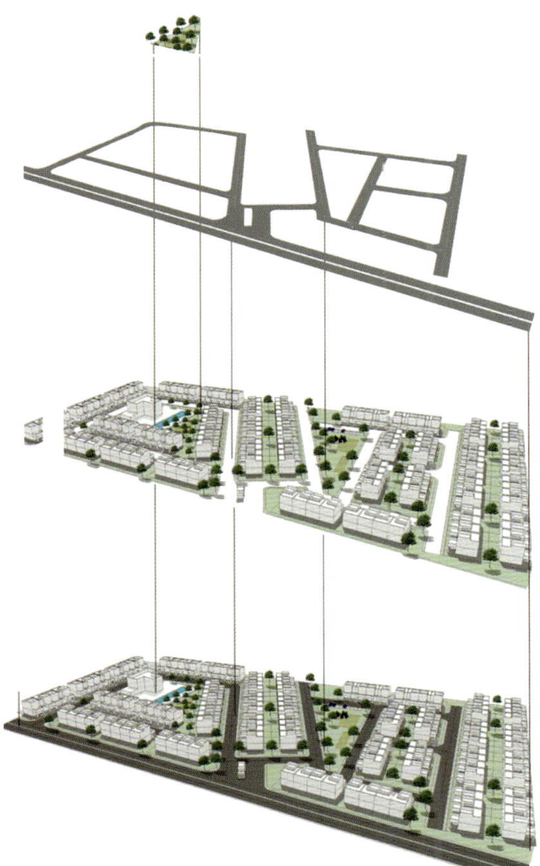

Open Space Strategies and Green Corridors

Project Phasing and Parcels

Place Vendôme

Place Vendôme

Lusail, Qatar

Expected completion date: end of 2017

Client: United Developers (UD)

Place Vendôme is a vast, multi-functional development project occupying a site of almost 190,000 square metres, and includes a shopping mall covering 148,000 square metres, with 207,870 square metres of hospitality facilities, with a total built up area of 835,903 square metres.

On completion in 2017, Place Vendôme will be the largest complex of its kind in Qatar, and will play a crucial role in attracting visitors to the rapidly expanding new city of Lusail.

To ensure the success and profitability of the operation, it was crucial to draw up a precise and appropriate functional programme in order to set a new standard for contemporary, state-of-the-art mall design, and to provide customers and visitors an engaging environment where they can spend their entire day.

With this in mind, the retail areas comprise a sophisticated variety of activities, ranging from high-end exclusive boutiques to mid-range outlets, alongside entertainment venues, media stores, and a wide range of eateries. The hospitality facilities include a luxury residence, a special family luxury hotel and fully serviced apartments.

In the midst of this, the elegant central concourse provides a welcoming, romantic gathering space. Assorted cafés and restaurants with terraces face onto a canal that runs through the entire complex.

Importantly, accessibility is guaranteed by a metro station, surface public transport, basement parking and multi-storey car parks.

The interiors offer a wide range of different aesthetic moods with a range of richly decorated interiors that take their inspiration from the Parisian original – such as the plaster-like decorations, arcades and pedestrian rotundas – all mindfully adapted to suit to the Middle Eastern environment.

Legend

1. Food & Beverage
2. High-End Retail
3. Retail Outlet
4. Hypermarket
5. Circulation
6. Parking (Multi-Storey)
7. Service Area
8. H1 Luxury Hotel
9. H2 Family Hotel
10. H3 Serviced Apartments
11. Water Feature

Upper Ground Floor Plan

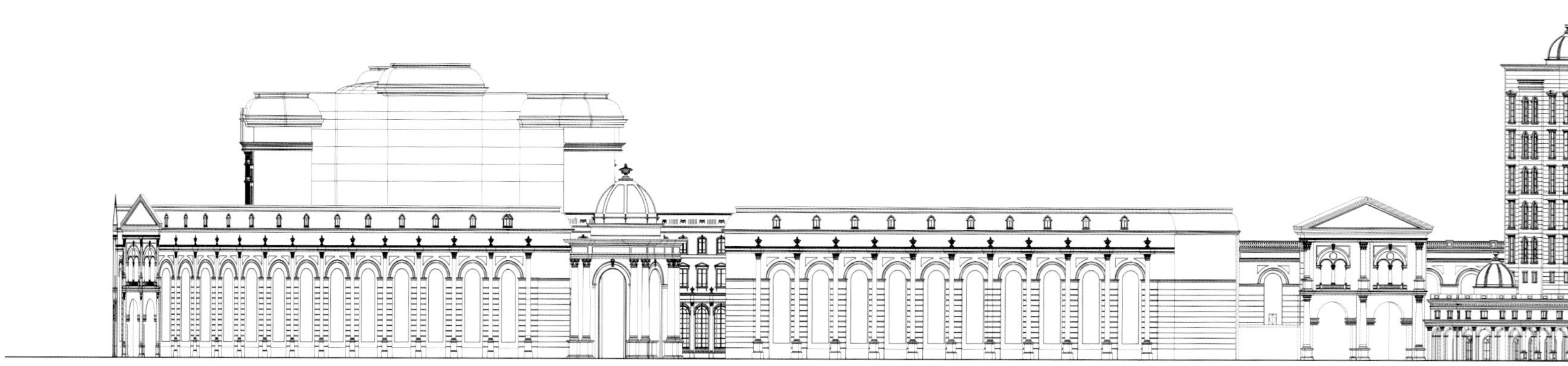

Front Elevation

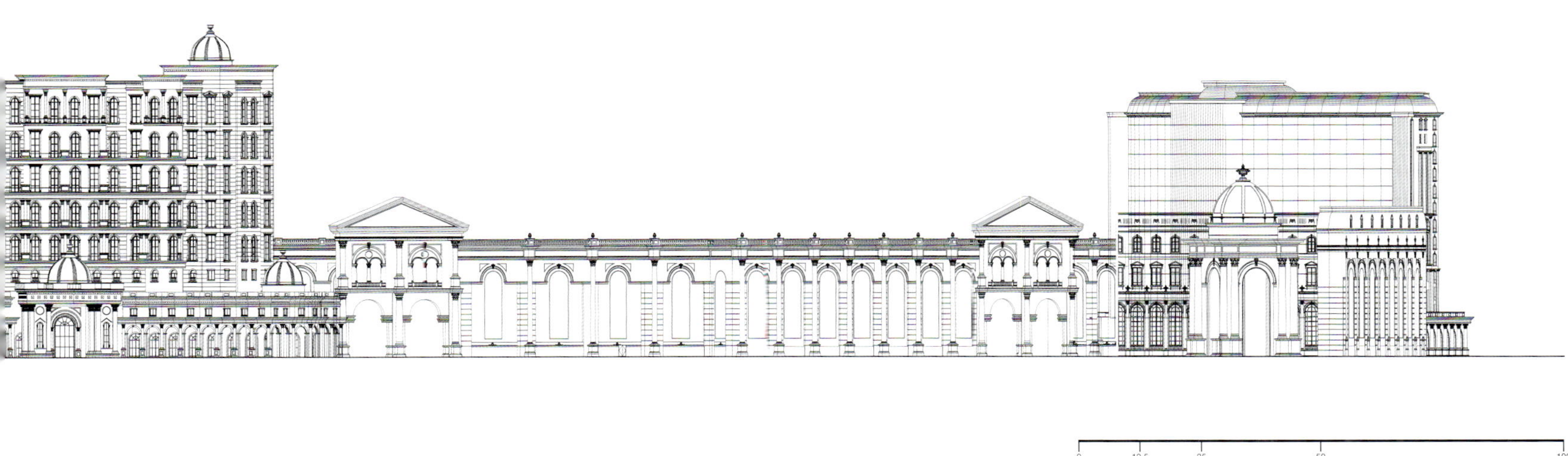

PLACE VENDÔME

Burj Alfardan

Burj Alfardan

Lusail Marina District, Qatar

Expected completion date: end of 2016

Client: Alfardan Properties Co.

In the case of Lusail, a brand new city rapidly developing 15 kilometres north of Doha, it was of crucial importance that planning requirements not only dealt with abstract figures concerning zoning, building areas and volumes, but could also formulate some guidelines to establish the image of the development as a whole.

In relation to this distinctive context, when AEB was commissioned to design the Burj Alfardan, in the local Marina District, the firm responded to the municipality's regulations by brilliantly re-inventing the typology of the common isolated tower.

By merging the vertical and horizontal surfaces, a hybrid building of an unprecedented organic shape is created, which effectively generates mixed-use spaces – as requested by the client.

A car showroom occupies the podium from the ground level up to the fifth floor, while commercial office spaces are planned for the upper block.

Taking inspiration from Qatari traditional architecture, the very clear and strong overall volume acts as a support for surprisingly abundant decorative features.

In fact the main expressive element of the complex is the continuous cladding surface that connects the high-rise section – seemingly composed of two towers, thanks to the set-back of its central volume – to the lower podium without any interruption, with the grid of windows of the vertical walls turning into the skylights of the showroom.

The cladding surface is entirely covered with a subtle engraved pattern, which is reproduced in the plot's open spaces and inside the entrance lobby.

In addition to its innovative aesthetics, the complex is equipped with certain state-of-the-art ecological features, in order to earn a GSAS 5-star rating.

The attention to all-round sustainability applies not only to the complex's architecture – in terms of its mechanical, electrical, sanitary, and acoustic features, among others – but extends to the entire process of construction (with recycled materials accounting for more than 20% of the total), and to landscape design, with rows of plants bound to buffer the region's strong north-west winds.

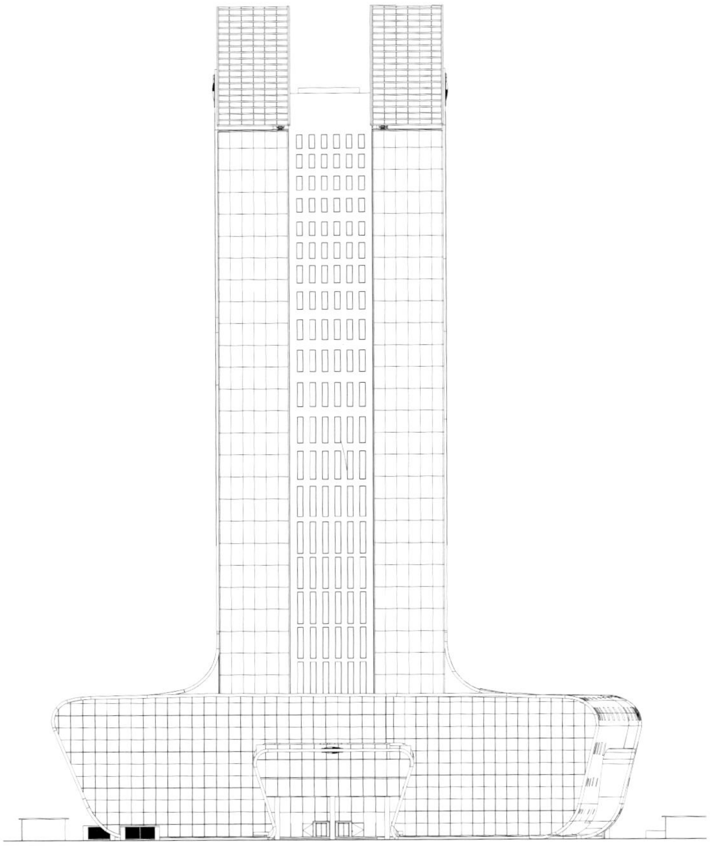

Front Elevation

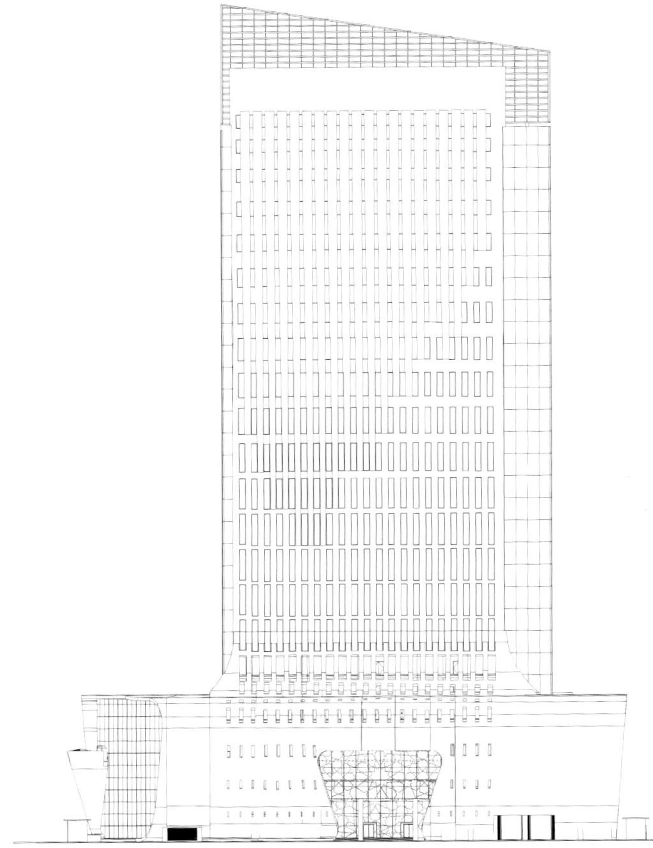

Right Elevation

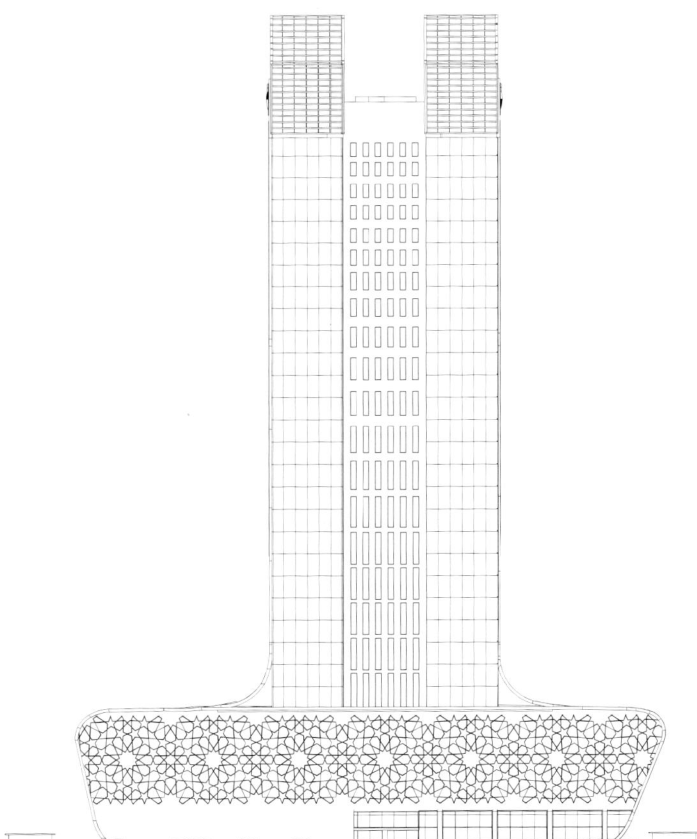

Rear Elevation

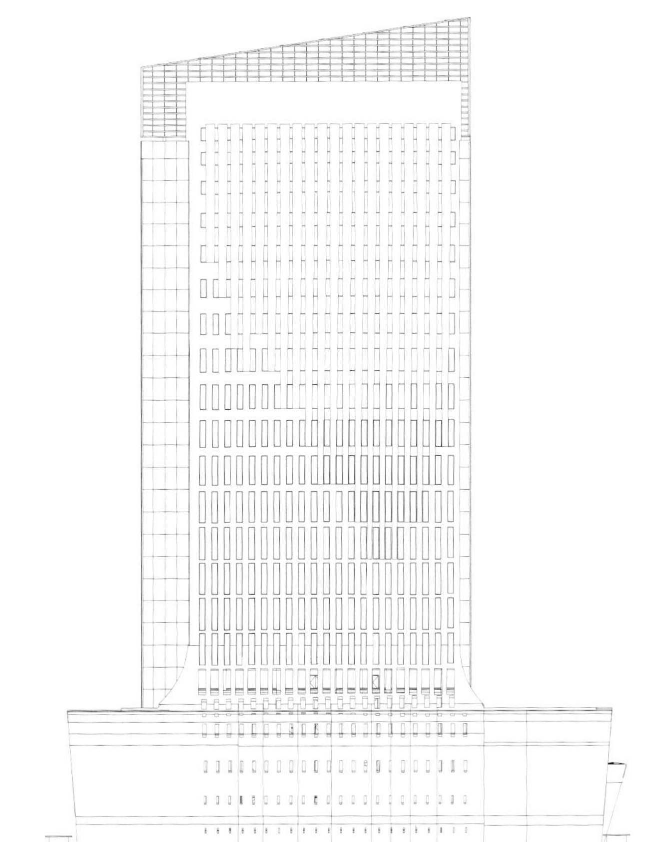

Left Elevation

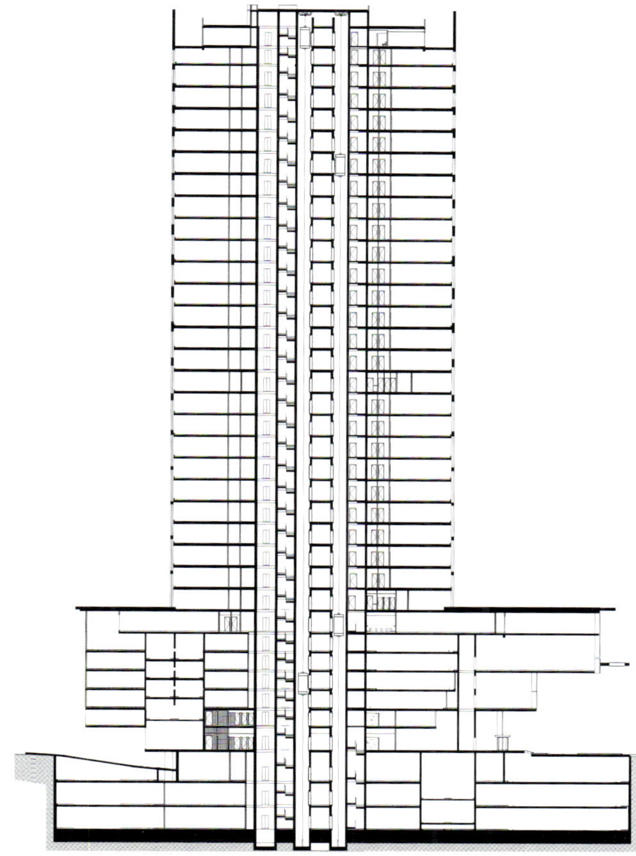

Cross Section

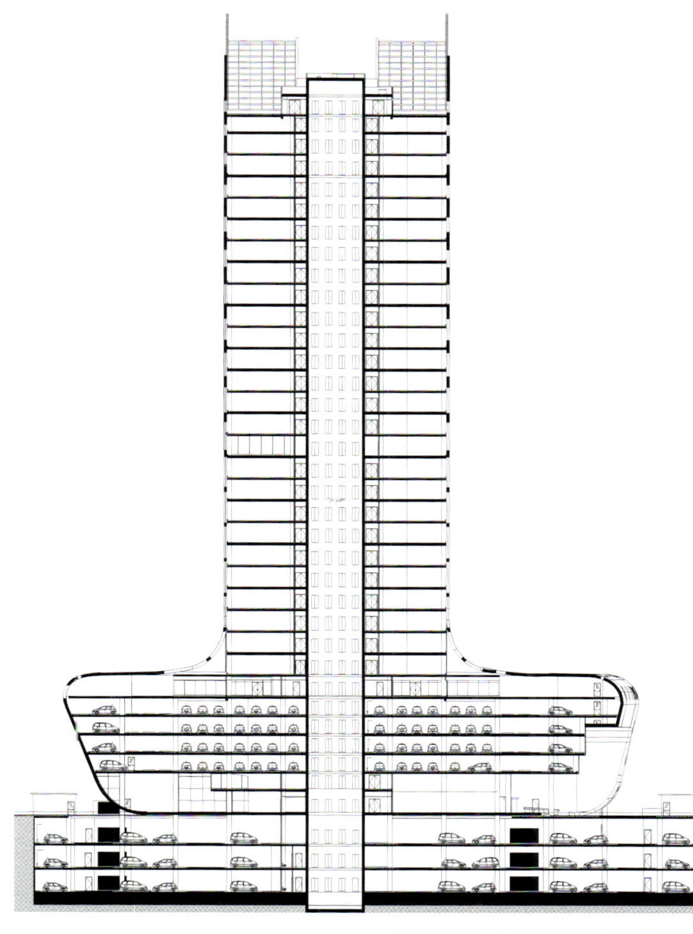

Longitudinal Section

QIMC Tower West Bay

QIMC Tower West Bay

West Bay, Doha, Qatar

Expected completion date: 2018

Client: Qatar Industrial Manufacturing Company

In many cases of modern urban development areas, a new high-rise office building is provided with a carefully calibrated second skin to enhance its identity, and make it a memorable presence in the urban landscape. Bearing this in mind, for its competition entry for a mixed-use tower for QIMC – submitted in 2013 for one of the few remaining underdeveloped sites on West Bay's waterfront – AEB devised two distinct patterns that wrap around the principal architectural masses. The podium is thus enveloped by a regular grid of rhombus patterns, while the three main tower wings employ an offset hexagonal screen resembling a honeycomb.

In the present case, AEB's ongoing research into ways of engaging the *masharabiya* leitmotif in its work is combined with a direct reference to QIMC's logo and the geometry of its manufacturing processes and final products. The impact of the hexagonal pattern is increased by integrating the façade lighting system with the screen itself, and by means of windows orchestrated at intervals emerging from the glazed surface to suggest solidity.

In terms of amenities, the five-storey podium includes retail space and restaurants, and functions as the central core of the complex, over and around which are clustered the three towers, the tallest of which rises 43 storeys and consists of hotel apartments, while the lower faces onto the Corniche and accommodates apartments for lease or sale, its rear wing hosting office spaces.

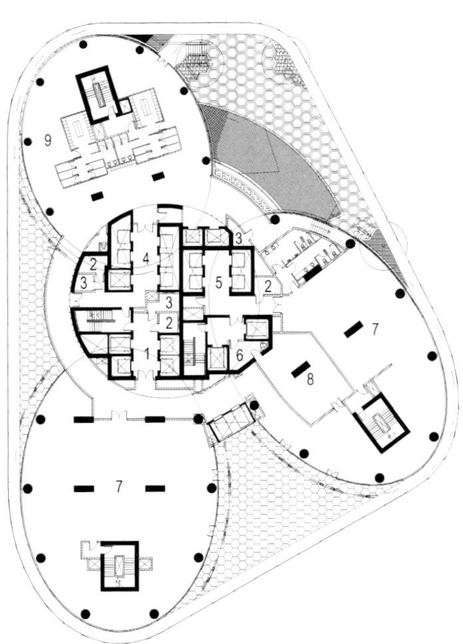

Podium Roof Floor Plan

Legend Podium Roof Floor

1. Apartment Elevator Lobby
2. Electrical Room
3. ELV Room
4. Office Elevator Lobby
5. Hotel Elevator Lobby
6. BOH
7. Restaurant
8. Kitchen
9. Gym

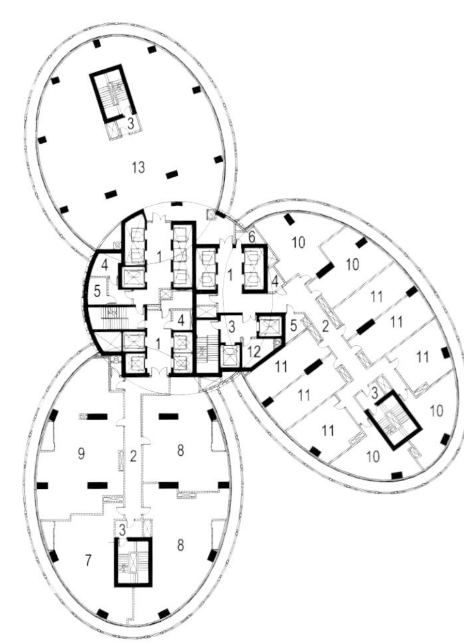

24th Floor Plan

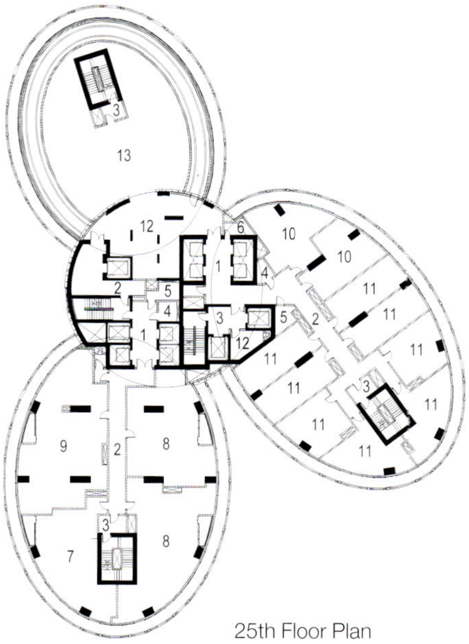

25th Floor Plan

Legend 24th–29th Floors

1. Elevator Lobby
2. Corridor
3. Smoke Stop Lobby
4. Electrical Room
5. ELV Room
6. Store
7. 1 Bedroom Apartment
8. 2 Bedroom Apartment
9. 3 Bedroom Apartment
10. Bedroom Suite
11. Studio
12. BOH
13. Refuge Area

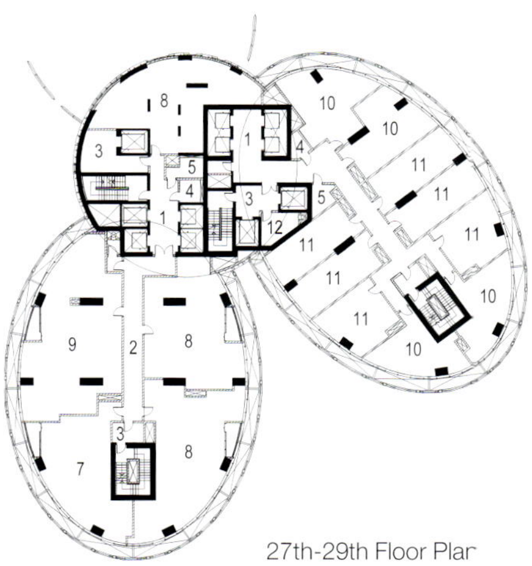

27th-29th Floor Plan

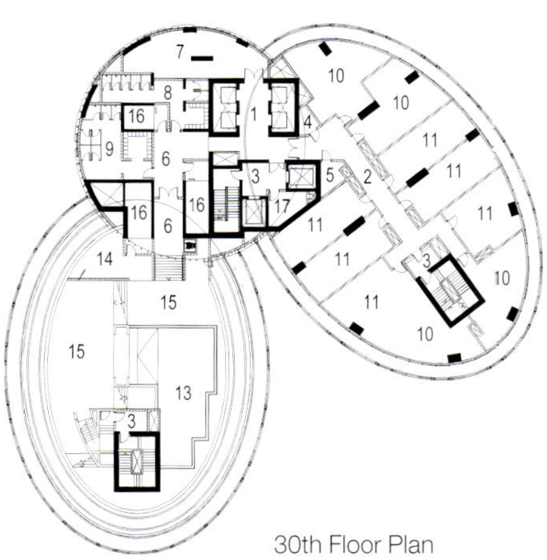

30th Floor Plan

Legend 30th Floor

1. Elevator Lobby
2. Corridor
3. Smoke Stop Lobby
4. Electrical Room
5. ELV Room
6. Lobby
7. Kid's Room
8. Male Changing
9. Female Changing
10. 1 Bedroom Apartment
11. Studio
12. 2 Bedroom Apartment
13. Swimming Pool
14. Pool Bar
15. Pool Deck
16. Mechanical Room
17. BOH

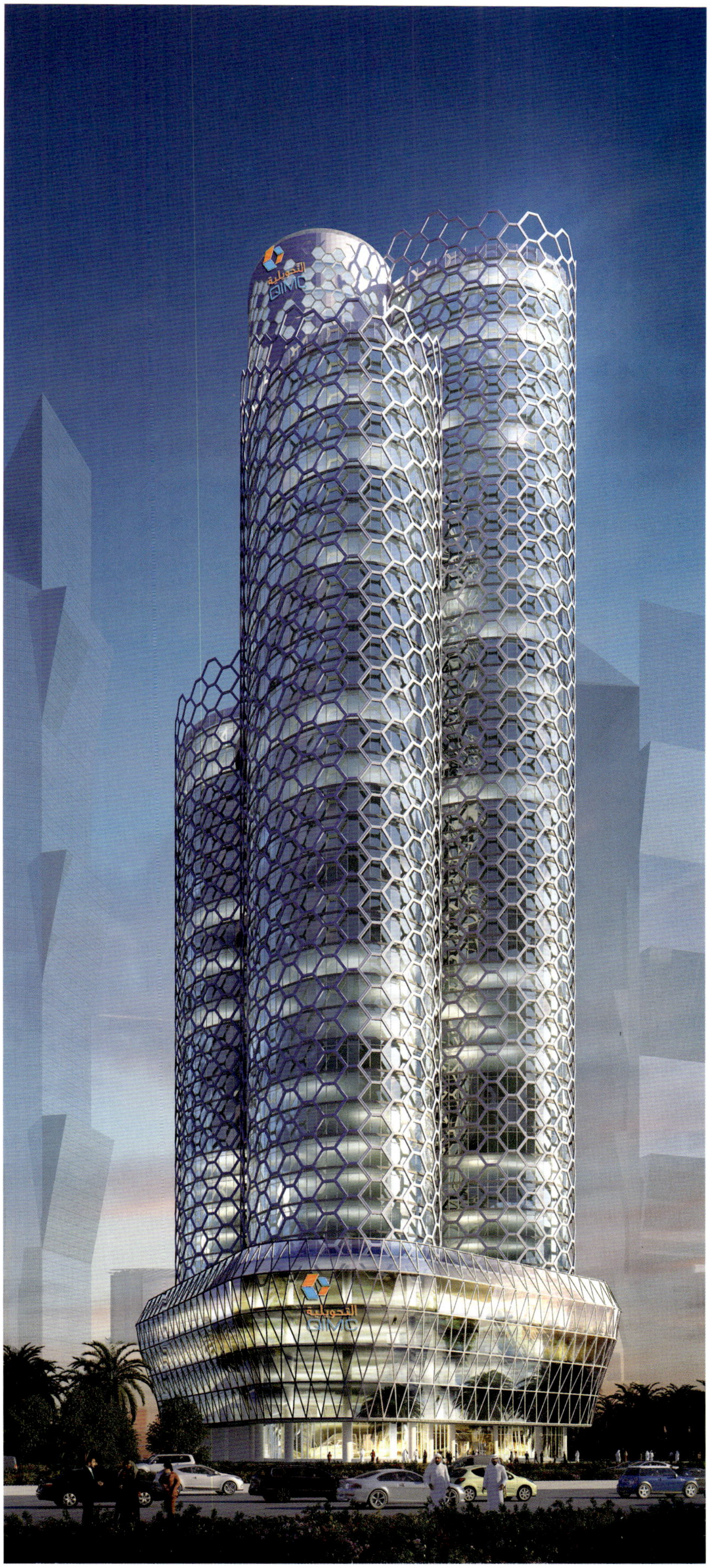

Cardita Shell Tower

Cardita Shell Tower

Lusail, Qatar

Expected completion date: 2018/19

Client: Al-Bandary Group

Located right on the Lusail City waterfront, the Cardita Shell Tower is one of AEB's many contributions to the area's rapidly developing landscape. By integrating a C-shaped podium with two separate high-rise volumes, here AEB is continuing its formal research into ways of blurring horizontal and vertical surfaces.

This is made possible by means of an oblique frame which emerges from one of the towers, crosses through the void between them, and folds around the podium; meanwhile, a multi-faceted second skin ascends to the crown of the two high-rises, featuring an original combination of a compact streamlined shell and a finely embroidered lattice that offers a reinvention of the region's traditional patterns; finally, a fully glazed sphere is nestled into the podium, and functions as the effective barycentre of the entire composition.

Contraco Headquarters

Contraco Headquarters

Lusail Energy City, Qatar

Design proposal

Client: Contraco WLL

Contraco WLL commissioned AEB to develop a design for the company's future headquarters, to be located in the Energy City of Lusail, on the northern outskirts of Doha.

The firm wanted to devise a contemporary office building with distinctive features that would both look global – as an acknowledgement of the international role played by the country today – and yet express the local heritage.

In order to establish a strong link with the region's identity, the basic concept of the building's design stems from the *dahal*, a vast sinkhole and complex of underground caverns that forms one of the most important historical and archaeological features in the country. In fact, the Contraco building is accessed through three main entrances: shaped as irregular cavities reminiscent of natural underground caverns, the entrances are carved into the building's masses and allow three main blocks to emerge from its compact volume.

AEB's concept of creating a multi-layering façade design originates from combining Taoist philosophy with the theories of autonomy in western architecture, as processed by Michel Foucault.

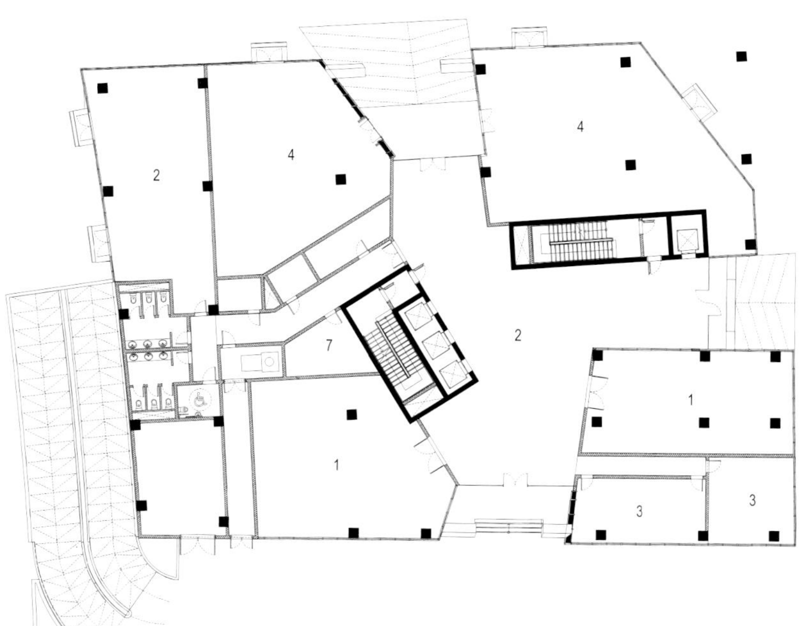

Legend

1. Office
2. Main Lobby
3. Meeting Room
4. Café / Lounge
5. Dinning Area
6. Prayer Room
7. Pantry

Ground Floor Plan

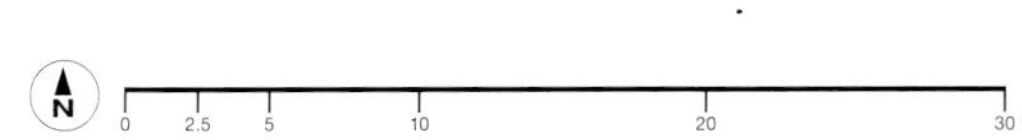

A richly embroidered lattice – a contemporary interpretation of one of the local architecture's most typical geometries – is superposed on the simple frames of the curtain wall, whereby the historical references are accentuated to enhance the building's character.

At street level, the filtering lattice gives way to an integrally transparent glazed surface, ensuring the highest grade of visual permeability, while blurring the boundaries between interior and exterior.

On the functional side, the Contraco includes two underground and five above-ground levels. All public areas – café lounge, dining area, prayer room, and meeting rooms – are located on the ground floor, clustered around the main lobby, a full-height representative space, the true core of the entire complex.

On the upper levels, offices are arranged in four separate blocks and connected through a system of suspended walkways.

Thanks to the combined use of "passive" and "active" energy systems, and the selection of locally sourced and recyclable materials, Contraco fully meets the sustainability parameters established by Global Sustainability Assessment System (GSAS).

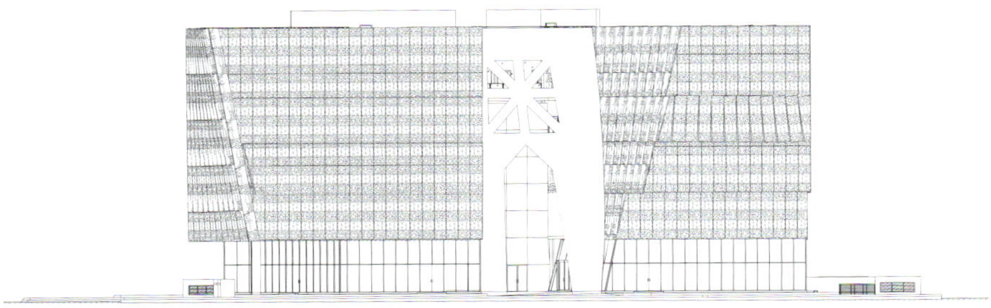

Front Elevation

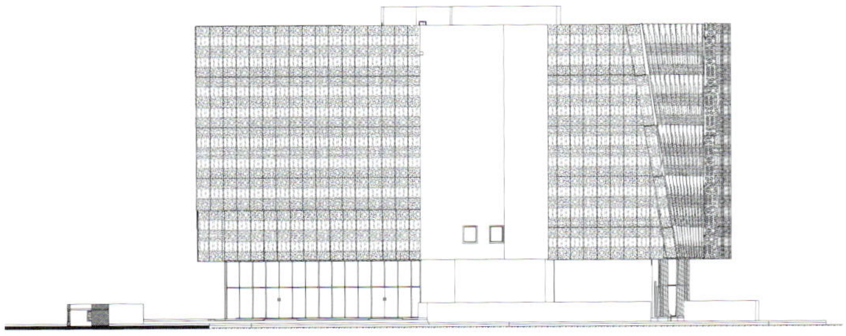

Left Elevation

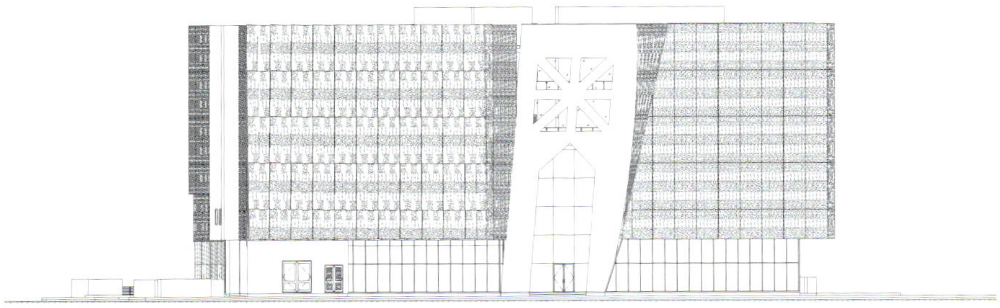

Rear Elevation

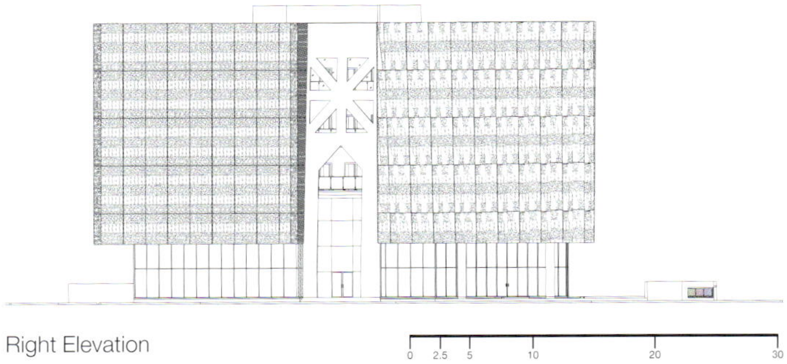

Right Elevation

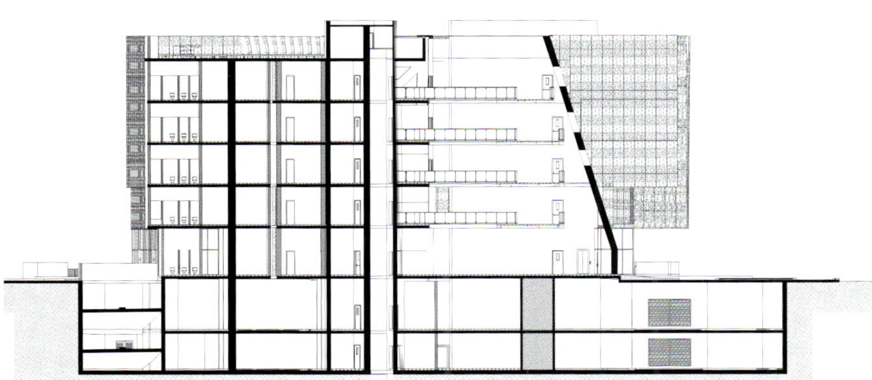

Longitudinal Section

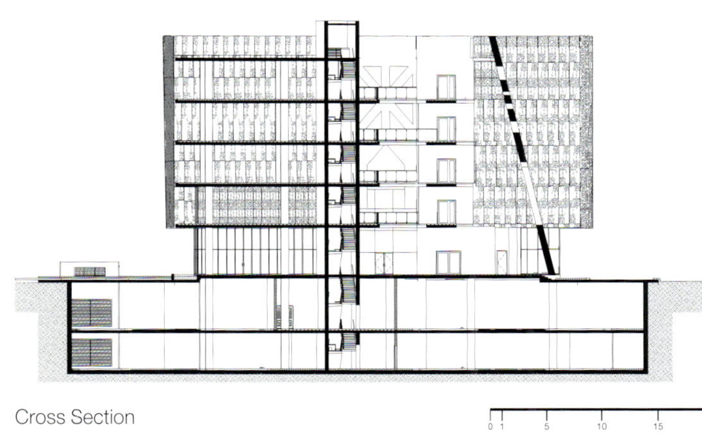

Cross Section

Erkyah Mixed-Use Development

Erkyah Mixed-Use Development

Lusail, Qatar

Expected completion date: 2020/21

Client: Ariane Real Estate

For the Erkyah Mixed-Use Development, which includes retail spaces, apartments, and a hotel, AEB has implemented a straightforward, contemporary design.

The sinuous plan of the complex features a continuous podium that links three main volumes and elegantly combines with the streamlined aesthetics of the buildings' façades.

The latter consist of uninterrupted glazed strips alternating with wrapping string-courses that smoothly merge to form an integral curtain wall.

Several high-end amenities, such as rooftop gardens and pools, have been provided to redefine the state-of-the-art for a contemporary mixed-use complex.

K-Hotel

K-Hotel

Lusail, Qatar

Expected completion date: 2020

Client: Falcon Real Estate

Situated in the Marina District of Lusail City and directly overlooking the new iconic Marina Mall, the K-Hotel stands out from its context as a complex sum of architectural masses.

A sequence of terraces retreats from the street level to the base of the tower, which is articulated in two main volumes. The latter rise to different heights, and are partially cantilevered from the lower podium, the projecting loads being supported by tree-shaped pillars.

The design concept and architectural morphology of the hotel are derived from the colourful and exhilarating world of the coral reef: the plentiful balconies, rooftop gardens and solariums, glass pools – plus a prominent waterfall feature – make the building blur almost seamlessly within the bay's natural landscape.

Adding to this, the extensive use of bow windows multiplies the glazed surface available for each room, and provides unobstructed views in all directions.

Qatari Diar Headquarters

Qatari Diar Headquarters

Lusail, Qatar

Expected completion date: end of 2018

Client: Lusail Real Estate Development Company

The design of the new iconic Qatari Diar Headquarters offers one of world's finest office building formulas in terms of usability, spatial quality, materials, and sustainability, and thus serves as a benchmark for the expectations of future Lusail developments.

An intricate interplay of mutually overlapping, shifting and retreating glass-boxes are the distinguishing features of the complex. Using this simple design concept as the basis for its design, AEB has enriched the neutral aesthetics of the curtain wall with three specific geometric patterns, each corresponding to a different level of shading, and hence enhancing the climatic sustainability of the buildings. They all draw inspiration from the geometries of traditional Qatari architecture, along with the overhead canopy partially protecting the complex from direct sunlight, and the solid cladding patterns – a contemporary reinterpretation of the local calligraphy.

Considerable attention has been given to the public space at the ground level, which features a covered drop-off bay and an elegantly landscaped pedestrian area. Featuring stone seats, pergolas, and abundant local flora, this gathering space overlooks a lower patio giving access to the building's underground levels.

Dune Stadium

Dune Stadium

Lusail, Qatar

Design proposal

Client: Supreme Committee for Legacy and Delivery

AEB's proposed concept design for the Dune Stadium addresses the necessity for providing the country with a wide variety of sports facilities, in light of the upcoming FIFA World Cup 2022. Located inside the strategic hub of Lusail City, the complex is designed not only to create a unique, premium-quality stadium experience, but also to function as a hub for the wide array of public and community activities located in the area. To achieve this a compact, self-sufficient urban environment is reproduced under the stadium's roof, comprising a set of complementary, interchangeable units that include a shopping mall, a hotel, exhibition spaces, and restaurants.

The project as a whole is dedicated to celebrating the sand dune – one of the country's most distinctive natural features – and takes its inspiration from the forms created organically by the wind's timeless interaction with the desert sands. The central pavilion rises gently but impressively from a car-free podium – which segregates pedestrian and vehicular circulation – assuming the form of a lowered parabolic curve that opens on one side to embrace and welcome its visitors. The formal principles of this central core of the composition are reiterated in the plentiful complementary design elements, such as the undulating canopies shading the walkways, the paving patterns that mimic sand-ripples, and the concentric layout of the parking lots. The final result is an impactful landscape feature designed to combine beauty with functional, forward thinking, and most importantly, conceived as a cogent example of architectural and urban sustainability.

Isometric view of the stadium components

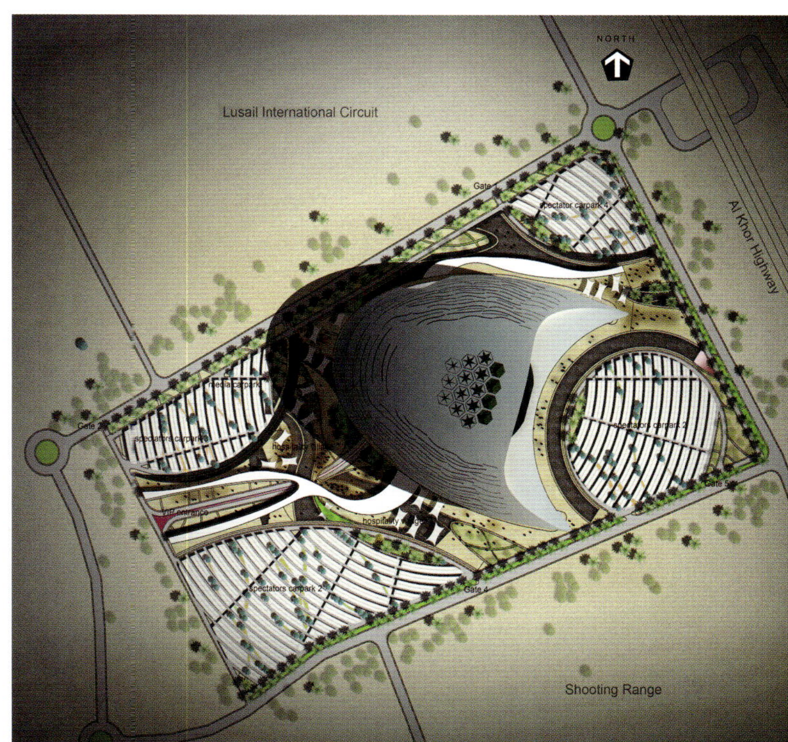

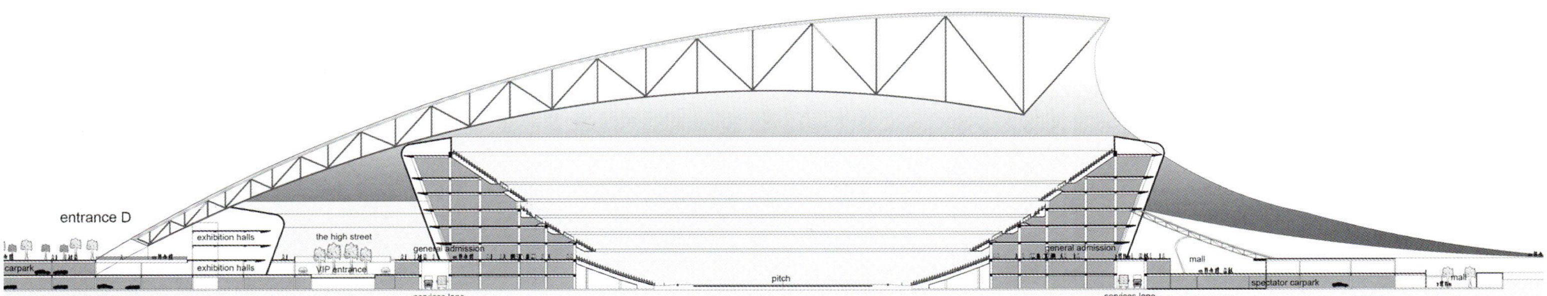

Cross Section

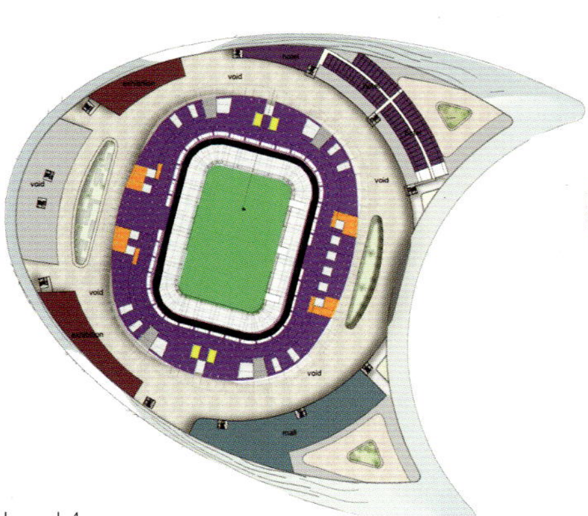

Level 4

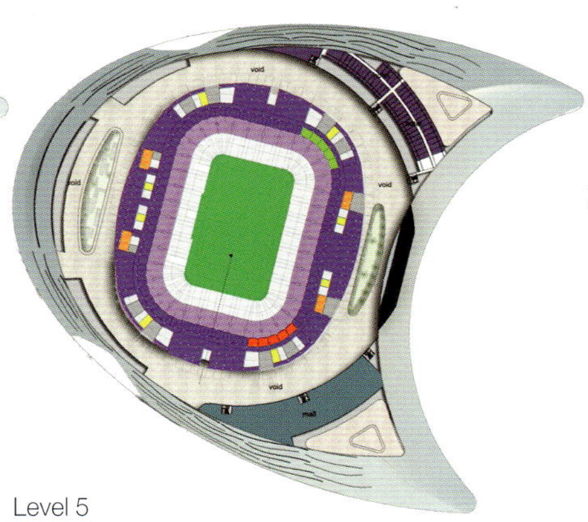

Level 5

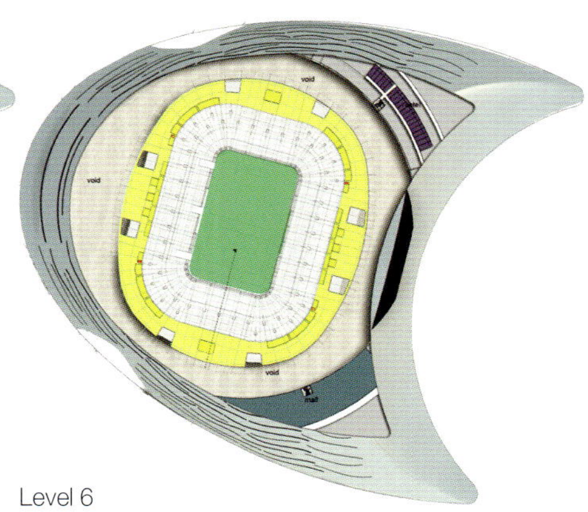

Level 6

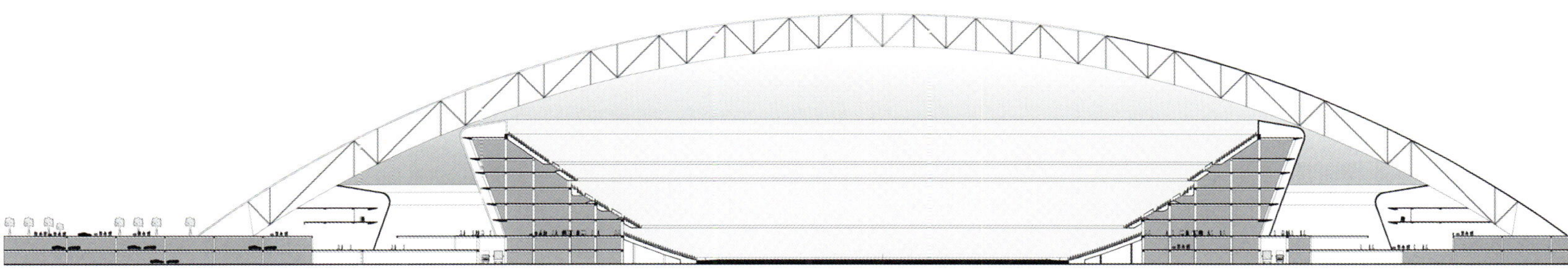

Longitudinal Section

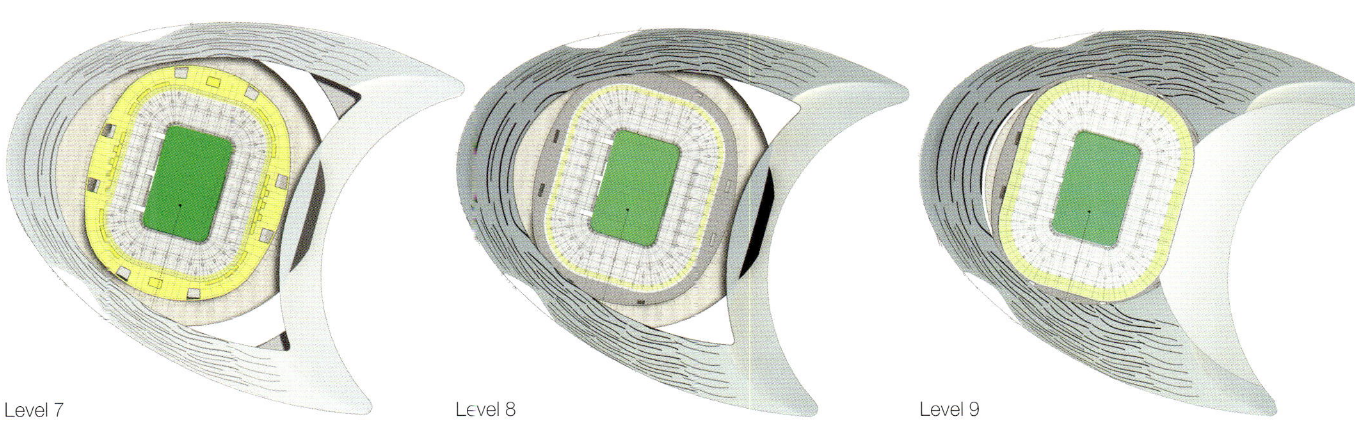

Level 7 Level 8 Level 9

The Inspiring Future

AEB – Multidisciplinary International Network

Luca Molinari
in conversation with
Ibrahim Jaidah

Luca Molinari: To your mind, what are the most relevant challenges that Qatari architecture will face in the near future, and how will your office interpret them?
Ibrahim Mohamed Jaidah: I would say it is the sustainability issue. We should definitively be sensitive to the environment. We have taken it for granted. At the moment energy is free – or let's say the cost of energy is very low – but we really need to create a sustainable city for our future. I think that in the next few decades you will see that a lot of buildings being completed now will turn out to be hugely energy-consuming.
Clients are becoming more aware of this, and even as a nation we can see already that sustainability is becoming a mandatory component of our urban planning. By default, all government buildings now have to go through the whole process.
So I think that is one of challenges we are facing, and something we have to be critically aware of. At the moment I tell the design firms – and the future architects – that although right now sustainability is a luxury, if you don't learn all about it you will not be able to practise your profession in the next decade. It's going to be the "ABC", the basics of any design, in which you have to prove that your design is the most efficient, that it makes most use of the natural resources, natural light, natural ventilation, and anything else to make the building more sustainable.

LM: I couldn't agree more. Up to now we have talked about the need to continue research unceasingly, about redefining the identity of Qatari architecture through historical references and awareness, about what it means to be contemporary today… But a further point to discuss is how your company focuses and develops these issues, like a machine, a clever machine. This is a critical matter, because I remember the first time we met you said: "When I acquired this company in the early 1990s there were only seven of us, and now we number around six hundred."
IMJ: Seven hundred, actually.

LM: Seven hundred. So this means that the company has been growing fast, making it a very complex machine to manage. Would you describe how the office organisation has changed from the beginning up until today? How has your work method evolved? Which are your firm's strongest features, and what allowed Arab Engineering Bureau to grow so fast?
IMJ: I think I was lucky. Key people started coming into my life and they became my colleagues and my friends, and helped me build the office. Nothing ever works perfectly,

but facing the challenges and changing our way of doing things is the secret of our success. Recently, I decided to make some dramatic changes in the office because there was a big risk of losing control, a situation in which projects and clients risked becoming just a number – and I don't want us to turn into a mere production machine. We have to be sensitive to what we are doing, and safeguard our brand message. We don't want to give birth to a "commodity".

There's a tendency to fall into this trap. It's really easy, because you create this huge dinosaur and keep feeding it with work to keep it alive, but soon you lose your awareness of what you want to pass on to the next generation, your name and the future. Over the years, we grew in line with market demand, and even created new departments to fill the gaps. As the office started growing I even created a non-profit research section which aided me in publishing the book… and now we are considered to be at our peak and many lessons have been learnt.

In practice, architectural consultants tend to feel the impact of an economic downturn after a few years. They don't feel it while it's actually happening, because they already have projects under way. In fact, it took us about two or three years to feel the impact of the recent economic downturn, during which we retained full employment, because we were committed to our ongoing projects and clients. Most recently we have divided the mother firm into individual "work firms".

LM: What do you mean?
IMJ: Before we had a more traditional structure, divided into distinct departments: concept, production, mechanical, electrical, structural, and so on. Now the firm is composed of four

studios working in unison, each one self-sufficient with a full-fledged team across all the disciplines.
The reason for this is simple: in the past we were once challenged by a client who insisted that he had to have the entire team present throughout the design.

LM: So you had to change the setup.
IMJ: At first I was very reluctant, and fought against it, but it turned out to be more successful, with big advantages to quality and client satisfaction – and even financially more profitable. We repeated the same formula for the New Port project, and that's become a wonderful successful story.
In this scenario, all the disciplines work together. Even the people managing the client are part of the working unit, so they talk the same talk, and it's easier to manage and deliver, to guarantee project quality.

LM: What's the most important change you made in the past twenty years? What were the key moments?
IMJ: Well, the first key moment was when I bought the firm and I realised I needed good architects, technologies, and there were no CAD workstations. So moving into my new location – which was elsewhere in Doha – was a big turning point because I still had mechanical tables and drawing boards. I also had my very first computer – which I won as a young trainee in the government – and that was the first one in the office. The physical change of location also played a fundamental role. Our offices at the time were in an apartment building, so I started by renting just one apartment. That became two, then three, then four... In all there

were six apartments in the building, and by the time I took over the sixth, I understood it was time to move out! So we moved to a more open place, and that's when the firm started really getting bigger. As more architects arrived, I began to delegate responsibilities. Along with two other guys I managed the clients: we went out to meet them and discuss the projects… But in time the firm became even bigger, so I began appointing project directors to act as the client's coordinators. The next step was to re-organize the studio offices.

I think that at some point in big firms, even though the work produced is beautiful, projects can very often become just numbers. Smaller work-groups mean more attention to the job under way. However, the key of successful individual groups is that you integrate the specialties – such as landscaping, interiors, acoustics, and so on – which ensures a comprehensive service, and teams share responsibilities, but also rewards and successes.

Other milestones that have changed my life are some of the projects that I've had the pleasure to work on. A special highlight is when, early in my professional career, I was invited by His Highness to the royal palace, where he gave me some old black-and-white photographs of Qatar and Doha, and told me to take inspiration from my country's history. This significantly influenced me.

Oh, and when I found out that my project was to be printed on the 100 *riyal* banknote, I began to tremble. When such things cross your own destiny with that of a nation, you feel a huge responsibility, and that's when you become concerned about how things will eventually turn out, how you'll be perceived later on in your life – or after you've gone. What sort of impact you have had, what legacy will remain…

LM: Absolutely. So let's take a look at your latest set-up. If I were a client and came to you with a new assignment, how would the project be developed and carried out? How does AEB function? What's the firm's working method?
IMJ: Well, first of all the design studio itself is separate from all the other departments, and it's here where the concepts happen, close to me. The clients come here to talk to me, and in 90% of the cases I'm the one who initiates the project. At that point I talk to the designers and choose the one most suited for the job. Because I am already familiar with the directions of the project and the clients' expectations, with this in mind I work with the designer whose mentality, ability and way of comprehension and creation best suits the project. Then I explain the project's background and core elements, sometimes with presentation sketches, sometimes just verbally and the sketches follow. Then we formulate the project's concept design and present it to the client. Once it's approved, we figure out a preliminary coordination scheme to ensure that everything will run smoothly. After that the project is ready and passes to the studios, at which point the project director becomes the main point of contact.

LM: But do you also follow the various construction phases?
IMJ: Well, on average we hand over at least one project every two weeks. That could be a skyscraper, a palace, a government building or a hotel…

LM: As I see it, you are in a position to handle everything yourself, to keep complete control over any project. You have the technical office, the environmental research department, the interior designers. How has your collaboration with international teams contributed to this comprehensive approach?

IMJ: Well, those international collaborations have been an important milestone in my career. Working in tandem with international firms has tremendously affected my way of working. I mean, imagine the pleasure of sitting with Arata Isozaki and discussing design with him.

Certainly, working with other international firms has taught me many lessons. Without all that, I wouldn't have become what I am now. You open your eyes to new ways of doing things. That's why it's always a must that twenty per cent of our work involves working in tandem with others. Currently we are working with Foster. Collaborating is always so exciting. You learn so much! You get better at what you do through working together. A lot of people are reluctant to participate in international joint projects, but when it works you exchange and combine local and global knowledge. And I believe there are no secrets in life: whatever you know now, you will know better by sharing it rather than keeping it to yourself.

LM: I couldn't agree more. So what's the most significant collaboration you have done with a big firm?

IMJ: I'd say this latest one with Foster. It's for a new stadium. I got really excited because I was in his office and we talked about what is local and what is not local, about what can be preserved and what cannot. So you see, he gets involved even in the workshops, and you feel that you are really giving an input.

In some cases a concept is originally created by someone else, and AEB takes over and develops the detailed design. This is when we ascertain that although a certain thing might work someplace else, it won't work here in Qatar. Likewise, such things as local engineering, methods of doing things, the mentality of our contractors… These are all traits of our specific work environment, and this is where we really assist international companies, by contributing our local knowhow.

LM: Very true… My final question is about the AEB network. You don't have only an office here, you have a network of offices in Asia that are interconnected. How does it work?
IMJ: Well, in the Middle East, besides Qatar, we have offices in UAE and Oman, each with a branch manager. However, the concept design is still done here in Doha.

LM: Right, here in your headquarters.
IMJ: Yes, and I am glad that the concepts are explored here, where our assets and strengths first started, where it all began.
The Malaysia office is a different story. A while back, we had a Malaysian architect working here who trained in France. After two years with us he decided to go back to his country, and I suggested we do something together. Initially the Malaysian firm was created to support the Qatari studio, but now it operates almost fully independently and is taking on projects from Malaysia.
The Philippines office mostly manages production. We complete the concept here, and our Manila colleagues – some of whom are former employees now living in the Philippines – detail the architectural and interior design. Currently there are sixty people, but hopefully they will become a hundred. This system is very efficient and practical, especially because of the time difference. They're working when we are sleeping. It is also easier to recruit there.
In Thailand we have a small way-finding design firm. In the beginning we collaborated, and then we realized we could do something nice together, so I became a 50% shareholder.

Just recently we won a project in Saudi Arabia. This doesn't mean that we have to open a branch everywhere we go, but we will do what we have learnt from international firms, which often gives better and wiser results. You keep the concept and design control, and you appoint local engineers that definitely add a relevant value. In this organisation I keep on learning as much as when I was the local expert.

My ambition is to be in North Africa, to add or reflect this identity within the different influences in North Africa. The same formula that I'm adopting here can potentially be adopted there, in a dialogue with their local architects. This is my ambition. But now with the boom in Qatar there is so much to do here, and it's a beautiful environment in which to create.

LM: This is the next global challenge, I guess: following and nurturing the new quality faces of the country's growth.

IMJ: Yes, it's very exciting, especially now as we are evolving and doing management changes. It gets me very excited, and I'm hoping that in the next few years I will have less of a management role, and be able to enjoy more time designing.

Appendix

Brief History of Qatari Traditional Architecture

Ibrahim Mohamed Jaidah

The climate and geographical nature of Qatar both have played a role in shaping of the country's architecture. Owning to its geographical positioning Qatar was for many decades a cross road for major trading convoys which crossed from Indian subcontinent towards Near East and from Persia to North Africa. This resulted for many architectural influences to be brought to the state from other regions such as India, Iran, Basra, Najd, and Oman; along with materials which have improved the way structures were built, especially wood from Zanzibar which was used for reinforcing the ceilings.

Due to the deterioration of materials over time, there are very few surviving architectural structures which we classify as old and which date back to the 19th century. Most of the information collected on the old structures, which no longer exist, comes from the narratives, hand drawings and paintings which were left behind and have been handed down from one generation to the next. Considering the lack of information, the history of Qatari architecture is only few centuries old and in my opinion History of Traditional Qatari Architecture can be classified in three distinctive eras: *Pre Oil Period, Beginning of the Oil Period, and Post Oil Period*.

Pre Oil Period

The Pre Oil Period era strongly reflects Islamic architectural influences. The traditional Qatari architecture in this period adopted philosophies of the traditional Islamic architecture which embodies principles of social organization and physical environment. In this period, which is evident up until the beginning of the 1950's, master mason was the main architect and builder. The materials used for construction were composed of whatever could be found in the surrounding (bamboo strips, mangrow leaves, compacted sand, cut coral blocks or lime stone) and I consider this to be the most sophisticated form of sustainable architecture.

Social Organization

The most important design consideration is privacy and territoriality. Spaces are segregated on the basis that male visitors are separated from the family, young men from young women, servants from others, and passer-by from residents.

Physical Environment Dimension

In the past the traditional physical environment was not based on the aesthetics of buildings and streets. The city of the past was built within the scope of very simple principles that are required to understand the gradual transformation of the urban pattern from the old Islamic cities where aim was to protect environment and to maintain the privacy of the people and their accessibility to public spaces.

City Developments

The major cities of Qatar developed on the coast for two reasons: fishing and trading. Qatari cities have been shaped not only by urban and architectural planning, but also by the social dimension. Urban development of Doha, Al Wakrah, Al Khor, and Umm Slal Mohammad was affected by the most typical characteristics of the traditional Islamic city: unity of architecture represented by the sequence of spaces in the mosque, souq, palace and private home. The growth of the collective form of housing arises from the extension and the subdivision of inherited properties, which creates an intensification of land-use.

The city of Doha used to be known as Al Beda'a, an important town on the east side of the Qatar peninsula. The ruling family built their palaces and mosques in the center of the city for the reason of symbolism, protection against climate, and military purposes. The layout accords with the Islamic urban traditions in which the ruler's palace lays at the center of administrative, political, and economic life. This formed the physical and functional core of Doha, from which city organically grew in different directions. Maps of Doha (created in 1937, 1947, 1952 and 1959) reveal the city's expansion northwards and southwards.

Qatari architecture from this period is often categorized as: religious (mosque), civil (palaces, houses, and souqs), and military (forts, tower and walls). Some great still standing examples of such architecture are: Al Ayouni Mosque (1935), Old Palace which has been turned into Qatar National Museum (1912). Sh. Hamad Abdullah House (1930), and Zubara Fort (1937).

Beginning of the Oil Period

Sudden burst in the economy with the discovery of oil resulted in large scale migration from the old houses into the new "modern villas". This changed social aspect of the urban development significantly as the organic growth was almost impossible to establish, since people resided in the cube-like houses surrounded by walls. On the other hand this period shows array of new architectural influences and decorative features.

As mentioned before throughout history the master mason was the architect. This way of designing and building structures remained unchanged at the beginning of the oil period. The master mason was still the designer even though the building materials have changed, especially with the introduction and availability of cement.

The time period of the late 1950's and early 1960's marked the architectural revival period with the arrival of new architects from Lebanon, Egypt, and the Indian subcontinent. They introduced the new decorative features, which primary roles was of aesthetic nature rather than the functional one as it was done in the past. This new look was welcomed by the Clients and the architects were even encourage to add more ornamental and colorful details that had a reference to what is liked and what was very often lacked in this part of the world.

This type of architecture was reflected in palaces, villas, and high-end apartment buildings. The new style was thriving and it was the birth of what I call the "Arabian Deco Era".

That particular era in architecture was never documented, and those building have never been recognized as part of the architectural history. As a result those buildings have not been listed and are still being demolished wherever they come in a way of new development.

It is important to document that era and list these buildings as a significant period of our "Old modern period". It would also be interesting to study the Region to see a similar architecture in that particular period and classify it as "Arabian Deco".

Post Oil Period
End of the 20th century marked economical shift in Qatar towards more intellectually based environment. Like any other metropolis, Doha down-town was beginning to take shape and new large developments started to emerge (The Pearl Qatar and Lusail). It is important to mention that recognized international architects have contributed to the development of Doha's skyline.

Most importantly this period marks emergence of contextually appropriate architecture and revival of Qatari vernacular.

End of 1990s depict Qatari vernacular in its original form as it is evident in the architecture of Diplomatic Club, QF headquarter building and Al Dana Club. On the other hand past decade is marked by the renowned architects taking elements of our traditional architecture as basis for their developments such as Museum of Islamic Arts by I.M. Pei, Qatar National Museum and Burj Qatar by Jan Nouvel, Liberal Arts and Science building at Education City by Arata Isozaki, and many more.

The new trend of architecture and urban development strongly reflects Qatari past, and is largely evident in one of the biggest developments, Msheireb; which is set to revive heart of Doha area. Part of the revival will also include conserving of four houses dating 1900-1910 which will be restored and preserved transforming Heritage Quarter into an important cultural destination within the development. These historic structures will become cultural centers, museums and exhibition buildings. This project is of a great importance as it will conserve some of the last remaining traditional and historic buildings in the city center.

Important to mention is also Al Dhayaan Municipality complex which is a key initiative in nation's growth and expansion of urban areas while striving to preserve cultural identity. Because of its geographical location and close proximity to the capital, The Government of Qatar decided to revive this village, hoping that it would serve as a matrix for potential of establishing new towns and cities in Qatar.

2A Architecture & Art
ISSUE No. 23 & 24
Spring & Summer 2013
"Brief History of Qatari Traditional Architecture"
Pages 8 to 13

The Future of Doha's architectural heritage
Ibrahim Mohamed Jaidah

The aim of the Qatar feature in 2A Magazine has been to present major trends in current architectural styles and art scene activities in constantly developing State of Qatar, while briefly reflecting on the history of architecture in this part of the world where due to the harsh climate conditions very few buildings from the past have survived to this day. The feature also shows how Qatari architecture, to this day is influenced by cultural, social and economic logic.

Looking back, in a short period of time of only 100 years, Qatar has gone through major shifts in architectural development from the times of humble abodes made out of clay and materials available in the nature to the current times of ultra-modern and sophisticated high-rise structures.

The time period of the late 1950's and early 1960's (Beginning of Oil Period) marked the architectural period of what I refer to as Arabian Deco era in Qatar where intricate decorative features were introduced and its thematic had no direct reference of the local culture. This era is still not being recognized nor documented as part of local architectural history and unfortunately it is not being protected.

The local identity, or better said survival of the local identity, was always an issue in the state that was developing at the fast rate. The Government of Qatar played a major role in the attempt to preserve the local character and merge it with the state of the art technologies.

In the period of 1970s-1990s when a lot of developing cities, especially from the region, went through major transformations, where through the development they diverted from their local history and identity, Doha has managed to hold tight on its tradition, and use it as foundation of modernization. Today Doha is a developing city with the signature architects taking part in shaping its skyline. The major difference here is that Qatar has managed to develop a local trend where it is desirable to have heritage of the traditional building forms, culture, tradition and religion be interwoven with modern simplistic designs.

Through examples featured here we can see that vernacular Qatari architecture can easily be adopted to meet the requirements of the modern functionality and high living standards while maintaining similarity with Qatari social and cultural values. With that being said and with the clear direction of the future developments, we can expect to see serious step taken towards creating an original contemporary Middle Eastern Architecture: architecture that is unique to its origin, yet global in thinking.

2A Architecture & Art
ISSUE No. 23 & 24
Spring & Summer 2013
"The future of Doha's Architectural Heritage"
Pages 66 to 69

Middle East
Landscape, City, Architecture
Chair Prof. Dr. Joseph Lluis Mateo, ETH Zurich

Qatari Vernacular…
Ibrahim Mohamed Jaidah
Surviving traditional buildings give us a glimpse of the life of the people of Qatar before the discovery and exploitation of oil and gas sparked off the modernization process. These buildings are endowed with elements that provide today's architect with lessons to guide contemporary design. Some architects in the Gulf region struggle to adapt to the process of the rapid change and to revive traditional architecture, thus it is of importance to look at these old buildings and learn about different spaces and their relationships, about why they were built and how they were used, and about their construction and materials. We are only just beginning to try to understand the relationships between spaces and openings-relations that will give us a much better appreciation of such factors as house form, building design, privacy and gender. These relationships are the bearers of messages, which, if succeed in

reading them correctly, may take us into the minds of the past and enable us to create contemporary vernacular architecture using modern solutions and materials.

The Gulf's architectural forms have, to some extent, been limited by two important factors: climate and the availability of building materials. The principal feature of Arabian residential architecture has always been based on measures taken to protect the inhabitants from the very hot climate of the Gulf's summer. This feature led to houses being built with thick walls for insulation, with few windows and with devices designed to take advantage of any potentially cooling breeze. Thick, well-insulated walls help minimize heat gain by conduction. Consequently, a common feature of indigenous Arabian architecture is the absence of windows on the exterior walls of a house. Another characteristic of traditional Gulf town-scapes was that the buildings tended to be closely clustered together, separated only by narrow, shaded alleyways. This meant that buildings offered each other mutual shading, but this may simply have been a by-product of building clusters for a greater security within some defensive perimeter or city walls. Compared with other areas of the Islamic world, there appears to be very little written about the traditional architecture of the Gulf, and even less about Qatar. Therefore, it is important to document what is there-and what can be remembered-as there is now very little left in Qatar that is truly original.

Historically, in the old architecture of Qatar the urban development of cities and villages was based on the creation of agglomerations of housing units. These agglomerations of housing units were the essence of traditional Qatari architecture, which can be defined as an architecture of social values. The Qatari urban development is a result of social factors, such as religion, privacy, and the notions of neighboring relatives and extended family. The climate and availability of materials and resources also played major roles dictating the shape of the city, the form of the streets, and also the overall shape of the buildings, their facades and openings.

... Arabian Deco

The vernacular style of Qatari Architecture was often created in response to cultural and climatic factors. Throughout history the master mason was the architect. The way of designing and building structures remained unchanged at the beginning of the oil period. The master mason was still the designer even though the building materials had changed, especially with the introduction and availability of cement.

The time period of the late 1950's and early 1960's marked an architectural revival period with the arrival of new architects from Lebanon and Indian subcontinent. They introduced the new decorative features whose primary role was of an aesthetic nature rather than a functional one as in the past. This new look was welcomed by the clients and the architects were even encouraged to add more ornamental and colorful details, which referred to what is popular yet very often absent in this part of the world.

This type of architecture was reflected in palaces, villas, and high-end apartment buildings. This style thrived and gave birth to what I call the "Arabian Deco Era".

That particular era in architecture was never documented, and those buildings have never been recognized as a part of the architectural history. As a result those buildings have not been listed and are still being demolished wherever they come in the way of new development.

I wish to document that era and list these buildings as an important part of our "old modern period." It would also be interesting to study the Gulf Region to see a similar architecture in that particular period and document it as "Arabian Deco."

Middle East: Landscape, City, Architecture
Josep Lluís Mateo, Krunoslav Ivanisin (editors)
Park Books – Architectural Papers
Zurich, 2013
"Qatari vernacular...", "... Arabian deco"

List of Projects

1.

Qatar Foundation HQ (Al Shaqab)
Education City, Doha, Qatar

- *Status*: Completed
- *Completion date*: 1997
- *Client*: HH The Emir's Office
- *Built area*: 3,702 sq.m
- *Typology*: educational
- *Scope*: design + supervision
- *Landscaping*: AEB
- *Contractor*: Al Rabban Contracting & Trading Co.
- *ID*: AEB
- *Cost* (Qatari *riyal*): 23.4 million
- *Awards*: Nominated for Aga Khan Award for Architecture (2001); 2nd place for Arab Towns Organisation Award (2002); Honoured on Qatari's 100 riyal banknote

Project Timeline
- *Design*: 1995
- *Start of construction*: 1996
- *End of construction*: 1997

2.

Barzan Tower
West Bay, Doha, Qatar

- *Status*: Completed
- *Completion date*: 2000
- *Client*: HE Abdullah bin Khalifa Al Attiyah
- *Built area*: 22,825 sq.m
- *Typology*: corporate
- *Number of levels*: B+G+M+21F
- *Scope*: design + supervision
- *Landscaping*: AEB
- *Contractor*: Contraco
- *ID*: AEB
- *Cost* (Qatari *riyal*): 80 million
- *Award*: Nominated for Aga Khan Award for Architecture (2004)

Project Timeline
- *Design*: 1997
- *Start of construction*: 1998
- *End of construction*: 2000

3.

Diplomatic Club
West Bay, Doha, Qatar

- *Status*: Completed
- *Completion date*: 2001
- *Client*: Ministry of Foreign Affairs
- *Built area*: 6,431 sq.m
- *Typology*: hospitality
- *Number of levels*: G+2F
- *Scope*: design + supervision
- *Landscaping*: AEB
- *Contractor*: Design 2000
- *ID*: AEB
- *Cost* (Qatari *riyal*): 80 million
- *Award*: 2nd place for the Organisation of Islamic Capitals and Cities in the Architectural Projects Category (2004)

Project Timeline
- *Design*: 1996
- *Start of construction*: 1999
- *End of construction*: 2001

4.

Jaidah Mosque
New Salata, Doha, Qatar

- *Status*: Completed
- *Completion date*: 2004
- *Client*: Private
- *Built area*: 498 sq.m
- *Typology*: religious
- *Scope*: design + supervision
- *Landscaping*: AEB
- *Contractor*: Al Seal Contracting Co.
- *ID*: AEB
- *Cost* (Qatari *riyal*): 7 million

Project Timeline
- *Design*: 2002
- *Start of construction*: 2002
- *End of construction*: 2003

5.

Najadah Mosque
Al Najadah, Doha, Qatar

- *Status*: Completed
- *Completion date*: 2005
- *Client*: Ministry of Awqaf
- *Built area*: 2,869 sq.m
- *Typology*: religious
- *Scope*: design
- *Cost* (Qatari *riyal*): 40 million

Project Timeline
- *Design*: 1998

6.

Lusail Visitors Centre
Lusail, Qatar

- *Status*: Completed
- *Completion date*: 2006
- *Client*: Qatari Diar
- *Built area*: 5,629 sq.m
- *Typology*: corporate
- *Number of levels*: G+M+1F
- *Scope*: design + supervision
- *Landscaping*: AEB
- *Contractor*: Arcon
- *ID*: Candy & Candy
- *Cost* (Qatari *riyal*): 39 million

Project Timeline
- *Design*: 2005
- *Start of construction*: 2006
- *End of construction*: 2006

7.

Qatar Financial Centre
West Bay, Doha, Qatar

- *Status*: Completed
- *Completion date*: 2006
- *Client*: Qatar Insurance Company
- *Built area*: 27,941 sq.m
- *Typology*: corporate
- *Number of levels*: B+G+M+20F
- *Scope*: design + supervision
- *Landscaping*: AEB
- *Contractor*: Gulf Housing & Construction Co.
- *ID*: AEB
- *Cost* (Qatari *riyal*): 75 million

Project Timeline
- *Design*: 2004
- *Start of construction*: 2005
- *End of construction*: 2006

8.

Alfardan Twin Towers
West Bay, Doha, Qatar

- *Status*: Completed
- *Completion date*: 2007
- *Client*: Alfardan Real Estate Co.
- *Built area*: 110,116 sq.m
- *Typology*: mixed-use
- *Components*: car showroom, offices, apartments
- *Number of levels*: Off=2B+G+M+29F Apt=2B+G+M+40F
- *Scope*: design + supervision
- *Landscaping*: AEB
- *Contractor*: Construction Development Co. (CDC)
- *ID*: PEIA Associates
- *Cost* (Qatari *riyal*): 430 million

Project Timeline
- *Design*: 1997
- *Start of construction*: 2004
- *End of construction*: 2007

9.

Al Sharq Village & Spa
Ras Abou Aboud, Doha, Qatar

- *Status*: Completed
- *Completion date*: 2008
- *Client*: Qatar National Hotels
- *Plot area*: 95,465 sq.m
- *Typology*: hospitality
- *Scope*: design + supervision
- *Landscaping*: Cracknell
- *Contractor*: United Construction EST. / Cybarco
- *ID*: Di Leonardo
- *Cost* (Qatari *riyal*): 600 million
- *Awards*: Arab Towns Organisation Award (2008); Winner in Tourism and Hospitality, CityScape Qatar Awards (2012)

Project Timeline
- *Design*: 2004
- *Start of construction*: 2005
- *End of construction*: 2008

10.

Al Qassar Tower
West Bay, Doha, Qatar

- *Status*: Completed
- *Completion date*: 2008
- *Client*: Alfardan Real Estate Co.
- *Built area*: 40,738 sq.m
- *Typology*: corporate
- *Number of levels*: 2B+G+24F
- *Scope*: design + supervision
- *Landscaping*: AEB
- *Contractor*: Construction Development Co. (CDC)
- *ID*: AEB
- *Cost* (Qatari *riyal*): 140 million

Project Timeline
- *Design*: 2005
- *Start of construction*: 2006
- *End of construction*: 2008

11.

Al Dhayaan Municipality
Al Dhayaan, Qatar

- *Status*: Completed
- *Completion date*: 2009
- *Client*: Public Works Authority
- *Built area*: 12,725 sq.m
- *Typology*: public/governmental
- *Components*: municipal headquarters, health centre, mosque, etc.
- *Scope*: design + supervision
- *Landscaping*: AEB
- *Contractor*: Al Balagh Trading & Contracting
- *ID*: AEB
- *Cost* (Qatari *riyal*): 350 million
- *Awards*: Organization of Islamic Capitals and Cities Award (2010); Arab Towns Organisation Award (2013)

Project Timeline
- *Design*: 2005
- *Start of construction*: 2007
- *End of construction*: 2009

12.

Al Rayyan Municipality
Al Rayyan, Qatar

- *Status*: Completed
- *Completion date*: 2009
- *Client*: Public Works Authority
- *Built area*: 17,442 sq.m
- *Typology*: public/governmental
- *Components*: municipal headquarters, theatre, archive, etc.
- *Scope*: design + supervision
- *Landscaping*: AEB
- *Contractor*: Al Sraiya Trading & Contracting Company
- *ID*: AEB
- *Cost* (Qatari *riyal*): 60 million

Project Timeline
- *Design*: 2007
- *Start of construction*: 2007
- *End of construction*: 2009

13.

Kempinski Residences & Suites
West Bay, Doha, Qatar

- *Status*: Completed
- *Completion date*: 2009
- *Client*: Alfardan Real Estate Co.
- *Built area*: 121,925 sq.m
- *Typology*: hospitality
- *Number of levels*: 2B+G+M+62F
- *Scope*: design + supervision
- *Landscaping*: AEB
- *Contractor*: Construction Development Co. (CDC)
- *ID*: PEIA Associates-Italy
- *Cost* (Qatari *riyal*): 700 million

Project Timeline
- *Design*: 2005
- *Start of construction*: 2006
- *End of construction*: 2009

14.

Awqaf Mosques
Various Locations - 18 Nos

- *Status*: Design completed
- *Client*: Ministry of Endowments and Islamic Affairs (Awqaf)
- *Built area*: 537 sq.m – 10,673 sq.m 115–5,000 worshipers
- *Typology*: religious
- *Scope*: design
- *ID*: AEB

Project Timeline
- *Design*: 2011

15.

Barwa Al Sadd
Al Sadd, Doha, Qatar

- *Status*: Completed
- *Completion date*: 2011
- *Client*: Barwa
- *Built area*: 202,996 sq.m
- *Typology*: mixed-use
- *Components*: 5 apartments buildings, 3 offices, 1 hotel, 1 recreational building, 1 car park building
- *Scope*: design + supervision
- *Landscaping*: AEB
- *Contractor*: MIDMAC
- *ID*: AEB
- *Cost* (Qatari *riyal*): 1.4 billion

Project Timeline
- *Design*: 2005
- *Start of construction*: 2009
- *End of construction*: 2011

16.

Business Park & Hotel
Airport Road, Najma, Doha, Qatar

- *Status*: Completed
- *Completion date*: 2011
- *Client*: H.E. Sh. Mohamed bin Hamad Al Thani
- *Built area*: 116,420 sq.m
- *Typology*: mixed-use
- *Components*: 6 office buildings, 1 hotel, 1 conference hall, 1 service apartments
- *Scope*: design + supervision
- *Landscaping*: AEB
- *Contractor*: Redco Construction Almana
- *ID*: AEB
- *Cost* (Qatari *riyal*): 700 million

Project Timeline
- *Design*: 2007
- *Start of construction*: 2009
- *End of construction*: 2012

17.

Oman Embassy in Qatar
West Bay, Doha, Qatar

- *Status*: Completed
- *Completion date*: 2011
- *Client*: Oman Ministry of Foreign Affairs
- *Built area*: 4,321 sq.m
- *Typology*: public/governmental
- *Components*: embassy building, ambassador's residence
- *Number of levels*: G+1F
- *Scope*: design + supervision
- *Landscaping*: AEB
- *Contractor*: Shelter Qatar
- *ID*: AEB

Project Timeline
- *Design*: 2007
- *Start of construction*: 2008
- *End of construction*: 2011

18.

Al Mirqab Souq Waqif Boutique Hotel & Amphitheatre
Souq Waqif, Doha, Qatar

- *Status*: Completed
- *Completion date*: 2011
- *Client*: Private Engineering Office
- *Built area*: 11,912 sq.m
- *Typology*: hospitality
- *Components*: hotel, amphitheatre
- *Number of levels*: B+G+3F
- *Scope*: design + supervision
- *Contractor*: Lotus
- *ID*: AEB KL
- *Cost* (Qatari *riyal*): 247 million

Project Timeline
- *Design*: 2007
- *Start of construction*: 2008
- *End of construction*: 2011

19.

Bukhamis Building
Lusail, Qatar

- *Status*: Design
- *Client*: Al Bukhamis Trading and Contracting Co. Ltd.
- *Built area*: 6,660 sq.m
- *Typology*: corporate
- *Number of levels*: 2B+G+M+3F
- *Scope*: design
- *Landscaping*: AEB
- *Cost* (Qatari *riyal*): 50 million

Project Timeline
- *Design*: 2013

20.

Private Villa at The Pearl
The Pearl, Qatar

- *Status*: Completed
- *Completion date*: 2013
- *Client*: Private
- *Built area*: 1,444 sq.m
- *Typology*: residential
- *Number of levels*: B+G+2F
- *Scope*: design + supervision
- *Landscaping*: AEB
- *Contractor*: RAMACO
- *ID*: PEIA Associates
- *Cost* (Qatari *riyal*): 15 million

Project Timeline
- *Design*: 2010
- *Start of construction*: 2010
- *End of construction*: 2013

21.

Fire Station Artists in Residence
Wadi Al Sail, Doha, Qatar

- *Status*: Completed
- *Completion date*: 2014
- *Client*: Qatar Museums
- *Built area*: 10,654 sq.m
- *Typology*: public/educational
- *Number of levels*: B+G+1F
- *Scope*: design + supervision
- *Landscaping*: Land Inc.
- *Contractor*: UrbaCon Trading & Contracting (UCC)
- *ID*: AEB
- *Cost* (Qatari *riyal*): 100 million

Project Timeline
- *Design*: 2013
- *Start of construction*: 2013
- *End of construction*: 2015

22.

State of Qatar Embassy in the Kingdom of Bahrain
Manama, Bahrain

- *Status*: Completed
- *Completion date*: 2014
- *Client*: Ministry of Foreign Affairs
- *Built area*: 7,016 sq.m
- *Typology*: public/governmental
- *Components*: embassy building, ambassador's residence
- *Number of levels*: B+G+1F
- *Scope*: design + supervision
- *Landscaping*: AEB
- *Contractor*: Kooheji Contractor
- *Cost* (US$): 17 million

Project Timeline
- *Design*: 2007
- *Start of construction*: 2011
- *End of construction*: 2014

23.

Kempinski Marsa Malaz Hotel
The Pearl, Qatar

- *Status*: Completed
- *Completion date*: 2014
- *Client*: Alfardan Hospitality
- *Built area*: 81,280 sq.m
- *Typology*: hospitality
- *Number of levels*: B+LG+G+5F
- *Scope*: design + supervision
- *Landscaping*: Cracknell
- *Contractor*: Construction Development Co. (CDC)
- *ID*: AEB
- *Cost* (Qatari *riyal*): 1.1 billion
- *Award*: Construction Week Qatar Hospitality Project of the Year (2014)

Project Timeline
- *Design*: 2008
- *Start of construction*: 2012
- *End of construction*: 2015

24.

Ghanem Holdings Headquarters
Salwa Road, Doha, Qatar

- *Status*: Completed
- *Completion date*: 2015
- *Client*: Ghanem Real Estate Investment and Development Co.
- *Built area*: 24,239 sq.m
- *Typology*: corporate
- *Number of levels*: 2B+G+M+7F
- *Scope*: design + supervision
- *Landscaping*: AEB
- *Contractor*: RAMCO Trading
- *ID*: AEB
- *Cost* (Qatari *riyal*): 904 million

Project Timeline
- *Design*: 2010
- *Start of construction*: 2011
- *End of construction*: 2015

25.

Gulf Mall
Al Gharafa, Doha, Qatar

- *Status*: Completed
- *Completion date*: 2015
- *Client*: H.E. Sh. Nasser bin Abdullah Al Thani
- *Built area*: 162,748 sq.m
- *Typology*: retail
- *Number of levels*: 2B+G+M+1F
- *Scope*: design + supervision
- *Landscaping*: AEB
- *Contractor*: IDC
- *ID*: AEB
- *Cost* (Qatari *riyal*): 600 million

Project Timeline
- *Design*: 2007
- *Start of construction*: 2009
- *End of construction*: 2015

26.

State of Qatar Embassy in Lebanon
Beirut, Lebanon

- *Status*: Completed
- *Completion date*: 2015
- *Client*: Ministry of Foreign Affairs
- *Built area*: 6,583 sq.m
- *Typology*: public/governmental
- *Number of levels*: 2B+G+2F+P
- *Scope*: design + supervision
- *Contractor*: Tabet Enterprises
- *Cost* (US$): 8 million

Project Timeline
- *Design*: 2007
- *Start of construction*: 2011
- *End of construction*: 2015

27.

Ministry of Interior Headquarters (MoI HQ)
Wadi Al Sail, Doha, Qatar

- *Status*: Completed
- *Completion date*: 2016
- *Client*: Private Engineering Office
- *Built area*: 244,967 sq.m
- *Typology*: public/governmental
- *Components*: main building, multi-storey parking
- *Scope*: design
- *Landscaping*: AEB
- *Contractor*: WTC Berhad
- *ID*: AEB

Project Timeline
- *Design*: 2008
- *Start of construction*: 2010
- *End of construction*: 2016

28.

Fraser Suites
West Bay, Doha, Qatar

- *Status*: Under construction
- *Completion date*: Expected end of 2016
- *Client*: Al Sarh Real Estate W.L.L.
- *Built area*: 79,430 sq.m
- *Typology*: hospitality
- *Number of levels*: 3B+G+M+46F
- *Scope*: design + supervision
- *Landscaping*: AEB
- *Contractor*: Construction & Reconstruction Engineering Co. W.L.L.
- *ID*: Studio Matteo Nunziati
- *Cost* (Qatari *riyal*): 565 million

Project Timeline
- *Design*: 2011
- *Start of construction*: 2012
- *End of construction*: Expected 2016

29.

Sidra Musalla
Education City, Doha, Qatar

- *Status*: Design completed
- *Completion date*: Expected end of 2016
- *Client*: OHL Contrack
- *Built area*: 581 sq.m
- *Typology*: religious
- *Number of levels*: G+M
- *Scope*: design
- *Landscaping*: Parsons
- *Contractor*: JV - MIDMAC & CCC
- *ID*: AEB

Project Timeline
- *Design*: 2011
- *Start of construction*: 2014
- *End of construction*: Expected end of 2016

30.

Abu Sidra Masterplan
Al Rayyan, Qatar

- *Status*: Ongoing
- *Client*: H.E. Sheikh Mohamed bin Hamad Al Thani
- *Typology*: masterplan, mixed-use
- *Scope*: design + supervision
- *Landscaping*: AEB KL

Project Timeline
- *Masterplan design*: 2013
- *Building design*: ongoing

31.

Place Vendôme
Lusail, Qatar

- *Status*: Under construction
- *Completion date*: Expected 2017
- *Client*: United Developers (UD)
- *Built area*: 835,903 sq.m
- *Typology*: mixed-use
- *Components*: mall, 3 hotels
- *Scope*: design
- *Landscaping*: AEB
- *Contractor*: CRC (Dorra Group)
- *ID concept*: AEB
- *Cost* (Qatari *riyal*): 2 billion

Project Timeline
- *Design*: 2012
- *Start of construction*: 2014
- *End of construction*: Expected end of 2017

32.

Burj Alfardan
Lusail Marina District, Qatar

- *Status*: Under construction
- *Completion date*: Expected end of 2016
- *Client*: Alfardan Properties Co.
- *Built area*: 114,566 sq.m
- *Typology*: mixed-use
- *Number of levels*: 3B+G+M+27F+P
- *Scope*: design + supervision
- *Landscaping*: AEB
- *ID*: AEB
- *Cost* (Qatari *riyal*): 550 million

Project Timeline
- *Design*: 2012
- *Start of construction*: 2015
- *End of construction*: Expected end of 2016

33.

QIMC Tower West Bay
West Bay, Doha, Qatar

- *Status*: Design
- *Completion date*: Expected 2018
- *Client*: Qatar Industrial Manufacturing Company (QIMC)
- *Built area*: 120,311 sq.m
- *Typology*: mixed-use
- *Number of levels*: 4B+G+M+3P+38F
- *Scope*: design + supervision
- *Landscaping*: AEB
- *Contractor*: Al Balagh Trading & Contracting
- *ID*: AEB
- *Cost* (Qatari *riyal*): 1.1 billion

Project Timeline
- *Design*: 2015
- *Start of construction*: Expected 2016
- *End of construction*: Expected 2018

34.

Cardita Shell Tower
Lusail, Qatar

- *Status*: Design
- *Completion date*: Expected 2018/19
- *Client*: Al-Bandary Group
- *Typology*: residential

Project Timeline
- *Design*: 2016

35.

Contraco Headquarters
Lusail Energy City, Qatar

- *Status*: Design proposal
- *Client*: Contraco WLL
- *Typology*: corporate

36.

Erkyah Mixed-Use Development
Lusail, Qatar

- *Status*: Design
- *Completion date*: Expected 2020/21
- *Client*: Ariane Real Estate
- *Typology*: mixed-use

Project Timeline
- *Design*: 2016

37.

K-Hotel
Lusail, Qatar

- *Status*: Design
- *Completion date*: Expected 2020
- *Client*: Falcon Real Estate
- *Built area*: 43,428 sq.m
- *Typology*: hospitality
- *Number of levels*: 3B+G+25F
- *Scope*: design + supervision
- *Landscaping*: AEB
- *ID*: AEB

Project Timeline
- *Design*: 2016

38.

Qatari Diar Headquarters
Lusail, Qatar

- *Status*: Under construction
- *Completion date*: Expected end of 2018
- *Client*: Lusail Real Estate Development Company
- *Typology*: corporate
- *Built area*: 89,190 sq.m
- *Number of levels*: QD1: G+8, QD2: G+6, Lusail Building: G+6 (QD1 and QD2 are for Qatari Diar1 and Qatari Diar2)
- *Scope*: design + supervision

Project Timeline
- *Design*: 2015
- *Start of construction*: 2016
- *End of construction*: Expected end of 2018

39.

Dune Stadium
Lusail, Qatar

- *Status*: Design proposal
- *Sports specialists*: ARUP Sport Venue Design (ASVD)
- *Client*: Supreme Committee for Legacy and Delivery
- *Typology*: sports and recreation

Map of AEB Projects Around the Globe

- Qatar
- UAE
- Oman
- KSA
- Iran
- Syria
- Sudan
- Yemen
- Bahrain
- Cyprus
- Egypt
- Lebanon
- Malaysia
- Mauritania
- Morocco
- Tajikistan
- Turkey

Turkey
Tajikistan
Cyprus
Syria
Lebanon
Iran
Bahrain
Qatar
Egypt
Oman
Saudi Arabia
UAE
Sudan
Yemen
Malaysia

Biographies

Arab Engineering Bureau

Founded in 1966, Arab Engineering Bureau is an award-winning full-service architectural design and consultancy firm with an outstanding international portfolio. AEB draws its strengths from the unique design methodology established by its GCEO and Chief Architect Ibrahim Jaidah, which expresses present-day developments in building design, while preserving and articulating traditional Qatari architecture wherever appropriate.

The firm considers every project it undertakes as a further element in ensuring a sustainable environment while benefiting the local economy and community. Through many of its projects, AEB has demonstrated an ability and vision that goes beyond the building as a physical form. Meanwhile, AEB actively participates in the development of projects devised to socially and culturally further the evolution of the State and its people.

The firm works across extensively divergent project scales, typologies and environmental conditions, adopting an approach grounded in the quest for contextually appropriate and environmentally sustainable solutions. Over the past 50 years AEB has played a leading role in building some of the most recognisable landmarks in the State of Qatar, one of which is Al Shaqab, the first building in the new Education City, whose design is honoured on the Qatari 100-*riyal* banknote.

Ibrahim Mohamed Jaidah

Ibrahim Mohamed Jaidah is Group CEO & Chief Architect of the Arab Engineering Bureau. In addition to his role at AEB, Jaidah is a researcher and the author of the *History of Qatari Architecture*, the first comprehensive study of the country's building legacy. Ibrahim grew up in the old neighbourhood of Al Jasra, and as a child showed an interest in photography and the arts, developing an eye for form and beauty that has accompanied him throughout his career in architecture.

Jaidah ranks as a pioneer of a new architectural movement, which combines the far-reaching influences of traditional Qatari architecture with modern style, creating memorable landmark structures that are helping to shape the developing State of Qatar.

Jaidah graduated from the University of Oklahoma (USA) in 1988, and acquired AEB in 1991. Since then his firm has completed more than 1500 projects, which he has overseen personally. In each project, Jaidah attempts to retain the identity of his culture, embrace the modern, and present the true potential and ambition of both Qatar and AEB. His focus on vernacular architecture has brought a new dimension to the region's architectural profession. Jaidah is widely considered a leading authority on traditional architecture, and in many instances he has been directly commissioned to create national landmarks.

Among the numerous accolades Jaidah has received for his architectural work are the Organisation of Islamic Capitals and Cities Award and the Arab Towns Organisation Award; and he has been nominated for the Aga Khan Award for Architecture. In 2005 Jaidah was honoured with the medal of the State of Qatar Encouragement Award.

Each of Jaidah's projects strives to reflect the cultural, historical and environmental context in which it arises. He is a dedicated advocate for sustainability, and is a co-founding member of the Qatar Green Building Council.

Awards

- *Construction Innovation Awards Qatar* Engineering Firm of the Year (2015)
- *Construction Week Qatar* Architecture Firm of the Year Award (2015)
- 9th place on MEP's Power 25 list (2015)
- RasGas HQ listed among the top 5 GCC Green Projects (2015)
- 1st place on *Qatar Project Magazine*'s "Top 10 architectural firms" list (2014)
- *Construction Week Qatar* Architecture Firm of the Year Award (2014)
- *Construction Week Qatar* Hospitality Project of the Year: Kempinski Marsa Malaz (2014)
- 14th place on Power 50 MEP list (2014)
- Al Dhayaan Municipality - Arab Towns Organisation Award (2013)
- *Construction Week Qatar* Architecture Firm of the Year (2012)
- Al Sharq Village & Spa – Winner in Tourism and Hospitality, CityScape Qatar Awards (2012)
- *Construction Week Qatar* Consultancy of the Year Award (2011)
- American School of Doha – MEED National Award for Social Project (2011)
- Al Dhayaan Municipality – Organization of Islamic Capitals and Cities Award (2010)
- Al Sharq Village & Spa – Arab Towns Organisation Award (2008)
- The Diplomatic Club – 2nd place for the Organisation of Islamic Capitals and Cities in the Architectural Projects Category (2004)
- Barzan Tower – Nominated for Aga Khan Award for Architecture (2004)
- Al Shaqab Institute for Girls – 2nd place for Arab Towns Organisation Award (2002). The same project was nominated for Aga Khan Award for Architecture in 2001 and is honoured on Qatari's 100 *riyal* banknote.

Furthermore, on an individual level, Ibrahim M. Jaidah was presented with the State Encouragement Award from the State of Qatar in 2005, for his work in the field of architecture. The State Encouragement Award, supervised by The Ministry of Culture and Arts, is awarded to distinguished and promising researchers and innovators.